#GENDER

AN INTRODUCTION TO Gendered Social Problems

SECOND EDITION

SARAH DEWARD
University of Michigan

ROWMAN & LITTLEFIELD
Lanham • Boulder • New York • London

Acquisitions Editor: Alyssa Palazzo
Acquisitions Assistant: Hannah Eveland
Sales and Marketing Inquiries: textbooks@rowman.com

Published by Rowman & Littlefield
An imprint of The Rowman & Littlefield Publishing Group, Inc.
4501 Forbes Boulevard, Suite 200, Lanham, Maryland 20706
www.rowman.com

86-90 Paul Street, London EC2A 4NE

British Library Cataloguing in Publication Information Available

Library of Congress Cataloging-in-Publication Data
Names: DeWard, Sarah, 1982– author.
Title: #Gender : gendered social problems through a social media lens / Sarah DeWard, Eastern Michigan University.
Other titles: Hashtag gender
Description: Lanham : Rowman & Littlefield, [2024] | Includes bibliographical references and index. | Summary: "A textbook that examines gendered social issues through the lens of social media"—Provided by publisher.
Identifiers: LCCN 2024024026 (print) | LCCN 2024024027 (ebook) | ISBN 9781538180631 (cloth) | ISBN 9781538180648 (paperback) | ISBN 9781538180655 (epub)
Subjects: LCSH: Sex role. | Gender identity. | Sex differences—Social aspects. | Sexism. | Women—Social conditions.
Classification: LCC HQ1075 .D49 2024 (print) | LCC HQ1075 (ebook) | DDC 305.3—dc23/eng/20240611
LC record available at https://lccn.loc.gov/2024024026
LC ebook record available at https://lccn.loc.gov/2024024027

Contents

Preface

WE'RE LIVING THROUGH A HISTORIC BATTLE of opposing ideologies in the United States. On one side, politicians, legislators, and religious leaders routinely undermine the human rights of women, people of color, and LGBTQIA+ people. They restrict public education curricula, whitewashing the shameful realities of slavery and the resultant privileges of whiteness. LGBTQIA+ and gender nonconforming people are criminalized for self-expression and are the focus of rising hate crimes. The overturn of *Roe v. Wade* and innumerable new state and federal legislations undermine basic legal protections, so much so that full bodily autonomy and the right to marriage can no longer be assumed. For the first time in several generations, our daughters have fewer rights than their mothers.

And yet, another movement is starting. Generations Z and Alpha, including my daughter Hannah, are deconstructing the idea of gender altogether. For them, gender is not just constructed, it is burdensome and unnecessary. They've found ways to decenter social identities, thereby diluting the power of gendered societal expectations. For them, gender is not a static identity with defined roles and responsibilities but a dynamic performance that can change at will. Not only do they embrace the fluidity and futility of gender, but they embody the change we must see in the world.

I have taught sociology and gender studies for nearly twenty years, and students have always resonated with real-life information about gendered social problems. Now, more than ever, we need our students to not only show academic interest in these concepts but also take the lead in fighting for a world where all people are valued equally. *#Gender* provides timely, accessible, real-world cases of gendered social issues so that students can easily see the impact of gender on society. I've purposely written the text with approachable language and social media examples to further connect with the lived experiences of students.

#Gender features several learning tools to assist students and teachers in the classroom, including the following:

- **Learning Goals** at the beginning of each chapter identify major concepts and provide students with a reading road map.
- **Bolded key terms** enable students to build a necessary vocabulary for discussing gendered issues.

- **"In the News" boxes** tie the contents of the chapter with real-world issues surrounding gender.
- **Moving Forward** sections highlight the efforts that activists and everyday people are making to offer solutions for current issues.
- **Key Takeaways** aid student discussion and engagement with the chapter material.

Instructors, we need you to inspire. Students, we need you to resist. It's my sincere hope that *#Gender* helps you on this journey.

—In solidarity, Sarah DeWard

1

INTRODUCTION
#LETSGETSTARTED

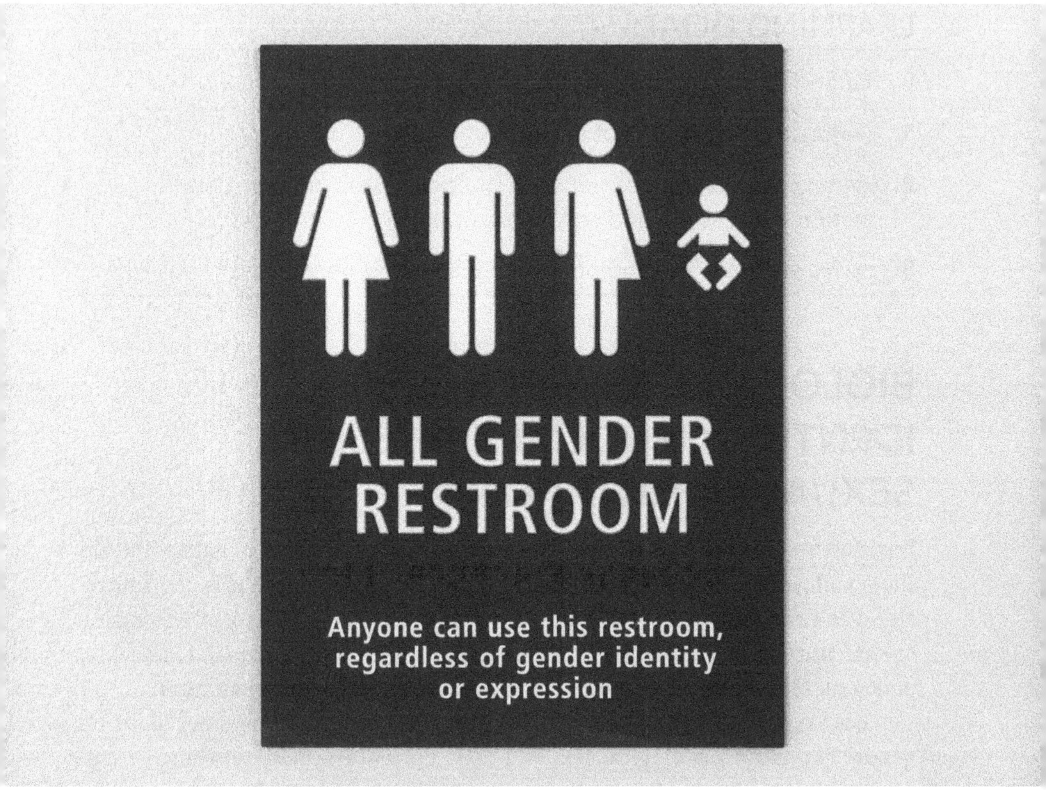

Figure 1.1 Gender-neutral bathrooms are more common as awareness about gender identity increases. iStock by Getty Images

ADVOCATES OF gender-neutral language, including the genderless pronouns "they" and "them," argue that use of gender-neutral language supports an inclusive society; however, others believe that gender is a biological trait, and therefore society should only use the binary terms "his/him" or "her/she." So who is right? If you look up this issue on the internet, you'll find a variety of opinions. One of the problems with debates about gender issues, especially those happening over social media, is that people don't always use the correct terms to express their ideas. This can lead to confusion and mixed messages. This chapter explains common terms used when discussing gender. Understanding these concepts lays a foundation so we can speak the same gender "language." There are a lot of terms, so it is easy to get confused. *Let's try to make things a bit clearer.*

LEARNING GOALS

By the end of this chapter, you should be able to

1. Deconstruct the concept of gender
2. Identify the differences between biological sex, gender identity, gender expression, and sexual orientation
3. Utilize accurate terminology when discussing gender sociologically

BIOLOGICAL SEX, GENDER IDENTITY, GENDER EXPRESSION, SEXUAL ORIENTATION

Envision four parallel lines. These lines have a countless number of data points on them and will never intersect. Each line represents a concept that is best understood as a **continuum**—or a range of locations subtly increasing or decreasing toward the end points. These four continuums represent four major concepts: biological sex, gender identity, gender expression, and sexual orientation.

Each concept is separate—its own line. That means that gender identity, gender expression, biological sex, and sexual orientation do not cause or create each other—they're stand-alone ideas (Killerman 2019). The lines are also parallel, which means they do not cross. While we can often make connections between these concepts, for example, predicting someone's sexual orientation by observing their clothing (a form of gender expression), the reality is that we cannot predict people's identity on one continuum based upon their location on another.

Biological Sex

Biological sex refers to external physical characteristics (i.e., penis, testicles, vagina, breasts) and internal reproductive structures (i.e., hormones, chromosomes) that can be measured or observed through medical testing. Many people misunderstand sex as a **binary**, or the belief that there are only two groups of biologically opposite people: male-bodied and female-bodied (Wade and Ferree 2019). Consider the many examples of society screwing this up, including your driver's license. Many will have to choose between two categories: M (male) or F (female). Biologically speaking, we know this is not the case. Intersex bodies are quite common—about 1.7 percent of the world's population (Moriarty 2023). Being **intersex** means having ambiguous sex organs, combinations of male and female sex organs, or chromosomal differences. This term and its definition are socially constructed—created by people. After all, who decides how much testosterone is "enough" to be labeled "male?"

In addition, while many people do exist toward the ends of the biological sex continuum (male-bodied or female-bodied), this location can change. Consider hormonal fluctuations throughout the life course or even the surgical intervention of breast implants. These changes can move a person back and forth on the biological sex continuum.

Despite inaccuracies and misunderstandings, the biological sex binary holds significant weight in our society. People who are female-bodied, or who are assumed to be women, experience sexism. **Sexism** refers to institutional and individual prejudice, discrimination, and belief of superiority against people based on their sex. Sexism is part of the social fabric of our society and is embedded in our social institutions. We'll discuss more examples of sexism later in the book.

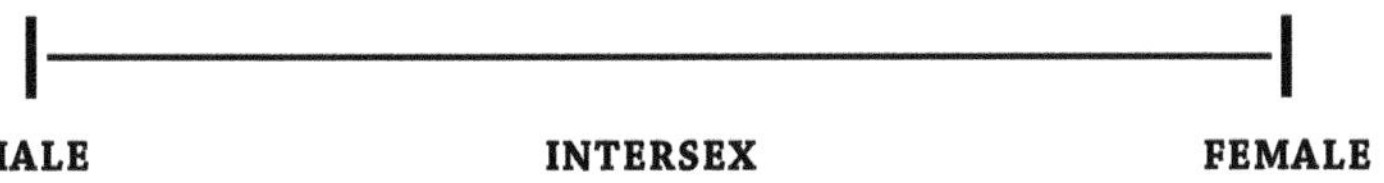

Figure 1.2 The biological sex continuum. Adapted from Killerman 2019

In the News . . .

In 2019, "Q" was developed as the first genderless virtual assistant. Q was created to utilize a gender-neutral voice, creating a balance between a low-tone masculine voice and a high-tone feminine voice. Developers insisted that this new assistant would provide the depth of information provided by other brands, while purposefully rejecting gender norms of the willing, female, secretary (Saguy and Williams 2019). In 2022, Apple developers followed this trend by introducing their users to "Quinn," the fifth voice available for use by virtual assistant Siri (Myers 2022).

Gender Identity

The definition of gender can be expanded into two parts: gender expression and gender identity. **Gender identity** is defined as a person's psychological sense of self related to gender. Currently, gender identity cannot be biologically measured, although many researchers are trying to find a way to do so. This means people report their gender identity—and we must believe them (Killerman 2019).

Gender identity is our second continuum, with many people identifying as men or women, boys or girls. However, gender identity is not binary. There is an ever-expanding list of terms people use to self-identify as **gender nonconforming**, including third gender, genderqueer, gender fluid, agender, enby, pangender, and bigender, among others. Gender identity is assigned at birth based on assumptions made from biological sex. Think about the delivery room when a baby is born: after the child is delivered, the doctor sees the external genitalia. Does the doctor say, "It's a female!" or "It's a male!"? Nope. The gender is assigned right then: "It's a boy!" or "It's a girl!"

Need another example? Think about the phenomenon of gender-reveal parties. The advent of ultrasound technology allows expectant parents to receive a picture of their unborn child, including genitalia.

Using this picture, the parents can predict the biological sex of their baby (at best); however, the parents (and society in general) also assume the gender identity of their child and assign a label. A picture of a male-bodied baby

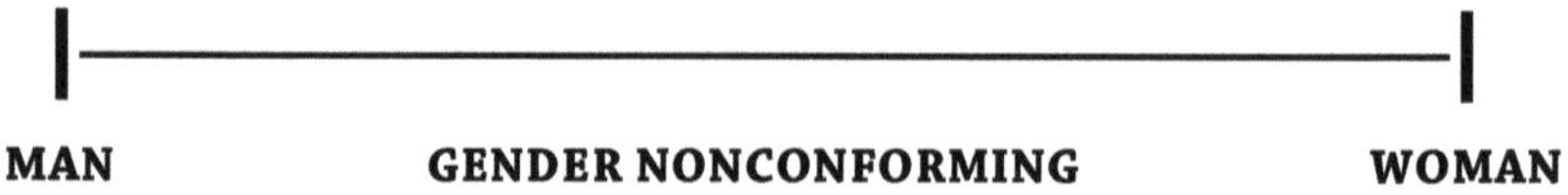

Figure 1.3 The gender identity continuum. Adapted from Killerman 2019

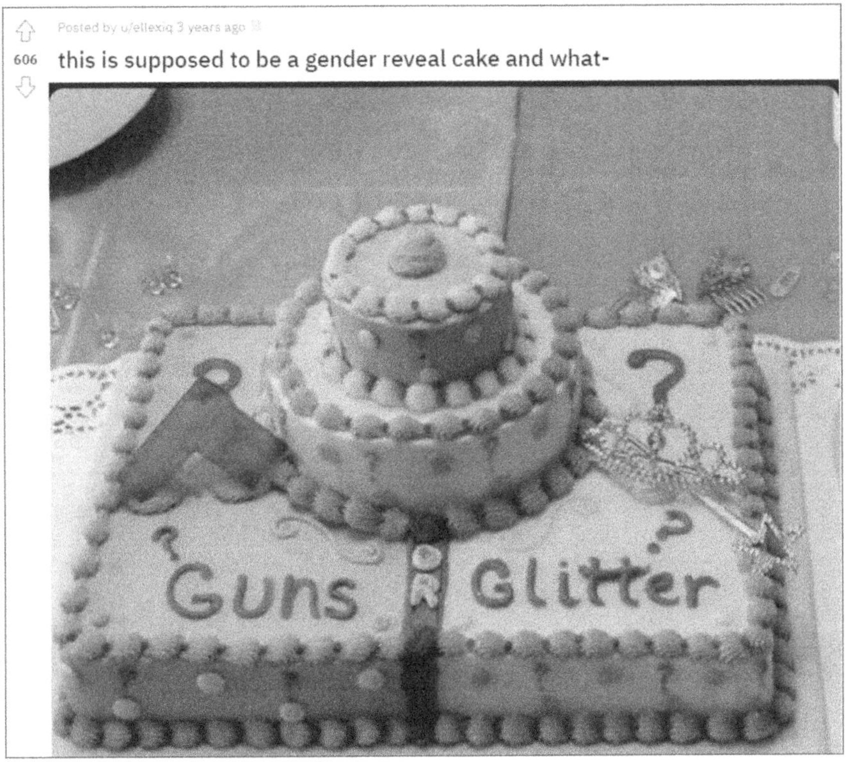

Figure 1.4 Gender reveal party themes often rely upon traditional gender norms.
REDDIT POST

suddenly translates to an avalanche of blue-colored décor, trucks, and sports-themed toys and apparel. Themes like "Pearls or Pistols" and "Tiaras or Trucks" flood Pinterest boards (King-Miller 2019).

At one gender reveal party in Arizona, expectant parents tried to shoot a target to release either pink or blue powder—of course, indicating whether their baby was a boy or a girl. The dad-to-be hit the target and accidentally started a wildfire that caused over 47,000 acres of damage (Vera 2018). The destruction caused by gender reveal parties has been so extensive that the woman credited with inventing the trend has expressed her regret and begged people to stop hosting them (Sparks 2020).

For many people, this assignment of gender identity fits their psychological sense of self. This is called being **cisgender**. However, transgender folks experience something different—they do not identify with their assigned gender at birth. They know that their gender identity, or their psychological sense of self, does not neatly fit into the gender binary.

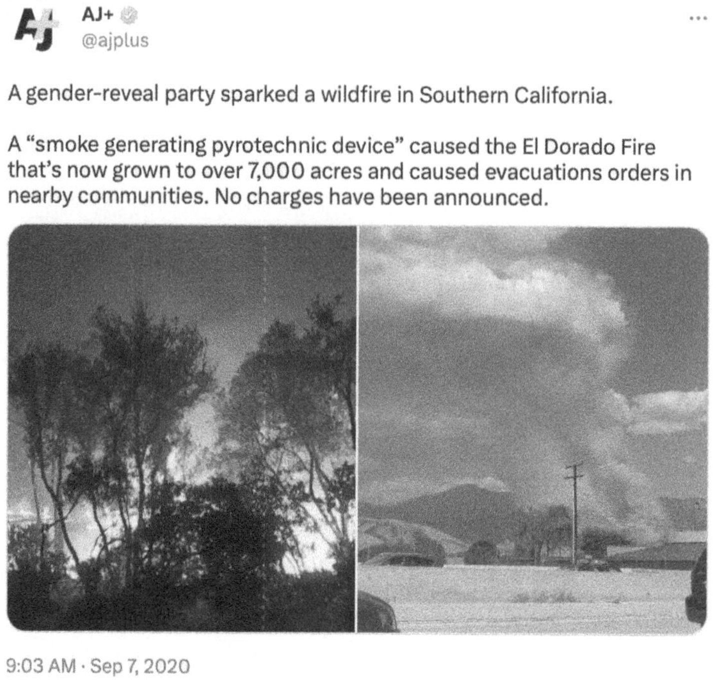

Figure 1.5 After this California forest fire was caused by a gender reveal party, advocates called for an end to gender reveal party stunts. Posted on X

The term **transgender** is an umbrella term for all people who do not identify with the gender they were assigned at birth. "Transgender" is an adjective. That means we say that a person "is transgender" not "transgendered." Also, be sure to use people-first language: say "transgender people" versus "transgenders." Many transgender folks do not go through sexual reconstruction surgery or hormone replacement therapy, and this choice is nuanced and personal. The availability of medical interventions is limited and extremely costly. Some trans folks feel comfortable in their bodies and have no desire to alter them. Their discomfort comes from society's labels and cultural norms—not their bodies.

Notice that we have yet to talk about sexual orientation. That's because gender identity (or being transgender) has nothing to do with a person's sexuality! Remember, we're discussing parallel lines here—they don't intersect. That means that if we know someone's gender identity, we cannot predict their sexual orientation. This is confusing because we often use the acronym LGBTQIA+

(lesbian, gay, bisexual, transgender, queer, intersex, asexual) which lumps together the "L, G, and Bs" with the "Ts." This is functionally inaccurate.

Gender Expression

Gender expression refers to the ways we actively communicate our gender identity to the world. We do this through our clothing, hairstyle, mannerisms, ways of speaking, roles we play, and social interactions. We can actively express our gender, like a bride dressed up as a princess on her wedding day. Gender expression can also be passive. Despite our personal preferences, cultural artifacts have been assigned to us, such as our names and our pronouns, which passively communicate our gender identity to the world. For example, someone might mistake your gender, or misgender you, because of your hairstyle. **Misgendering** is the act of addressing someone by pronouns that do not reflect their gender identity. We'll discuss these concepts in depth in chapter 4.

This continuum includes **masculine**, the social and cultural expectations linked to men and manhood, on one end. On the other end is **feminine**, or the social and cultural expectations linked to women and womanhood. Keep in mind, our definitions of masculinity and femininity are created by society and change over time. For example, your woman professor wearing a business suit might still be feminine in our historical context, but a hundred years ago, this gender expression would have been distinctly masculine. In our imaginary midpoint of the gender expression continuum is the category **androgynous**, or an expression that is neither masculine nor feminine or combines elements of both (Killerman 2019). Again, what we determine to be gender nonconforming or androgynous changes based on societal and historical context. We'll explore societal definitions of gender in the next chapter.

Most people feel strongly about expressing themselves in a way that is consistent with their gender identity and will go to great lengths to present an image of themselves that corresponds with their psychological sense of self. However, gender expression is not always a personal decision; it can be forced. Transgender people are often asked to dress or behave in a manner consistent

MASCULINE | **ANDROGYNOUS** | **FEMININE**

Figure 1.6 The gender expression continuum. Adapted from Killerman 2019

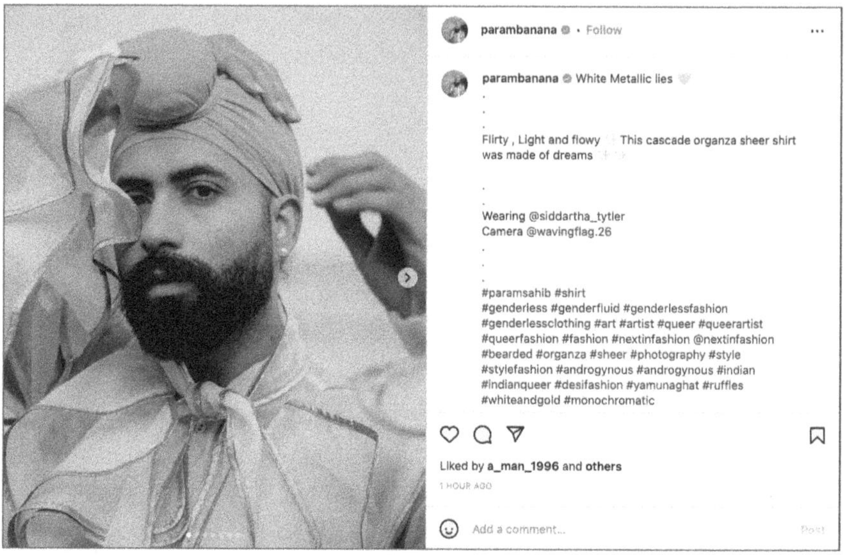

Figure 1.7 Social media is a place for many to showcase their gender expression. Posted on Instagram

with their biological sex, not their known gender identity. As previously stated, this is discriminatory to individuals and oppressive to trans people as a group.

Sexual Orientation

Sexual orientation is our final continuum and refers to a person's romantic or erotic response to others. These erotic attractions are based on internal feelings. One does not need to have sexual interactions with others to understand one's sexual orientation (Kimmel and Messner 2013). The opposing sides of this category include "attracted to women" and "attracted to men" or labeled **gay** or **lesbian**. **Bisexual**, attracted to both men and women, can be found as the fictional midpoint of the continuum (Killerman 2019). While the term "homosexual" was used in the past, we're seeing more changes in terminology. Because of the derogatory use of this label, GLADD (formerly Gay and Lesbian Alliance Against Defamation) listed "homosexual" as a term to avoid (GLADD 2019).

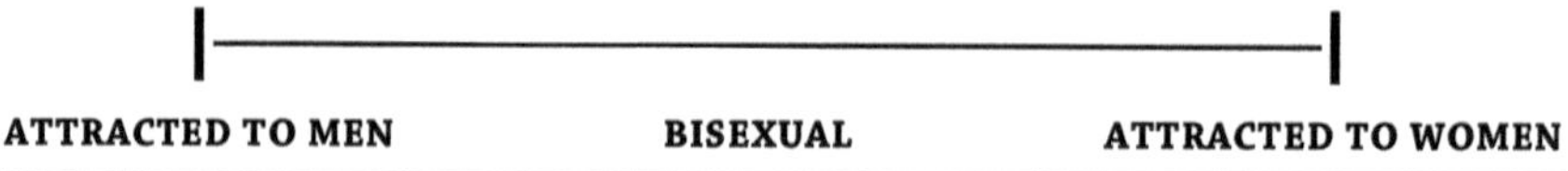

Figure 1.8 The sexual orientation continuum. Adapted from Killerman 2019

In the News . . .

The majority of LGBTQIA+ social media users state that they have been targets of menacing or violent comments online (Seitz 2022). A recent report published by GLAAD states that social media companies, like TikTok, YouTube, Facebook, and X (formerly Twitter), have policies against hate speech on their platforms. However, advocates argue that the removal of hateful comments and suspension of offender accounts is lacking (Seitz 2022). For people in the LGBTQIA+ community, social media continues to be a space rife with harassment and discrimination.

GLAAD (formerly Gay and Lesbian Alliance Against Defamation) is a nonprofit organization in the United States that works for cultural change to ensure fair and accurate representations of LGBTQIA+ people (GLAAD 2023).

Other categories are being added all the time, including **asexual**, or having no sexual feelings or desires; **demisexual**, a person who does not experience sexual feelings until a strong personal connection is developed (Iqbal 2019); and **pansexual**, a person who is sexually attracted to a person regardless of sex, gender, or gender identity. The acronym LGBTQIA+ stands for lesbian, gay, bisexual, transgender, queer, questioning, intersex, asexual and all other non-dominant sexual orientations.

Historically, our labels and categorizations of sexual orientations have changed over time. While people's sexual desires have always been diverse, it wasn't until 1930 that the terms "heterosexual" and "homosexual" entered the public consciousness. On April 30, 1930, the *New York Times* published a book review that referred to sexuality as a hetero/homo dyad (Katz 1995). While this wasn't the first time these terms were used, it was the first time they got public attention. A public fear of "turning homosexual" emerged as a result. Society hunkered down into a **heterosexual hegemony**—a period where heterosexual dominance was expected and unchecked (Katz 1995). However, in 1948, Alfred Kinsey published the first substantial scientific study about human sexuality, presenting sexual orientation as an evolving continuum (Kinsey 1948). Kinsey (1948) stated that most people can be found within the middle portion of the sexuality continuum, having at least some attraction to the opposite and same sex. Kinsey's work is still being used today to study human sexuality.

Recently, a study published in the peer-reviewed journal *Science* deepened our understanding of the biological component of sexual orientation. Researchers found that there are genetic components to sexual attraction, but that DNA is not the only component to sexual orientation (Phelps and Wedow 2019). Personal histories, social context, and historical location all play a role in the development of sexuality (Ganna et al. 2019).

Although the US Supreme Court ruled in 2015 to allow same-sex marriage, our society is still steeped in **heterocentrism**—the assumption that everyone is heterosexual, and by implication, *should be* heterosexual. We see these **heteronormative** beliefs exhibited in most of our major institutions. Religious entities focus on heterosexual marriages, and most television shows depict romances between men and women. Of course, there has been progress, but our society is largely heterosexist. **Heterosexism** is the cultural and societal bias against non-heterosexual people. Heterosexism comprises both institutional (macro-level) and individual (micro-level) prejudice and discrimination. **Homophobia** is the individual-level hatred, hostility, and/or general disapproval of LGBTQIA+ folks. **Sexual prejudice** is the general attitude one might have against LGBTQIA+ folks and is usually the mindset that promotes discrimination.

MOVING FORWARD

Terminology can seem unnecessary and boring, but we will apply these academic terms to real-world scenarios. After reading this chapter, you should know the key terms related to the study of gender.

Key Takeaways

- Gender identity is a person's psychological sense of self and may or may not correspond to the gender assigned at birth.
- Biological sex, or internal and external reproductive structures, differs from gender.
- Gender expression is the way that people communicate their gender identity to the world.
- Sexual orientation is on a continuum with many possible locations.

2

CONSTRUCTING GENDER
#GENDERISFAKENEWS

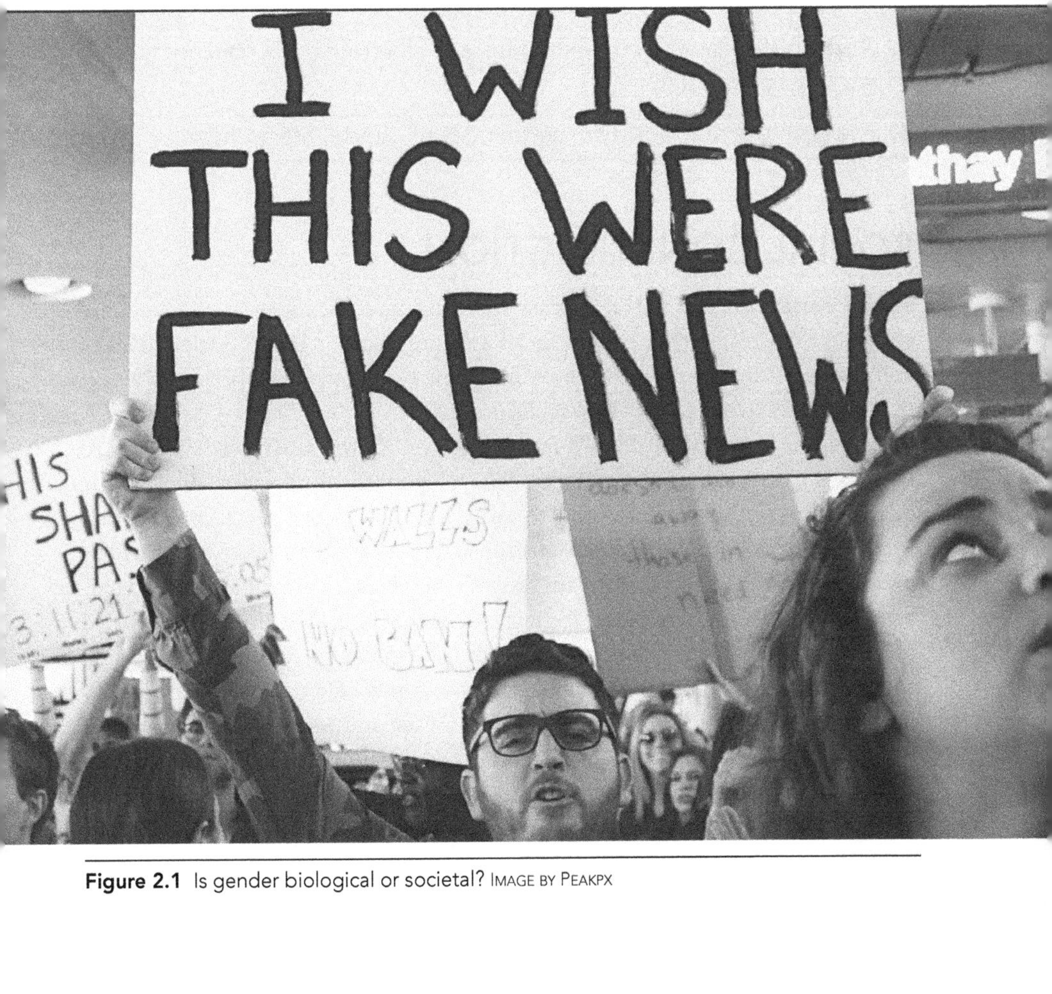

Figure 2.1 Is gender biological or societal? Image by Peakpx

THE SOCIAL CONSTRUCTION of gender has become controversial. You've probably heard people incorrectly say that gender is biological or genetic. Some might argue that men are hardwired to be fighters, leaders, or providers. Others insist that women are genetically nurturing, gentle, or passive. However, scientists understand that biology does not create our gender norms; society does. How do we determine which concepts are biological and which are created by society? *We first must understand the concept of social construction.*

LEARNING GOALS

By the end of the chapter, you should be able to

1. Explain the social construction of gender
2. Apply historical and contextual tests to determine if a concept is socially constructed
3. Evaluate the real-world consequences of gender hierarchy

SOCIAL CONSTRUCTION

Social construction is the process by which specific ideas or concepts are assigned a definition that creates social meaning (Lorber 1994). Society tries to make sense of our world—this is nothing new—so it creates a fictional "story" that allows us to put people into social groups.

Imagine a row of cardboard moving boxes. All the stuff needs to fit into the boxes in an organized way, so we take a big marker and write labels on the outside flaps so that we know how to sort them. This is how social construction works. Societies (or the humans within societies) want to make sense of the people around them, so they create "boxes" (or labels) to attach to certain characteristics. Each of these labels is given social meaning. The meaning attached to an idea (or label, term, concept) exists only because that definition fits within society's current **hegemonic norms**, the commonly held beliefs about inequality situated within a current place and time (Wade and Ferree 2019).

One of these created labels is "gender." You've already learned that gender and biological sex are different. Gender is assigned at birth based on characteristics that society deems important—in this case, reproductive organs. But the word "gender" doesn't mean anything significant in our culture until we say it does; gender is socially constructed. Once we understand social construction, we're empowered to critically evaluate the cultural categories that affect the

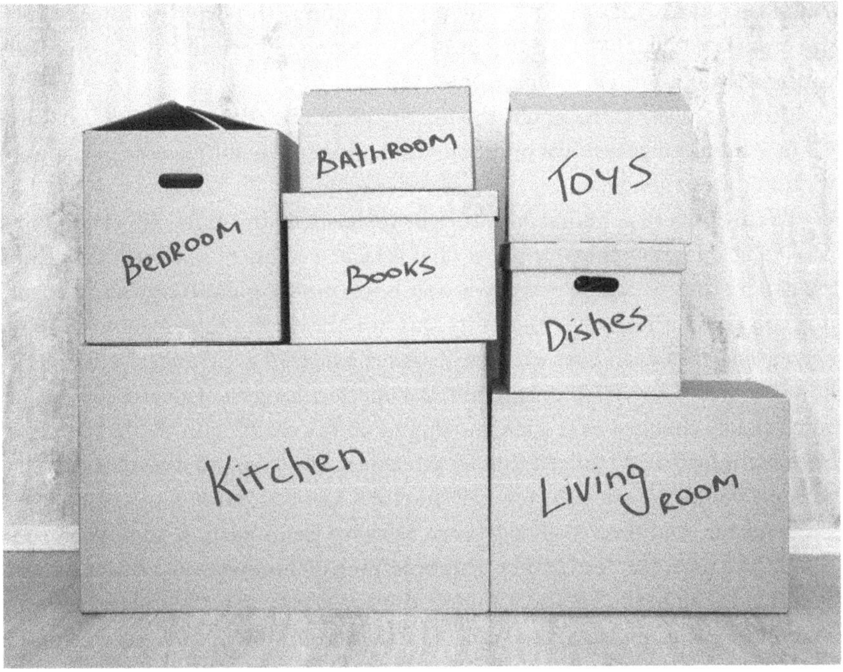

Figure 2.2 Labeling moving boxes—a lot like social construction! iSTOCK BY GETTY IMAGES

world we live in (Ryle 2018). You might be asking yourself, "How do I know if an idea is socially constructed?" Good question. There are two easy tests you can apply to any concept. If the concept question passes either of these two tests or analyses, you know that it is socially constructed.

Historical Analysis

Even though this is not a history textbook, we still need to look at the past or the historical context. When we stop learning about the historical background of concepts, we start to assume that today's ideas are defined in the same way they were in the past. We make the critical error of assuming that a concept is immutable, unchanging, or static. Now, you know what assuming does, right? It makes us stubbornly think we undeniably know something that is untrue.

If an idea is indeed unchanging, static, or immutable, then society would have been observing, analyzing, and discussing this concept in the same way across time. For example, we know that grass is green (or sometimes brown). This is a concept that we believe to be true in the present time. When we look at historical literature and scientific analysis, we see the same observations.

There isn't a text that says, "The grass is maroon with purple polka dots." No, the grass is green, and this concept is unchanging historically; it is *not* socially constructed but rather biological.

However, let's think about the history of gender. Can you think back fifty years, a hundred years, five hundred years and see any differences in the ways we think about gender?

Walk down the children's clothes or toy aisle in any major US retailer and you'll quickly notice that our society has attached colors to sex (well, they think it's gender, but we know better). Blue = boys, pink = girls. Historically speaking, this "blue is for boys" mentality was not always the case. Pink had always been associated with boys because it was considered a "stronger" color. Blue, however, was seen as dainty and prettier—perfect for girls (Paoletti 2012). This trend slowly changed over time, moving to unisex clothing in the 1970s. However, manufacturers realized that by attaching new colors to different genders, parents would buy entirely new clothes, toys, and decorations to assimilate to these norms, and then likely purchase all these items again if an opposite-sex sibling was born (Paoletti 2012). This blue/pink dichotomy was a business decision that began in the 1980s. Manufacturers guessed correctly, and their profits soared. At the same time, they created new gender norms related to color. Of course, this is starting to change again.

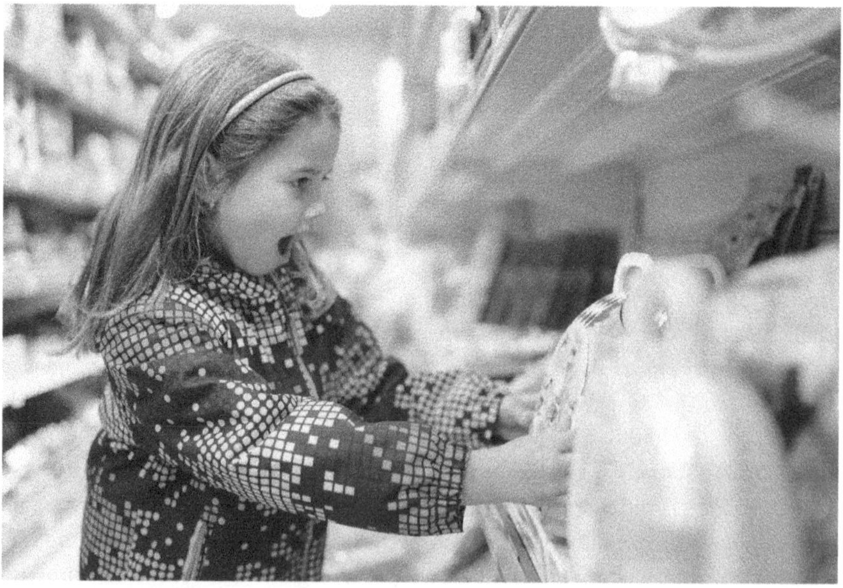

Figure 2.3 Although toy aisles cannot be labeled "boy" or "girl," we still see gendered toys.
iStock by Getty Images

Another big moment in the history of gender was when women began entering the paid workforce en masse in the late 1960s–1970s. Before the second-wave feminist movement, which focused on equal rights and women's inclusion in the workforce, women (particularly white, middle-, and upper-class women) followed the strict gender roles of taking care of the home and children while men completed paid labor and provided monetarily. The gender roles attached to masculinity and femininity were clear, and severe social stigma awaited anyone who deviated from these norms. Thanks to the hard work of

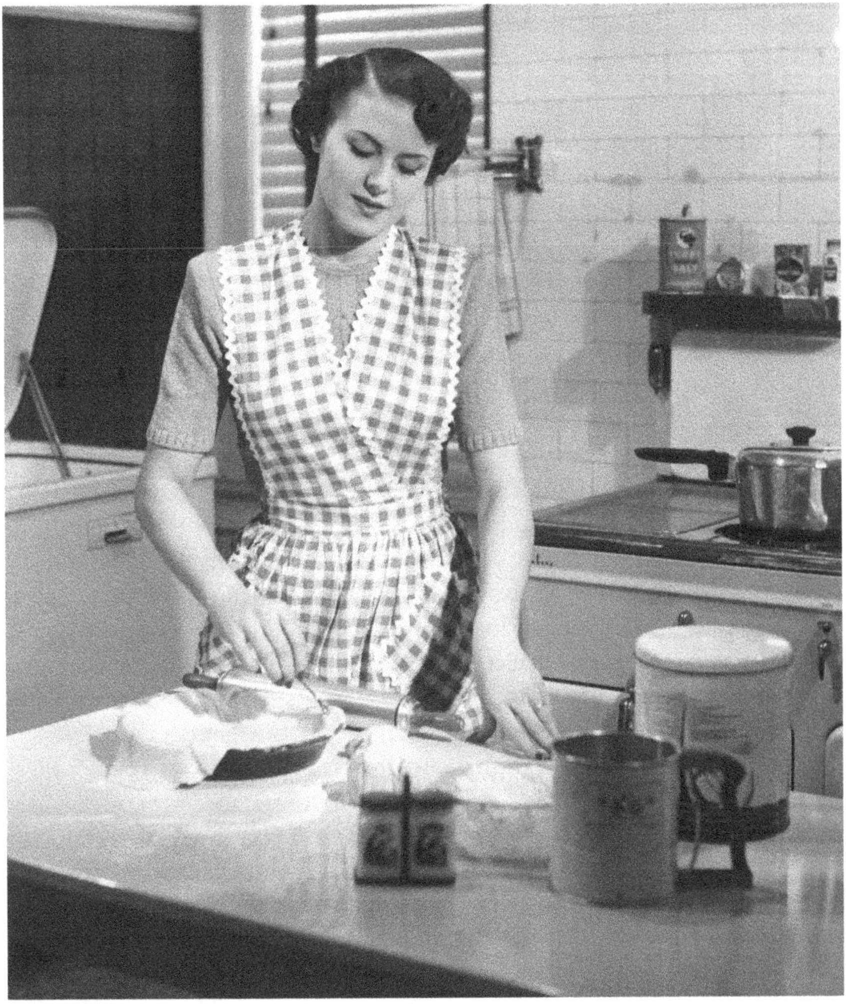

Figure 2.4 Traditional gender roles leave women spending plenty of time in the kitchen.
ISTOCK BY GETTY IMAGES

many activists, those gender norms have changed. Well, maybe not completely, but we know that women are in the workforce more than ever, are enrolling in colleges at higher rates than their male peers, and are actively engaging in all spheres of our society (see chapter 11 for more information) (Bureau of Labor Statistics 2019; National Center for Education Statistics 2018).

The point? The ways we think about gender have changed! Because our understanding of gender has changed across history, we know that the concept is socially constructed.

Social Contextual Analysis

The second test you can apply to a concept to determine whether it's socially constructed is an analysis of social context. **Social context** refers to the varying micro (personal, individual level) influences and macro (societal, institutional level) forces that constantly shape our individual experiences and interactions with others. We need to understand that our personal beliefs do not simply originate within us but are socialized into us through formal and informal interactions with others. **Socialization** is the way we learn the norms of a particular society. The primary agents of socialization are family, peers, school, religion, and the media. This means that we are always learning the expectations of society, either formally or informally, through interactions with our social world. Social context matters because our cultural norms and values help us create the stories we tell ourselves to make sense of the world.

Gender socialization is the process through which we learn society's definitions of masculinity and femininity. For example, sociologist Patricia Collins discusses the concept of controlling images. Controlling images are created to make forms of oppression, like poverty, racism, and sexism, appear normal and expected parts of life (Collins 2004). For example, in the United States, the media typically depicts Black women as "bitches" (i.e., loud, aggressive) or hypersexual, and Black men are shown as thugs, athletes, or pimps (Golash-Boza 2021). These images do not reflect the reality of Blackness in the United States; however, the prevalence of these depictions alters the way that we think about race. They socialize us into the assumed norms of gender, race, and social class.

What happens if we fail to analyze the social context in which a concept or idea resides? We assume that the way we make sense of an idea (through our individual lens) is the same way that others think of the idea. Again, assumptions are doing us no favors here. We know that peoples' perspectives of the world are largely influenced by the culture in which they're embedded. For example, have you ever studied abroad and made a seemingly harmless gesture

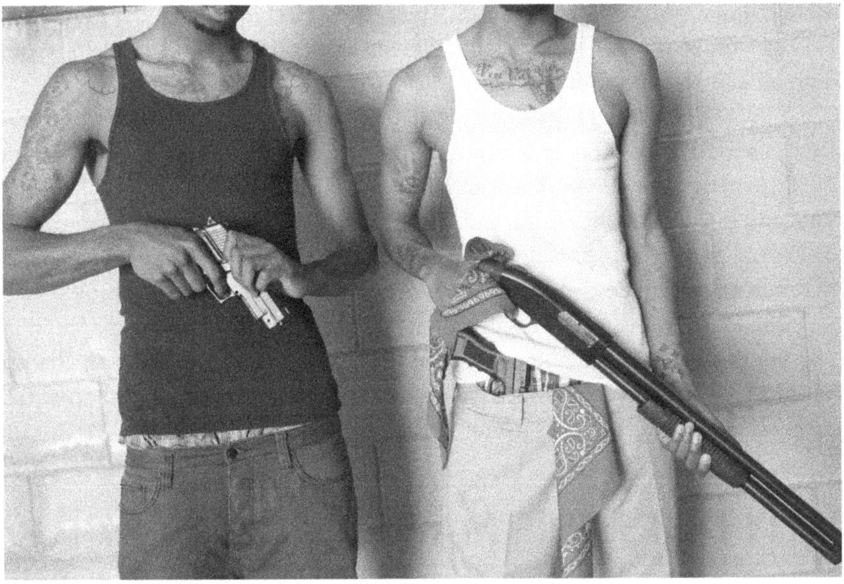

Figure 2.5 Portraying Black men as aggressive and dangerous is a common controlling image. iStock by Getty Images

that offended everyone around you? Have you ever traveled to another region of the United States and felt deeply uncomfortable because you did not "fit in"? Most of us can relate to these awkward experiences. Although this text focuses primarily on the United States, let's take a moment to think about gender from a cross-cultural (or social contextual) perspective.

In 2018, a major news headline was that women in Saudi Arabia were given the right to drive (Specia 2019). Yes, women were not allowed to drive until 2018! Women's rights activists in Saudi Arabia were imprisoned and put on trial for their advocacy work to lift the driving ban (Perez-Pena and Yee 2019). Many Americans were shocked at this cultural difference between the Middle East and the United States. As of 2022, the male guardianship system is still in place in Saudi Arabia, which requires a male guardian to consent before a woman can travel abroad, marry, receive a passport, or be released from prison (Human Rights Watch 2023). Despite international pressure to increase women's equality in this country, these oppressive policies remain intact. Most see the United States as much different, a beacon of equality.

However, the United States' political system tells a different story. Rwanda, a country in central Africa, has the largest number of women elected representatives in the world at 61.8 percent (UN Women 2019). How does the United

States compare? As of 2024, only 28.2 percent of elected seats in Congress were held by women (Center for American Women and Politics 2024). This is a record high for US women serving in these roles.

How about elected heads of state (like presidents or prime ministers)? Sri Lanka, an island country in South Asia, elected their first woman president in 1960; Argentina in 1974; Pakistan in 1988; Haiti in 1995; Peru in 2003; and Thailand in 2011 (Wills, Smith, and Hicks 2019). The United States? No woman has ever been elected president of the United States. This analysis shows us that our American ideas about gender are not as equal as we might think.

The experiences we have with gender, the ways that we define masculinity and femininity, and the norms that we associate with those labels all change based on cultural context. Because we can see these changes based on social context, we know gender is socially constructed.

WHY DOES THIS MATTER?

At this point in your reading, you might be asking yourself, "So what?" That's a legitimate question. If gender is socially constructed (it is), then the concept has no true meaning. In a perfect world, that would be true; however, in our society, socially constructed labels have deep and impactful meanings. That's because our society uses these labels to place groups of people in hierarchies. A **hierarchy** is the societal differentiation of power based on one's social grouping. People are labeled based on historically relevant, societally determined criteria. Next, people are put into groups based on those labels, and those groups are ranked. This means that some social groups, based solely on their societal label, have access to more power, wealth, and societal prestige than others.

To help visualize a hierarchy, consider a ladder. A ladder has rungs that are steps used to get to the desired "top." Our societal hierarchies operate like this because groups of people (in their socially constructed categories) are placed on a fictional rung on society's ladder. From the very beginning, some groups begin on the lower rung of the ladder. Is it possible for these lower-placed groups to get to the top? Sure, but they have farther to go, and will likely have more obstacles in their way. Remember, these obstacles have nothing to do with individual personalities or inadequacies but are only the effect of macro-level social hierarchy. Conversely, those higher on the social hierarchy will reach the top of the ladder much easier, as they have access to social privileges to assist their trip. This, again, isn't a result of any personal traits—just an outcome of the hierarchy.

When people say that they "reject" labels and don't like to categorize people, I often agree; however, even if we do not embrace a particular grouping,

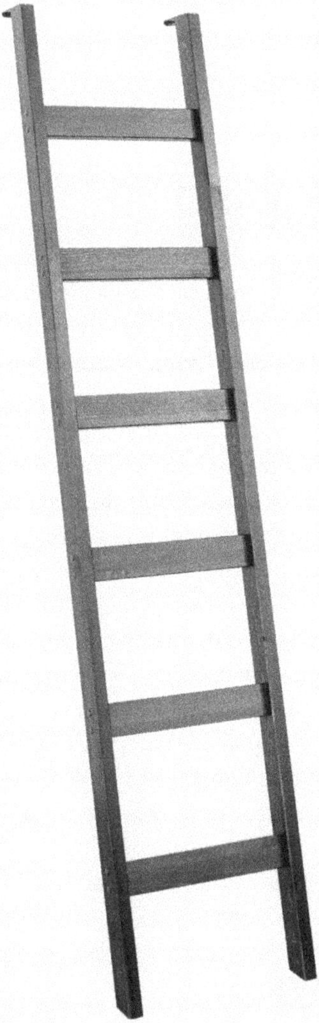

Figure 2.6 Social hierarchy can be illustrated using a ladder with each rung representing a relative amount of power and privilege allocated to a specific social identity group.
iSTOCK BY GETTY IMAGES

society still does. Like it or not, we are members of a hierarchal society, and our individual experiences and opportunities drastically change based on our social location. Some people are inherently advantaged, while some people are inherently disadvantaged simply because of their social categorization.

Hierarchy creates structured inequality in the allocation of societal rewards, privileges, and resources. Social scientists continue to empirically measure the effects of individual and institutional discrimination and have found that being in an oppressed social category negatively affects many life outcomes. This book outlines multiple examples of structural inequality and discrimination.

MOVING FORWARD

To truly understand the social construction of gender, we need to hold two seemingly contradictory concepts in our heads. **First, gender is a socially constructed label.** Gender labels do not inherently have any meaning. Society has determined who is labeled "man," "woman," or "other" and defines what those labels mean. Definitions of masculinity and femininity have changed over time and are likely to continue to evolve. Across cultures, the ways that people perform gender are drastically different, and each culture employs differing narratives to justify their perspectives. These differences will likely remain intact. In this regard, we could say that gender is not actually "real."

We must also remember that the hierarchy imposed on socially constructed categories is real in its effect (Ryle 2018). **Gender labels are real in their consequences.** Because our society has decided to rank the category of "man" or "masculine" above "woman" or "feminine," women as a group experience oppression and inequality. Women's lower social location on the hierarchy means that they receive unequal distribution of power, wealth, and prestige. Scientists have measured this impact, and we'll discuss many examples of this later in the text. Gender norms, since they are socially constructed, are changing all the time. The significant impact of allowing children to express themselves as they are comfortable cannot be understated.

Key Takeaways

- Gender is socially constructed since we can see that our definitions of masculinity and femininity have changed across history and societal contexts.
- Gender labels matter because our society ranks social groups into a hierarchy.
- Social hierarchies unequally distribute power, wealth, and prestige, inherently advantaging men over women.
- While gender labels are socially constructed and without inherent meaning, their consequences are real in their effect.

3

REPRODUCTIVE JUSTICE
#MYBODYMYCHOICE

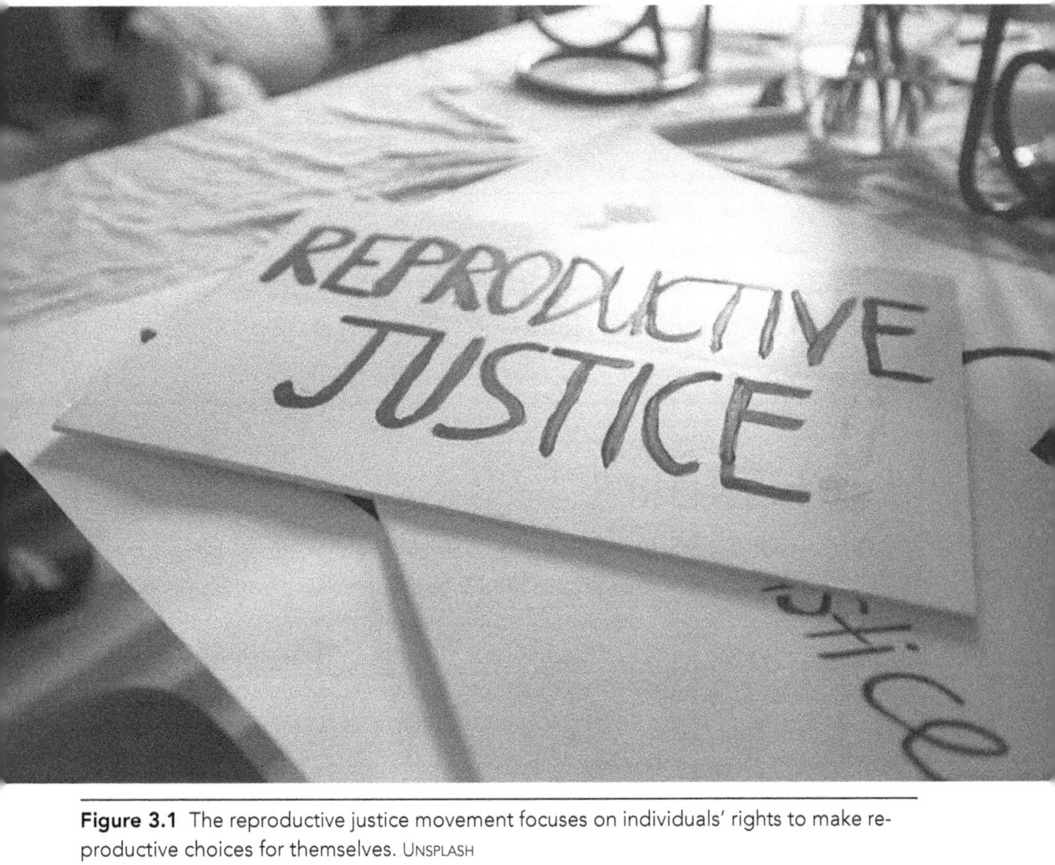

Figure 3.1 The reproductive justice movement focuses on individuals' rights to make reproductive choices for themselves. UNSPLASH

DESPITE YEARS OF activists and politicians lobbying for change, pregnancy discrimination is alive and well in the United States. Research indicates that regardless of occupation, pregnancy often marks the end of many women's careers (Kitroeff and Silver-Greenberg 2019). Top companies often sideline women when pregnant, deny raises or promotions, and fire them when they complain (2019). Given this context, some women have chosen not to have children.

The **reproductive justice movement** finds its roots in the human rights perspective, arguing that women have the right to make all reproductive health choices for themselves without interference. This includes access to affordable birth control, abortion, and other reproductive healthcare as well as pregnancy and childcare support (Ko 2016). Further complicating ideas about reproduction are micro-level individual relationships since women are not getting pregnant alone. We also know that reproductive health often intersects with racism and classism. No wonder this is a controversial topic! *Let's take this chapter to understand the historical and social implications of reproductive justice.*

LEARNING GOALS

By the end of this chapter, you should be able to

1. Define key elements of the reproductive rights debate
2. Explain the historical and present-day status of abortion rights
3. Assess social change efforts for reproductive justice

BIRTH CONTROL

Birth control is a method used to prevent pregnancy before it begins. Historically, men have controlled reproductive policy, and despite years of reform, those policies often do not meet the unique needs of women (Andersen 2015). Many assume that birth control methodology is a private choice; however, since birth control methods regulate both births and sexuality, the impact is more far-reaching. While many take for granted the availability of birth control methods, it was not until 1965 that the Supreme Court (*Griswold v. Connecticut*) established that using birth control was legal—for married women, at least (Andersen 2015).

Before the Supreme Court established the right to birth control, individual states could determine who had access to birth control and under which circumstances. This created long-lasting social norms about who gets to make reproductive health decisions. Instead of men and women making individual decisions with the support of medical professionals, the political climate and judicial leanings determined reproductive decisions (Andersen 2015).

Presently, the use of birth control is more popular than ever. According to the National Survey of Family Growth sponsored by the Centers for Disease Control and Prevention, most women utilize some type of contraception (Daniels and Abma 2020). Teens are more likely to use contraceptives at their first sexual experience—specifically 78 percent of women and 85 percent of men (Guttmacher Institute 2020). The most common types of birth control used by women are female sterilization, the pill, the male condom, and long-acting reversible contraception (i.e., IUDs) (Daniels and Abma 2020). The contraceptive method used varied based on age and race. Use of the pill decreased with age: 21.6 percent of females aged 20–29 use the pill compared to 6.5 percent of females aged 40–49. White women were most likely to use the pill (17.8%), while Hispanic and Black women utilized male condoms more frequently (11%) (Daniels and Abma 2020).

In 2022, the teen birth rate in the United States decreased to its record low (Centers for Disease Control and Prevention [CDC] 2023b). Researchers suggest that the declining birth rate is due to economic recession, easier access to contraception, less sexual intercourse, and more information about pregnancy prevention (Livingston and Thomas 2019). Abstinence-only education has proven widely ineffective (Mark and Wu 2022). Researchers estimate that only 3 percent of Americans wait until marriage to have sex (Khazan 2016).

Some religious institutions promote the signing of so-called purity pledges—or a formal document teens sign and vow to abstain from sex until

In the News . . .

In January 2019, Andrea Anderson, a mother of five children, called her gynecologist for a prescription for the morning-after pill after a "condom mishap" the night before. When Anderson went to her local Minnesota pharmacy for pickup, the pharmacist refused to fill the prescription due to personal "beliefs." Anderson sued the pharmacist for a violation of civil rights and gender discrimination (Sheperd 2019).

A 2022 Minnesota jury found that the pharmacist did not discriminate against Anderson but did offer a $25,000 judgment for emotional damages. Gender justice advocates express concern over the precedent this ruling sets, citing the dangers of politicizing a highly personal healthcare decision (Asma-Sadeque 2022).

marriage. However, research suggests that those pledges have alarming unintended consequences. Of those teens who pledge abstinence, 27 percent contracted the sexually transmitted infection HPV (human papillomavirus), and 18 percent had an unplanned pregnancy outside of marriage (Khazan 2016). Conversely, data show that funding comprehensive sex education reduced the teen birth rate by more than 3 percent (Mark and Wu 2022).

ABORTION

Abortion, or terminating a pregnancy before birth, is a highly controversial topic. On one side of the debate (self-defined as "**pro-life**"), proponents believe that a fetus is a human life at the time of conception, and ending that life is tantamount to murder. On the other side (self-defined as "**pro-choice**"), proponents believe that the right to **bodily autonomy**, or the ability to make choices about one's own body, is a critical human right. Allowing a woman to end her pregnancy is a personal choice, not a government decision.

Historically speaking, abortion was not as polarizing of a topic. In the early 1800s, ending a pregnancy within the first four months was commonplace

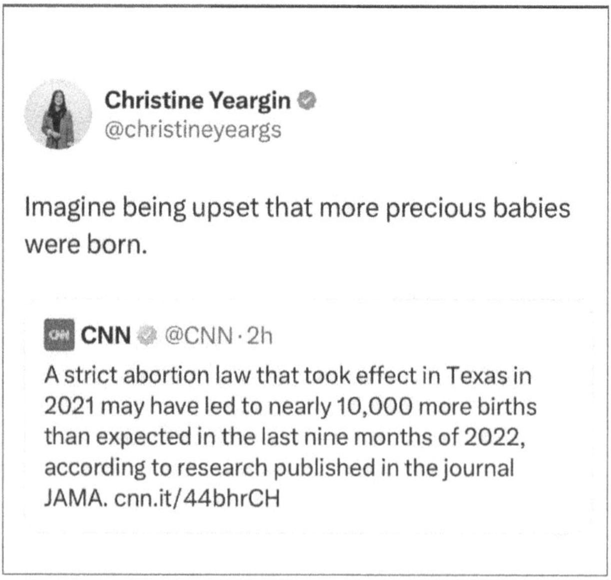

Figure 3.2 Pro-life activists respond to legislation changes.
Posted on X

and not seen as a moral decision (Andersen 2015). Colonial American church officials frowned upon the practice but treated it as evidence of premarital sex (Blakemore 2023a). The procedure was routinely provided by midwives and other physicians using herb tinctures and other manual methods. Abortion providers at this time could earn significant profits for their services. Abortion was not illegal until the mother felt the "quickening"—an ambiguous term signifying the movement of the fetus in utero. Even the Catholic church believed that no human life existed until this time (Blakemore 2023a; Reagan 1996).

Without the availability of birth control, women would give birth on average six times in their lifetime (Blakemore 2023a). Maternal death during childbirth was common, so women sought to reduce this risk. White middle- and upper-class married women were the largest group of women obtaining abortions (Andersen 2015). For enslaved women, abortion was more tightly regulated because they and their unborn children were considered property (Perrin 2001). However, Black midwives were known to practice folk medicine, providing education and support with ending pregnancy (Blakemore 2023a).

When did the social norms around abortion shift? In the late 1800s, doctors began protesting the commercialization of abortion procedures. At the same time, physicians and politicians began to worry that people of color (non-white immigrants) would begin having more children than white women (Reagan 1996). Remember, white women were having the bulk of abortions, so their birth rates were lower. Racist ideology won out, and the antiabortion platform was created (Andersen 2015). Abortion was now framed as immoral and illegal. After abortion became illegal, women still had abortions, but the difference was practitioners now worked behind closed doors. Women who could not afford such help often resorted to dangerous, life-threatening measures to end a pregnancy (Ravitz 2016).

FORCED STERILIZATION AND EUGENICS

Since the late 1800s, reproduction continued to be a means to control the population and enact racist ideologies. In the early twentieth century, scientific racism was rearing its ugly head under the guise of the eugenics movement. **Eugenics** is the practice of controlling "breeding" with the intent of decreasing undesirable traits and increasing desirable traits in future generations. Scientists believed that along with physical and cognitive capacities, social and behavioral traits were passed down genetically. Laziness, poverty, a tendency toward crime, and sexual promiscuity were all traits that scientists believed were passed down through DNA. Therefore, they recommended that the "biologically unfit" be sterilized (Golash-Boza 2021). **Sterilization** is a permanent medical procedure that eliminates a person's ability to reproduce.

Beginning in the early 1900s in the United States, approximately 60,000 people were forcibly sterilized, a third of whom were girls under the age of eighteen (Golash-Boza 2021; Ko 2016). Thirty-two states enacted federally funded sterilization programs throughout the twentieth century. People who were deemed "unfit" were mostly poor people of color and women. In a process referred to as a "Mississippi appendectomy," women of color in the South were subjected to unnecessary hysterectomies as practice for medical students (Ko 2016). In 1926, Carrie Buck was sterilized without her knowledge or consent in the state of Virginia. Her mother was involuntarily institutionalized for being "feeble-minded" and since it was believed that these traits were inheritable, Carrie was sterilized soon after she was born.

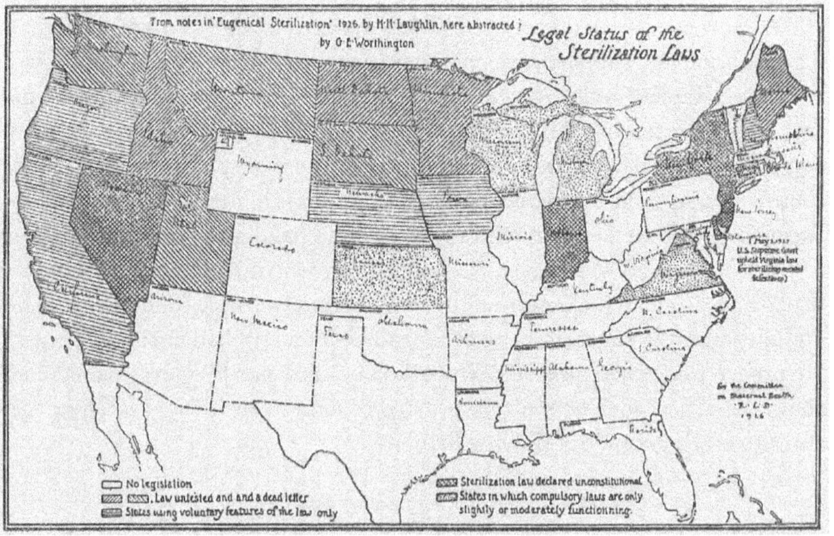

Figure 3.3 Eugenic sterilization map of the United States, 1926. WIKIMEDIA COMMONS

Victims who were illiterate were instructed to sign an "X" on consent documents. You're right if this sounds like a page out of Hitler's Nazi Germany. Published in 1916, the book *The Passing of the Great Race* by American Madison Grant outlined the requirements for a "master race." Later, Adolf Hitler referred to this book as his bible (Golash-Boza 2021). Most sterilizations stopped after the horrors of World War II, but North Carolina continued this practice through the 1970s.

Forced sterilization sounds like a tragedy of the past; however, in September 2020, a whistleblower complaint was filed claiming that women detained in a Georgia immigration facility were undergoing hysterectomies without their knowing. The complaint states that women, immigrants who often do not speak English, would wake up from surgery asking, "What happened to me?" or "Why did they do this to me?" (Dickerson, Wessler, and Jordan 2020).

House Speaker Nancy Pelosi and 173 fellow members of Congress wrote a letter condemning these actions and calling for an investigation. Pelosi stated that, if true, the conditions are a "staggering abuse of human rights" (McEvoy 2020). The initial review by five gynecologists found that the reasoning for the immigrant women's hysterectomies were "poorly supported" and that they were medically unnecessary (Dickerson, Wessler, and Jordan 2020). The White House agreed to pause any planned deportations of the women who experienced the abuse (Dwyer 2020). The investigation concluded that immigrant women were subjected to "excessive, invasive and often unnecessary gynecological procedures" (Montoya-Galvez 2022).

ABORTION PREVALENCE

Since the mid-1990s, abortions have generally decreased in the United States (Diamant and Mohamed 2023). The CDC collected abortion data from forty-eight states between 2007 and 2016. They found that the abortion rate had decreased by 26 percent over that period (Glenza 2019b). According to the Guttmacher Institute, a reproductive rights nonprofit agency, the current abortion rate is at its lowest since 1973 (Glenza 2019a).

The Centers for Disease Control and Prevention (CDC) states there were 11.2 abortions in the United States per 1,000 women (ages 15–44) in 2022 (Diamant and Mohamed 2023). Fifty-seven percent of women who obtain abortions are in their twenties, and 31 percent are in their thirties (Kortsmit et al. 2022). The majority (86%) of women who accessed abortion care were unmarried. When analyzing abortion care by race in 2020, 39 percent of all women who had abortions were Black, 33 percent were White, and 21 percent were Hispanic (Diamant and Mohamed 2023).

Despite controversial political interventions, researchers attribute the declining abortion rate to the decreasing fertility rate of US women (Glenza 2019a). After the COVID-19 pandemic, there was a marked decline in births, which then stabilized in 2022. Women are electing to have children later in life, which accounts for fewer births overall (Matthews 2023). American women are now predicted to have an average of one child over their life course (Bendix and Murphy 2023). Most women who access abortion services are already mothers, are in their twenties, and have never had a previous abortion (Glenza 2019b).

The CDC reports 58 percent of women who had an abortion in 2020 were getting one for the first time. The vast majority of abortions happen during the first trimester (93%), at or before the thirteenth week of pregnancy (Diamant and Mohamed 2023).

MATERNAL MORTALITY

Maternal mortality is the term used when a woman dies because of pregnancy-related complications (Katella 2023). Among high-income countries, the United States has one of the highest levels of maternal mortality (second only to Mexico) (OECD 2022). Maternal deaths are highest in the following states: Arkansas (43.5 deaths per 100,000 live births), Mississippi (43.0 deaths per 100,000 live births), and Tennessee (41.7 deaths per 100,000 live births) (KFF 2023). Over two million women live in **maternity care deserts**, or locations without access to birthing centers or general maternal care (March of Dimes 2022). The Maternal Vulnerability Index (MVI) is a tool developed to identify the locations in the United States where mothers are at the most risk for negative pregnancy-related health outcomes. The index compiles risk factors including personal, clinical, and environmental context (Surgo Ventures 2023). A higher score indicates a higher risk (see table 3.1).

Mothers are most at risk in Southern states and high-poverty areas. Across the United States, however, women of color are more likely than white women to live in areas lacking resources for maternal care (CDC 2023a). The data shows that Black women in the United States are four times more likely to die from pregnancy-related causes than white women (41 maternal deaths per

TABLE 3.1 Maternal Vulnerability Index Scores by State, 2021

0 = the least vulnerable, 100 = the most vulnerable

State	Maternal Vulnerability Index Score (0–100)
Colorado	0 (Very Low)
Vermont	2 (Very Low)
Illinois	50 (Moderate)
Alaska	54 (Moderate)
Mississippi	98 (Very High)
Alabama	100 (Very High)

TABLE 3.2 Maternal Vulnerability Index Scores by Race, 2021

0 = the least vulnerable, 100 = the most vulnerable

Maternal Race	Maternal Vulnerability Index Score (0-100)
Black	52
American Indian/Alaska Native	50
Hispanic/Latino	42
White	40
Pacific Islander	29
Asian	28

Source: CDC 2023a; adapted from Surgo Ventures 2023

100,000 live births versus 14 maternal deaths per 100,000 live births) (CDC 2023a). Women of color consistently experience higher MVI scores than white women, as shown in table 3.2. With all other factors being equal, a low-risk Black mother is more likely to die from childbirth than a low-risk white woman (Katella 2023).

REPRODUCTIVE JUSTICE AND PUBLIC POLICY

According to a July 2022 survey, 62 percent of Americans believe that abortion should be legal in all or most cases (Pew Research Center 2022). The watershed legislation related to abortion is ***Roe v. Wade***. Before this ruling, states severely regulated the use of abortion and focused legislation against practitioners seeking to offer abortion. The idea was that pregnant women needed to be protected from harmful medical interventions (Pew Research Center 2013). As women's movements began changing social norms, beliefs about women's sexuality began to shift. By 1970, twelve states, including Colorado, New York, and Hawaii, had decriminalized abortion during the early stages of pregnancy. In January 1973, the US Supreme Court ruled in *Roe v. Wade* that women have the constitutional right to terminate their pregnancy (Pew Research Center 2013). In this 7–2 ruling, the Supreme Court ruled that a woman's constitutional right to privacy and liberty granted her the right to abortion. However, as Supreme

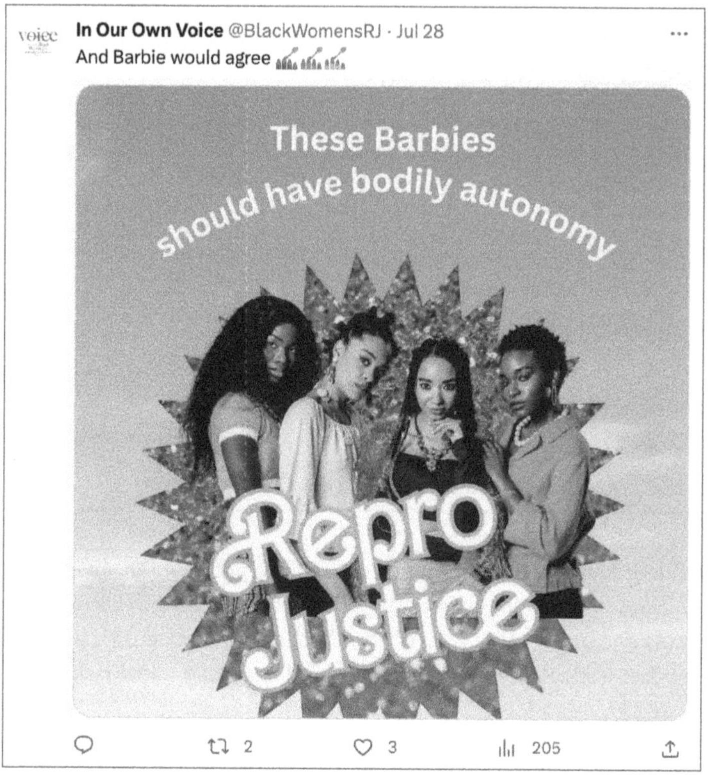

Figure 3.4 In Our Own Voice: a reproductive justice organization for women of color. Posted on Instagram

Court justices began to retire, the political leanings of new justices began to shift the court.

On June 24, 2022, the US Supreme Court reversed *Roe v. Wade* and removed the constitutional right to abortion (Totenberg and McCammon 2022). Data show 57 percent of Americans disapprove of this court ruling (43% strongly disapprove, 41% approve, 25% strongly approve) (Pew Research Center 2022). These responses are largely divided by political affiliation, with 82 percent of Democrats disapproving of the court decision, and 70 percent of Republicans approving of the court decision. For Americans under the age of thirty, 69 percent disapprove of the ruling; among Asians 72 percent disapprove, and for Black Americans, 67 percent disapprove. Adults in these groups are most likely to disagree with the ruling as well as those with a college education (60% disapprove). White Evangelical Protestants are most likely to approve of the Supreme Court's ruling (71% approve). Women (62%) are more likely to disapprove than men (52%) (Pew Research Center 2022).

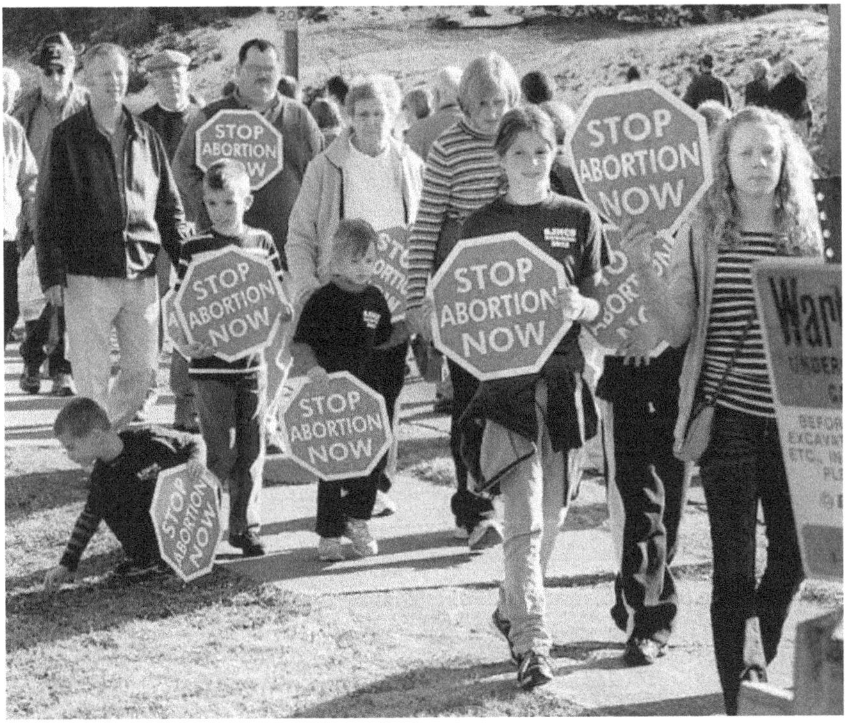

Figure 3.5 Pro-life "Stop Abortion" rally. UNSPLASH

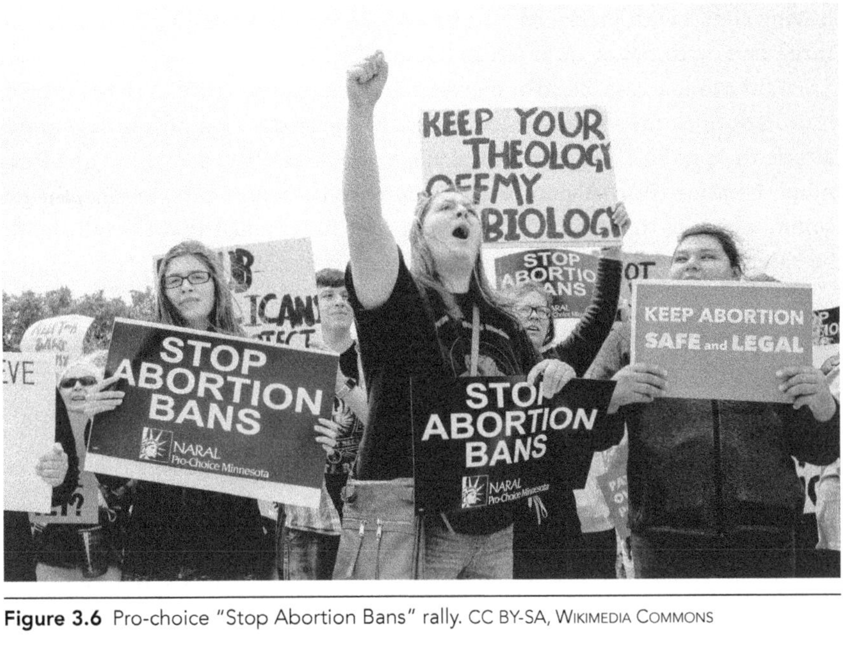

Figure 3.6 Pro-choice "Stop Abortion Bans" rally. CC BY-SA, WIKIMEDIA COMMONS

In the News . . .

In fall 2022, twelve-year-old Ashley was playing outside her Mississippi home when she was attacked and raped. Not knowing what to do, Ashley remained silent about the assault. When the physical symptoms became overwhelming, Ashley's mom took her to the emergency room. It was there that Ashley learned she was pregnant as a result of the rape (Alter 2023).

When Ashley's mother inquired about terminating the pregnancy, she was told that the nearest abortion clinic was in Chicago. Since the overturn of *Roe v. Wade*, Mississippi enacted an abortion ban. Although the ban does provide exceptions for rape, Ashley was too scared to discuss the trauma of the assault with the medical provider. Ashley's mother was unable to afford the long trip to Chicago, so the pregnancy continued. At thirteen years old, Ashley gave birth to a baby boy. With family support, Ashley started seventh grade in the fall of 2023 (Alter 2023).

With the federal protections removed, individual states now have the right to enforce state-level abortion "**trigger bans**"—abortion laws that become active in the absence of federal prohibitions (Totenberg and McCammon 2022). Fifteen states currently prohibit abortion (as of August 2023): Idaho, North Dakota, South Dakota, Wisconsin, Missouri, Indiana, Kentucky, West Virginia, Tennessee, Alabama, Mississippi, Arkansas, Louisiana, Oklahoma, and Texas (*New York Times* 2023). Patients have flooded to states where abortion is legal, leaving clinics with increased wait times for care—in some cases, from two to three days up to two to three weeks (Quinn 2023).

With clinic access illegal or inaccessible, women often turn to at-home medication options for abortion care. Access to these abortion pills is now under attack. In April 2023, a Texas federal judge ruled that the federal Food and Drug Administration (FDA) had incorrectly approved the use of mifepristone, the pill commonly used to terminate pregnancy. The judge ruled that the pill should be banned (Boodman 2023). However, soon after, a Washington federal judge

In the News . . .

A twenty-one-year-old woman from Oklahoma was convicted of first-degree manslaughter after experiencing a miscarriage. Pregnant at nineteen, Britney Poolaw miscarried at fifteen weeks gestation. An autopsy confirmed several abnormalities and the presence of methamphetamines and amphetamines. A jury deliberated for less than three hours and found Poolaw guilty of first-degree manslaughter. She was sentenced to four years in prison (Cruz 2021).

ruled that mifepristone should be available. Because of these dueling decisions, a federal appeals court determined that mifepristone should remain legal until the Supreme Court responds (Belluck and Liptak 2023).

MOVING FORWARD

Reproductive rights—access to abortion, birth control, and pregnancy prevention—are at the center of political ideologies, religious worldviews, and social movement activism. Activists in this movement fight equally for the right to have or not have a child, to parent those children, and to control personal birthing options (Ross 2020). Again, the idea of bodily autonomy is key for this movement—every individual has the right to make unimpeded decisions about their own bodies. Of utmost importance to this movement is centering the needs and experiences of traditionally marginalized people: poor, women of color, and immigrants.

Access to safe and affordable reproductive healthcare is a primary concern for activists. Many online clinics and pharmacies are used to address this concern. For example, Aid Access is an organization that allows women to consult with a doctor online and receive medical abortion prescriptions through the mail (Aid Access 2020). The pills are meant for women who are ten weeks pregnant or less. Since the overturn of *Roe v. Wade*, women have been using virtual clinics more than ever—an increase of 137 percent since the Supreme Court decision (Society of Family Planning 2023). Reduction of telehealth abortion access is most likely to negatively affect the care of low-income people and communities of color. The Protecting Access to Medication Abortion Act of 2023 (H.R.767) would require the FDA to allow telehealth providers to prescribe mifepristone.

Other activists are fighting against misinformation disseminated locally. Faith-based clinics that advertise access to free sexually transmitted infection (STI) and pregnancy tests are not healthcare providers. Therefore, they are not covered under the Health Information Portability and Accountability Act (HIPAA) and can disclose personal information at any time. Usually funded by local churches and faith-based nonprofits, these clinics meet extensively with young women, oftentimes sharing their religious beliefs. These include abstinence from sexual behaviors before marriage, the ineffectiveness of contraception, and the danger of abortion (Hutchings 2019). One college student in Colorado started an awareness campaign to expose the actions of a local clinic offering testing, but which provided fellow students with misinformation and shame (Hutchings 2019).

More misinformation is refuted in the newly published "Turnaway Study," which scientifically examined the effects on women who received or were denied abortion services (Bixby Center for Global Reproductive Health [BCGRH] 2020). Researchers recruited one thousand women from thirty abortion clinics and conducted eight thousand interviews (Baker 2020). This study overwhelmingly found that abortion does not harm women, but rather 95 percent of women were confident in their choice (BCGRH 2020). Lack of abortion access disproportionately affects poor families. Women who were denied abortion services were four times more likely to have a household income below the federal poverty level (BCGRH 2020). Their existing children were also less likely to achieve developmental milestones (Baker 2020). Writing for *Ms. Magazine*, Carrie Baker has one main takeaway message: trust women (2020).

Key Takeaways

- Although access to birth control varies, the use of contraception is more popular than ever.
- Popular opinion about the morality and legality of abortion has changed over time.
- Eugenics was a racist pseudoscience meant to regulate the population, which included condemning white women for abortion but forcibly sterilizing women of color.
- The Supreme Court overturned *Roe v. Wade*, thus removing federal protections to abortion access.
- The reproductive justice movement uses a social justice framework to advocate for individual choice regarding pregnancy, birthing, and parenting.

4

TRANSGENDER AND NONBINARY IDENTITIES
#PRONOUNSMATTER

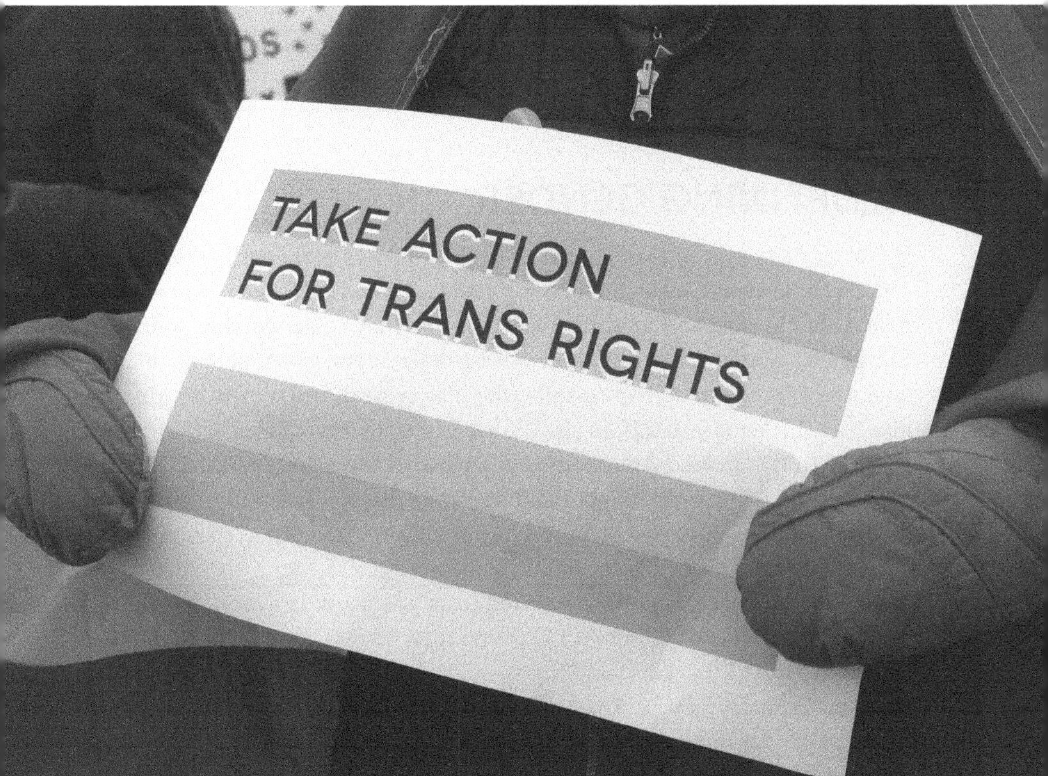

Figure 4.1 Take Action for Trans Rights Rally. Marc Nozell, CC BY 2.0, Wikimedia Commons

IT'S HARD TO ENVISION a social world beyond a person being a "man" or "woman." Indeed, gender is a key sorting mechanism in our society, so most have a hard time imagining a world that is nonbinary. Social change is happening, however. Gen Zers are rejecting the gender binary altogether (Edelman 2019). They are quick to define gender identity as a social construction and more openly accept nonbinary or transgender friends (Edelman 2019). *What does it mean to be a person who is transgender or nonbinary? Why is there so much legal debate about pronouns? Let's go!*

LEARNING GOALS

By the end of this chapter, you should be able to

1. Summarize the key terms related to gender identity.
2. Analyze the political landscape and legislative restrictions against equality for transgender people.
3. Evaluate the social change efforts meant to support transgender people.

REDEFINING GENDER

Historians cite examples of gender nonconformity as early as the seventeenth century. In ancient Greece and Rome, priests (*gala* and *galli*), who were assigned male at birth, routinely appeared as women so they could worship goddesses. Indigenous communities recognize third-gender or two-spirit people. In South Asia, the *hijra* are nonbinary people who play critical, ritual roles within communities (Blakemore 2022). In the United States, however, it wasn't until 1952 that the first transwoman obtained gender-affirming surgery. Christine Jorgensen, a US Army veteran, obtained hormone therapy and multiple surgeries in Denmark. The publicity surrounding Jorgensen's transition led to the widespread use of the term "transgender" (Blakemore 2022).

Being **transgender**, often referred to as just *trans*, is a term describing a person's experience of disconnect between their sex assigned at birth and their gender identity. Clinicians label this feeling of discomfort as **gender dysphoria** (American Psychiatric Association 2023). To be clear, the desire to deviate from the gender binary is not an illness or dysfunction; however, many people experience individual and societal distress when breaking away from gender norms (American Psychiatric Association 2023).

Remember what we covered in our first chapter? We learned about the differences between biological sex, gender identity, gender expression, and sexual orientation. Upon birth, we are assigned a sex. Some are **assigned female at birth** (or AFAB) and others are **assigned male at birth** (or AMAB). Those who have reproductive structures of both male and female bodies are labeled **intersex** or **differences in sex development (DSD)**. "Hermaphrodite" is an outdated term that assumes that a person is both fully male and fully female; this is biologically impossible. Many intersex people find this word offensive and stigmatizing, and it should no longer be used (Cleveland Clinic 2023b).

The assumptions don't end there. Our society has falsely assumed that a person's assigned sex also indicates their **gender identity** or their internal gender identification. People assigned male at birth are also assigned the gender of "boy." People assigned female at birth are assigned the gender of "girl." Sometimes, this works out. As the person develops, they may realize that their gender identity and assigned sex reflect their true sense of self. Those people are called **cisgender**—the connection between their assigned gender identity and biological sex follows societal conventions.

However, not everyone has the privilege of this experience. Some people learn that their gender identity does not reflect the assumptions assigned at birth; their gender identity and assigned sex are not correlated as originally defined. Those people are called **transgender**—the connection between their gender identity and biological sex does not follow societal conventions. People who identify as men, despite their female sex assignment, are called **trans men.** Those who identify as women, despite their male sex assignment, are called **trans women**. People who do not identify with the traditional gender binary are called **gender nonconforming, genderqueer,** or **nonbinary.**

What about people born intersex? In the United States, experts estimate that 1 out of 100 people are intersex (Cleveland Clinic 2023b). Some variations can be detected in the fetus before delivery using ultrasound technology or amniocentesis (a diagnostic test where the fluid surrounding the fetus is tested for genetic abnormalities) (Boyd-Barrett 2023). However, the exact hormonal, genetic, and internal organ makeup is not yet known in those early moments in a delivery room. These assignments are a best guess based on external genitalia. Indeed, some intersex variations are not noticeable until puberty (Boyd-Barrett 2023).

Until recently, intersex children often underwent medically unnecessary surgery to conform their genitals to the gender binary. These children grew up being told that their biological sex and gender identity were both natural and aligned, but many kids knew differently. This caused undue anxiety, confusion, and for some, suicidal ideation. At present, medical professionals and surgery survivors continue to advocate for gender assignment surgery delay until the child can express their own wishes.

GENDER-AFFIRMING CARE

Some trans people decide to pursue **sex reassignment** or **gender confirmation surgery.** This may include top surgery, bottom surgery, and/or facial surgery completed with the goal of their physical bodies matching their gender identity (Cleveland Clinic 2023a). **Top surgery** is another term for chest feminization or masculinization and includes the removal of breast tissue or the addition of breast implants. **Bottom surgery** (metoidioplasty, phalloplasty, or vaginoplasty) includes rearranging tissue in the genital area to create a vagina or penis (Liang 2023). People might also take hormones (estrogen, testosterone blockers, and/or progesterone) to feminize or masculinize their bodies. The term to describe this process is called **transition** or **transitioning**.

Jazz Jennings told her parents at six years old that she was a girl, although she was assigned male at birth. Her willingness to discuss her experiences as

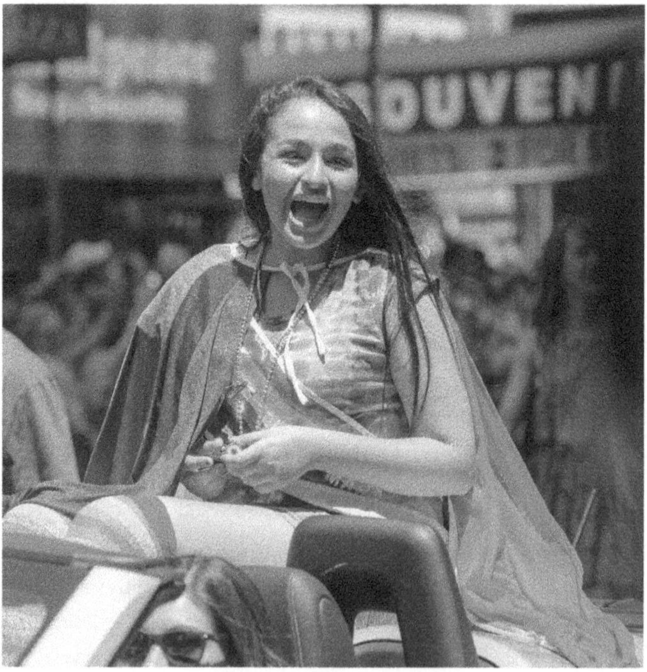

Figure 4.2 Activist Jazz Jennings continues to elevate the visibility of trans people at the NYC Pride Parade.

a transgender girl has increased trans visibility in the United States. Jennings coauthored a children's book titled *I Am Jazz*, which was also the name of her television show on TLC. She has been on the cover of multiple magazines, including *Time* and *Variety*. Jennings continues to be a tireless advocate for trans-inclusive policies. After being banned from playing her favorite sport after her transition, she successfully sued the US Soccer Federation to adopt more inclusive policies (Framke 2021).

Many transgender people never engage in these changes, however. Some trans folks argue that their problem isn't with their bodies; the problem is with others' perceptions and assumptions about their bodies. Other people can't afford the incredible costs associated with surgery, or don't have access to quality gender-affirming medical care.

PERFORMING GENDER

Whether we're cisgender, transgender, or nonbinary, we all perform gender every day. We might change the way that we sit in public spaces—tightly crossing our legs to convey femininity, or widely opening our knees (or manspreading) to convey masculinity. We might choose to soften our facial features and smile when passing a stranger, or harden our face and focus our eyes into a glare instead. Our gender identity often is reflected in our **gender expression** or our performance of gender.

Understanding the experience of transgender and nonbinary people requires a deeper understanding of gender as a social construct (Barnes 2023). Transgender men have spoken about the drastic changes to their relationships after transitioning—the distancing of male friendships, and the lack of physical touch among friends. They also discuss the freedom of their new bodies—the male privilege of moving through the world without pepper spray (Barnes 2023).

One interesting example of transforming gender expression is the presence of **drag queens** and **drag kings** —men and women who dress in a stereotypically gendered manner. They might act in these traditionally gendered ways for entertainment or pay (Wade and Ferree 2019). Some have made a career out of these performances.

Several states have tried to pass legislation banning drag performances. North Dakota, Arkansas, Tennessee, and Montana have enacted laws about "adult performances," which they link to drag. Tennessee and Montana have passed laws that target drag performers specifically (Millhiser 2023). However, the federal courts have blocked these laws from passing, stating that the First Amendment protects such performances as free speech.

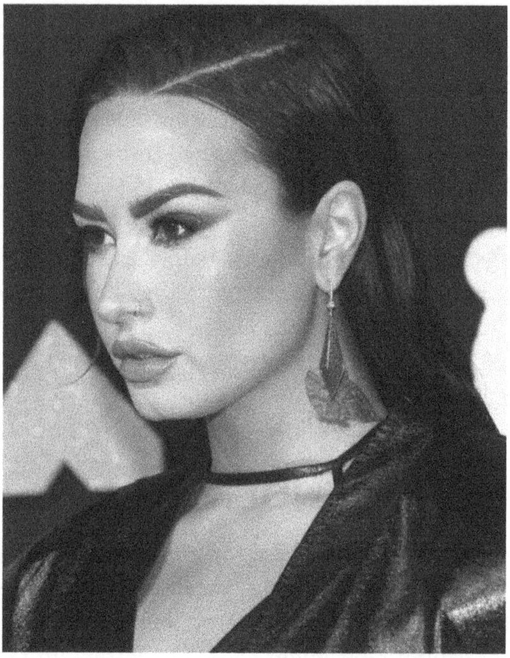

Figure 4.3 Actor and singer Demi Lovato at the 2023 MTV Video Music Awards. In 2021, Lovato came out as nonbinary using they/them pronouns. However, in 2023, she readopted she/her pronouns because explaining they/them was "exhausting" (Paul 2023).
POSTED ON INSTAGRAM

Beauty brands have increasingly marketed to gender nonconforming and trans consumers. Gender nonconforming models were prominently featured in Lady Gaga's 2019 launch of her makeup line Haus Laboratories (Riley 2019). Other product lines have followed with gender-neutral makeup products (see M•A•C and Morphe, for example). Makeup is used to play with gender norms and create an image that better reflects one's identity. Some critics, however, argue that this form of marketing is just another way for corporations to cash in on the LGBTQIA+ consumer (Riley 2019).

Generally, people feel strongly about expressing their gender in a way that is congruent with their identity. This is a privilege, however. Many trans and nonbinary people are unable to authentically express their gender identity. This may be for fear of ridicule or harassment, or concern about losing their jobs, friends, or family support. Increasingly, trans or nonbinary people might not express their gender identity because of fear of violence. According to the FBI's Uniform Crime Report (UCR), 4 percent of hate crimes were motived by a person's gender identity, and approximately 1 percent were motivated by gender (FBI 2022). The UCR collects data from law enforcement to disseminate this data, but we know that many violent acts of hate are never reported. While gender identity is not the same as sexual orientation, many make assumptions about a person's sexuality based on appearance. Seventeen percent of hate crimes were motivated by a person's perceived sexual orientation (FBI 2022).

PRONOUNS—WE ALL USE THEM!

We all use pronouns to refer generally to a person without using their name. When a person decides to come out as transgender or nonbinary, a change in their preferred pronouns typically follows. Traditionally, pronouns have preserved the gender binary: **she/her/hers** and **he/him/his**. Recently, trans and nonbinary people adopted singular "they" pronouns: **they/them/theirs.** As more awareness is brought to gender nonconforming identities, the sharing of personal pronouns and nongendered technology is becoming more popular. United Airlines announced that it will allow people to choose "Mx." as a nongendered honorific when booking flights (Saguy and Williams 2019).

The American Psychological Association maintains one of the leading style guides for writing and research. In the seventh edition of the APA style guide, the association embraced the singular use of the pronoun "they" in all forms of writing. This reflects an institutional change in the academic writing's acceptance of nonbinary identities (Lee 2019). The singular "they" was Merriam-Webster's "Word of the Year" in 2019. And while one author counted over 200 gender-neutral pronouns adopted across the ages, the singular "they" seems to be sticking (Steinmetz 2020).

Our information systems operate to keep trans and nonbinary people invisible. Computer code created in the 1990s and earlier coded "GENDER" as Boolean code: 0 = Male and 1 = Female. By coding this data field as binary, only two answers are recognized by the system. Changing this can become complex, as multiple sources utilize many databases' information. Changing this code would lead to errors in multiple forms of use. For example, university student data found in a portal will also be accessed by the registrar, financial aid, and advising. If the gender code is broken, all those departments will see errors in their reports. It can be done, however. New York University was the first higher education institution to allow students to manually change their gender identity in their student records (Broussard 2019).

Forty-four percent of US adults believe that online profiles and forms should provide an option besides male and female for those who don't identify

In the News . . .

Jonathan Van Ness is well known for his iconic role on *Queer Eye*, a Bravo then Netflix series which features the "Fab 5" team of gay fashion and lifestyle experts providing makeovers. In an interview with *Out Magazine*, he acknowledges that he never had to come out as gay—it was obvious to himself and others at an early age. However, it wasn't until 2019 when he publicly shared his gender identity, describing himself as genderqueer and nonbinary (Tirado 2019). While Van Ness uses he/him pronouns, he does not identify as a man.

as either (Parker, Menasce Horowitz, and Brown 2022). In 2014, Facebook was the first social media platform to allow over fifty custom gender options, including gender fluid, trans person, and two-spirit (Oremus 2014). However, despite all these options, the code remains a Boolean, with "null" appearing in the database for a person identifying as anything but male or female (Broussard 2019).

Awards ceremonies, such as the Oscars (film), Emmys (television), and Tonys (theater), traditionally have gendered awards categories. Best Actor or Best Female Artist have long been seen as prestigious, sought-after honors. But what happens when an artist is nonbinary and uses they/them pronouns? In 2019, Sam Smith, a popular English pop artist, publicly came out as nonbinary, yet he was nominated by the Brit Awards in the Top Male Artist category. Despite spokespeople for the major awards ceremonies claiming to celebrate inclusiveness, there have been no official changes to major award categories (Doyne 2023). However, several awards shows have removed gendered award categories, including the Grammys and MTV Video Music Awards (Buckley 2019).

Remember, always use the name, pronouns, and terminology as requested by the individual. Only 47 percent of US adults believe it is extremely or very important to use a person's new name and pronouns (Parker, Menasce Horowitz, and Brown 2022); however, advocates understand that proper pronoun use is critically important. Using a pronoun that does not reflect a person's gender identity is termed **misgendering**. Being misgendered can be invalidating, exhausting, and devaluing (Katz-Wise 2021).

Deadnaming is the act of calling a transgender person by a name they no longer use, most often their given name at birth. Using a name that reflects their gender identity is a critical part of a person's well-being, so it is important to always use the name as referenced by the person. What should you do if you misgender or deadname a person? Unfortunately, mistakes like this are going to happen. When learning of the offense, fight the urge to make excuses. Instead, quickly apologize and correct yourself (National Institutes of Health 2023).

PREVALENCE OF PEOPLE WHO ARE TRANSGENDER AND GENDER NONCONFORMING

A 2022 nationally representative survey found that 1.6 percent of US adults are trans or nonbinary. Among adults under thirty, 5.1 percent are trans or nonbinary, including trans men (2%), trans women (3%), and nonbinary (3%) (Brown 2022a). Twenty-six percent of adults say they know someone who uses they/them pronouns (Minkin and Brown 2021). Research indicates that approximately 3 percent of kids identify as transgender, gender nonconforming, or nonbinary (Rider et al. 2018).

Forty-four percent of US adults indicate that they personally know a transgender person, while 20 percent know someone who is nonbinary (A. Brown 2022a). People's understanding of gender identity, however, continues to shift in the opposite direction. Sixty percent of US adults believe that a person's gender identity is determined by their sex assigned at birth; this means more than half of American adults fully conflate the ideas of biological sex and gender identity. Interestingly, that percentage is an increase from previous data—it was 54 percent in 2017 (Parker, Menasce Horowitz, and Brown 2022). Not surprisingly, there is a strong correlation between beliefs that biological sex and gender identity can be different and opinions about transgender inclusion. Those who believe gender and sex can be different are also more likely to see discrimination against trans people and state that inclusion efforts haven't gone far enough (Parker, Menasce Horowitz, and Brown 2022).

Research indicates that attitudes about gender identity are largely correlated with age. Young adults ages 18–29 are most likely to understand the

In the News . . .

In 2021, a Colorado resident sued the US Department of State, saying that as a nonbinary person, there was no third gender option for US passports that reflected their gender identity. In April 2022, the Department of State responded to that request by adding a third gender option (Hernandez 2022b). Passport applications now allow male (M), female (F), or "unspecified or another gender identity" (X) (US Department of State 2023). Applauded by many, the State Department consulted feedback from the LGBTQIA+ community, Centers for Disease Control and Prevention, and the public before making the change. This is the first federal agency to adopt the third gender marker (Hernandez 2022b).

differences between gender identity and sex assigned at birth (50%), while US adults 50 and older are least likely to espouse those beliefs (30%) (Parker, Menasce Horowitz, and Brown 2022).

Americans are divided on the current legal and public policy inclusion responses. About 38 percent of US adults believe that our society has gone "too far" in accepting transgender people, while approximately the same amount (36%) claim that society hasn't gone "far enough" in acceptance (Parker, Menasce Horowitz, and Brown 2022).

TRANSGENDER IDENTITY AND PUBLIC POLICY

As awareness continues to spread about gender identity and transgender rights, people in the United States express complex feelings about the nonbinary community. Approximately 80 percent of US adults believe that there is at least some discrimination against transgender people (Parker, Menasce Horowitz, and Brown 2022).

Political affiliation is the most striking predictor of attitudes toward nonbinary people and trans-inclusive laws and policies. Democrats are four times more likely than Republicans to recognize the differences between gender identity and sex assigned at birth (Parker, Menasce Horowitz, and Brown 2022).

A return to legal protections for transgender people has been a recent priority. On January 20, 2021, the day that President Joe Biden took office, he signed an executive action that prohibited federal agencies from practicing sex discrimination, a definition that includes both sexual orientation and gender identity. As a result of this action, healthcare providers or other organizations that receive federal funding may not deny services to transgender individuals (Goldstein 2021). However, anti-trans legislation has been a key focus of Republican state lawmakers, proposing over 150 pieces of legislation in twenty-five states in 2022 (Astor 2023).

Bathroom Bills

While inclusion advocates spoke about this issue for years, the national debate began in March 2016, when North Carolina's House passed Bill 2. This legislation required transgender people to use the bathroom and locker rooms in public buildings that correspond with the gender assigned at birth (Phillips 2016). It also prohibited local governments from adopting antidiscrimination policies that support the LGBTQIA+ community (Levin 2019). Lawmakers

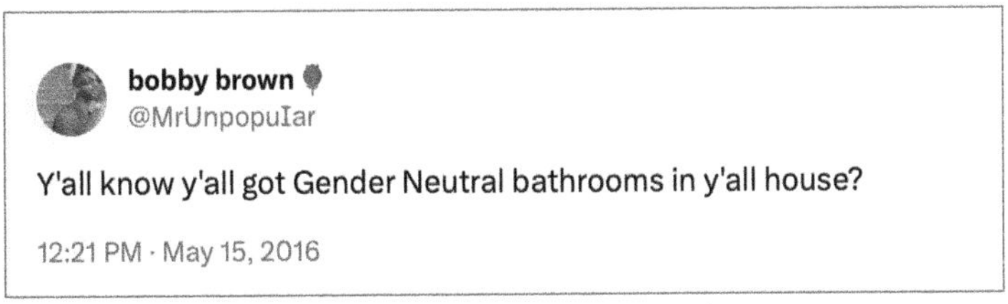

Figure 4.4 Gender-neutral bathrooms are commonplace in our homes. Why not in public spaces? POSTED ON X

contended that the bill was meant to protect women and children not just from transgender people but also from biological males entering women's bathrooms (Phillips 2016).

The response was immediate. Trans people spoke out about the dangers of entering bathrooms that do not match their gender identity, fearing that their lives would be in danger in those spaces (Phillips 2016). Corporations like PayPal stopped planned expansions in the state, and the NBA and NCAA moved events outside of North Carolina. These boycotts were predicted to cost North Carolina billions of dollars. In 2017, the state legislature passed a law that repealed House Bill 2 (Levin 2019), but the issue continues to be debated.

Under particular attack is the Obama-era interpretation of antidiscrimination legislation Title IX. **Title IX** is an educational amendment that forbids a publicly funded school from excluding from participation, denying benefits, or discriminating against a student based on their sex. The US Department of Education interpreted Title IX to mean that schools should treat transgender students in a way consistent with their gender identity (Williams 2021). This applied to school bathrooms and locker rooms. Despite this interpretation, individual school districts have adopted different policies. This was the case in a Virginia school district when the school board enacted a policy requiring students to use a bathroom consistent with their biological sex. After a string of legal battles, the Supreme Court ruled that students have the right to utilize the bathroom consistent with their gender identity (Williams 2021).

Transgender Athletes

A 2023 Gallup Poll found that 69 percent of US adults think that transgender athletes should be allowed to compete only on teams that match their birth sex (Jones 2023). This issue is being debated among local school districts, athletic governing bodies, and legislative bodies across the United States. Twenty-three states have passed legislation that limits transgender athletes participating on teams corresponding with their gender identity (K. Barnes 2022).

The issue made headlines when Idaho passed HB 500, barring transgender girls from playing on women's teams at publicly funded schools (K. Barnes 2022). Several national and global sports associations followed suit, including the International Olympic Committee. The protests continued as Lia Thomas, a transgender woman and swimmer at the University of Pennsylvania, won the Division I championship in 2022 (K. Barnes 2022). Protests continued with the filing of multiple Title IX complaints.

On April 6, 2023, the Biden administration released a list of new rules regarding transgender athletes in school sports (Tumin 2023). The U.S. Department of Education rule prohibits the blanket ban on transgender athletes in school sports as a violation of Title IX. However, it does allow individual school districts to restrict specific transgender athletes from participation if issues of fairness arise (Tumin 2023). This new rule has been criticized by both sides of the political aisle and has elicited hundreds of thousands of public comments (Knott 2023).

Restriction of Gender-Affirming Medical Care

Most US adults (64%) support laws that protect transgender and nonbinary people from discrimination (Parker, Menasce Horowitz, and Brown 2022). However, there is also a significant backlash to proposals codifying such ideas. Since 2020, thirty-six states have tried to pass legislative action restricting access to gender-affirming care, each with varying degrees of success (Redfield et al. 2023). Forty-six percent of US adults support making it illegal for medical professionals to provide gender-affirming healthcare (Parker, Menasce Horowitz, and Brown 2022).

As of March 2023, eleven states have passed legislative bans on gender-affirming care for kids and young adults (Redfield et al. 2023). That's approximately 78,000 trans youth that must live in those states without full access to medical care (see tables 4.1 and 4.2). Some of these bans would prohibit full access to care for adults as old as twenty-six (Redfield et al. 2023). In August 2023, a bill was passed that prohibited medical professionals from providing puberty-blocking drugs, hormone therapy, and gender-transition surgery to patients under the age of eighteen. Similar bans in Arkansas, Indiana, Kentucky, and Oklahoma have been temporarily blocked from enforcement by federal judges (Schoenbaum 2023). A US judge struck down a Florida law that banned state Medicaid payments for transgender healthcare. The judge stated that the law violated the constitutional right to equal protection under the Fourteenth Amendment (Trotta 2023b).

TABLE 4.1 States with Bans/Executive Orders Prohibiting or Restricting Access to Gender-Affirming Care (March 2023)

Georgia	Iowa
Mississippi	South Dakota
Tennessee	Utah
Alabama	Arizona
Arkansas	Florida
Texas	

Source: *Redfield et al. 2023.*

TABLE 4.2 States with Pending Legislation to Prohibit or Restrict Access to Gender-Affirming Care (March 2023)

Hawaii	Idaho
Indiana	Kansas
Kentucky	Michigan
Missouri	Montana
Nebraska	New Hampshire
New Jersey	North Carolina
North Dakota	Ohio
Oklahoma	Oregon
South Carolina	Washington
West Virginia	

Source: *Redfield et al. 2023.*

A growing number of medical professionals continue to publicly condemn such bills that restrict access to gender-affirming care for transgender youth (Andrew 2020). The American Medical Association, the American Academy of Pediatrics, and the Endocrine Society all state that gender-affirming care is safe, effective, and medically necessary (Redfield et al. 2023). Data show that gender-affirming care improves patient mental health and well-being (Cornell

University 2016). This connection is so well-supported that many consider gender-affirming care as suicide prevention (Boerner 2022).

The impact cannot be understated. A 2020 study of 300 youth whose gender identity was different than their sex assigned at birth found a significant increase of psychological distress (i.e., self-harm, suicidal thoughts, depression) at onset of puberty. Of the 187 trans youth aged sixteen or older, 46 percent were diagnosed with depression, 52 percent thought about suicide, and 17 percent had attempted suicide (Sorbara et al. 2020). These numbers are much higher than found in cisgender teens and trans youth prepuberty. One study found that access to gender-affirming care in adolescence had a protective effect even into adulthood. Access to hormone therapy as a teen was correlated with a 60 percent decrease in suicidal thoughts (Turban et al. 2022).

A poll by the Trevor Project found that 86 percent of transgender and nonbinary youth had their mental health negatively impacted by the debates surrounding anti-trans bills. A majority (55%) said the debate affected their mental health "very negatively." Eighty-six percent of trans and nonbinary youth say that state laws that restrict or prohibit the rights of LGBTQIA+ youth have negatively affected their mental health (Sylvester 2023).

MOVING FORWARD

Early organizing efforts for trans rights in the United States began in the 1960s, with the most notable protests taking place at the Stonewall uprising in 1969. The **Stonewall rebellion** happened in the early morning of June 28, 1969, in Manhattan. At this time, police officers would routinely raid so-called "gay bars" where trans and nonbinary folks met, assaulting bar staff and patrons and arresting those who left the building. A similar raid took place at the Stonewall Inn, but this time the patrons resisted by fighting the police. The protest continued for several days with thousands coming to the Stonewall Inn to confront police (Blakemore 2023b). Despite the tireless efforts of trans rights activists, there is still much work to be done.

With so much legislation restricting the rights of transgender people, strong political advocacy is necessary to fight back. The Human Rights Campaign focuses on mobilizing people who oppose these laws to support a society that treats all people equally. The organization runs a trans equality campaign called "Count Me In." The campaign provides fact sheets and videos for people to learn more about the cause. They also ask people to sign a pledge voicing support for the trans and nonbinary community as well as contact information for state legislators to send letters of support (Human Rights Campaign 2023).

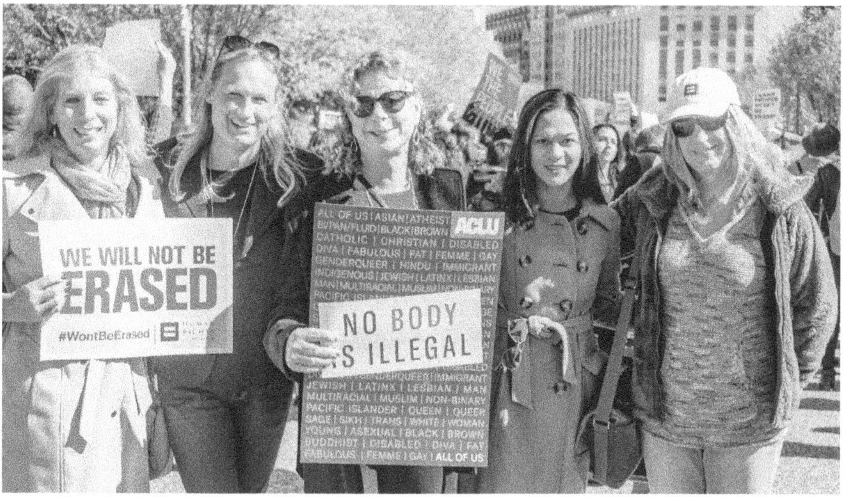

Figure 4.5 Rally for Trans Rights. TED EYTAN, CC BY-SA 2.0, WIKIMEDIA COMMONS

In addition to legislative advocacy and political lobbying to address policies and laws, many nonprofit organizations are doing incredible work on behalf of transgender and nonbinary people. The Trevor Project is a nonprofit organization working to address the suicide epidemic among LGBTQIA+ youth. They provide 24/7 crisis counseling services for those struggling with depression, identity, and suicide. Volunteers are extensively trained to navigate these calls with empathy and care. The organization also participates in research studies and public education and awareness campaigns to support people in being better allies to trans youth (The Trevor Project 2023).

The Gay, Lesbian, and Straight Education Network, or GLSEN, has championed the rights of LGBTQIA+ students since 1990. They provide a national network of ally educators, students, and parents to work in individual communities supporting LGBTQIA+ kids (GLSEN 2023). In addition to developing public awareness and educational materials, they support organizations like Gay/Straight Alliance (GSA) clubs and GLSEN Solidarity Week. This campaign asks teachers, administrators, and students to stand in solidarity with LGBTQIA+ students to build personal empathy and community solutions. The annual Day of Silence is a student-led nationwide demonstration where LGBTQIA+ students and allies take a vow of silence to protest discrimination and harassment of LGBTQIA+ people. The organization provides virtual resources for advocacy and guides to support students, educators, and corporations (GLSEN 2023).

Key Takeaways

- Being transgender means that you reject the gender identity and sex you were assigned at birth. Being nonbinary means you reject the gender binary.
- We perform our gender expression every day, and many people want to clearly express their gender identity, although this is not always possible.
- The use of the singular they/them pronouns is used for nonbinary people who don't identify with the gender binary. Always use the pronouns as requested by an individual to avoid misgendering.
- The political backlash against transgender people is fierce, with many laws and policies restricting full inclusion of transgender people in multiple facets of society.
- Political activists and nonprofit advocacy organizations work tirelessly to support the equality of transgender and nonbinary people.

5

GENDER AND POVERTY
#POVERTYISSEXIST

Figure 5.1 While individuals are often solely blamed for poverty, sociological research shows that institutional discrimination significantly contributes to economic inequality. iStock by Getty Images

ECONOMIC STABILITY is a cornerstone for overall well-being. In the United States, women continue to increase their labor force participation, college education rates, and earning potential; however, research still indicates that one in six US women are living below the US federal poverty line (Institute for Women's Policy Research [IWPR] 2016). *Why are women so affected by poverty? What can be done to end poverty?*

LEARNING GOALS

By the end of this chapter, you should be able to

1. Summarize the unique circumstances that make women and children more vulnerable to poverty.
2. Analyze societal interventions that assist women who live in poverty.
3. Evaluate the effectiveness of social welfare policies to end poverty.

WHAT IS SOCIAL CLASS?

Sociologists continue to study the influence of money and wealth on people's life outcomes. These scientists are studying the impact of social class. **Social class** or **socioeconomic status** refers to socioeconomic variations among groups of people that impact their access to money, wealth, and power. When scientists study social class, they usually consider income, wealth, occupational prestige, educational attainment, and family lineage. That means there's no uniform way to define social class groupings; however, we usually see the categories of upper class, upper middle class, middle class, lower middle class, working class, and poverty class.

According to a 2022 survey, about half (52%) of US adults self-identify as middle class. Two percent identify as upper class. Forty-two percent of US adults categorize themselves as being in the working class or lower class, that is, they experience economic hardship or insufficient access to employment, food, or housing (Jones 2022).

Social class is highly connected to the likelihood that people will have fulfilling experiences, enjoy goods and services, and have opportunities to live healthy and long lives. Social class also determines lifestyle—or the magnitude and manner of consumption of goods and services. This connection is probably obvious to you—those who have more money and wealth generally have

In the News . . .

In October 2023, Netflix launched a limited series about soccer legend David Beckham. He is famously married to '90s pop star Victoria, otherwise known as Posh Spice in the English power group the Spice Girls. In the series premiere, Victoria is interviewed about her relationship with David, saying they were attracted to each other because they both came from working-class families. David interrupts the interview and says, "Be honest!" and follows with the question: "What car did your dad drive?" Victoria replies, "Okay, in the '80s my dad drove a Rolls-Royce" (Weisholtz 2023). To put this in perspective, a Rolls-Royce in 1983 cost $156,000, the equivalent of $400,000 in 2023 (Hemmings 2023).

Fans were shocked by Victoria Beckham's blindness to the realities of truly being working class. This interaction, however, illustrates how beliefs about social class are socially constructed. People routinely think of themselves as a social class position reflecting the image they want to convey.

better life chances. You probably understand this from your own life. Do you know someone who is navigating college without the need to work while taking classes? Perhaps that person can take an unpaid internship in the summer since all their expenses are paid. Students who can focus solely on their studies without being concerned about basic living expenses have a fundamentally different college experience than those who must work to pay bills.

Class privilege is the advantages afforded to people in the middle and upper classes. Examples of class privilege include legacy admissions to universities, inherited wealth, good childhood healthcare, and quality education. Class privilege also includes the knowledge of how systems operate. For example, if your parents or siblings attended college, they are likely to share their knowledge about standardized tests and admissions essays, university scheduling, and course workload. This information provides an understanding of the college admissions process in advance, helping to ease the transition from high school to college.

Classism includes individual beliefs and attitudes as well as systems of policies that benefit the upper class at the expense of the working class and the poverty class. Classism is the rationale that supports these systems of unequal valuing and the culture that perpetuates them. Research shows that people who are perceived as middle and upper class are also seen as smart, articulate, and superior. These assumptions are used to justify class privilege (Friedersdorf 2022).

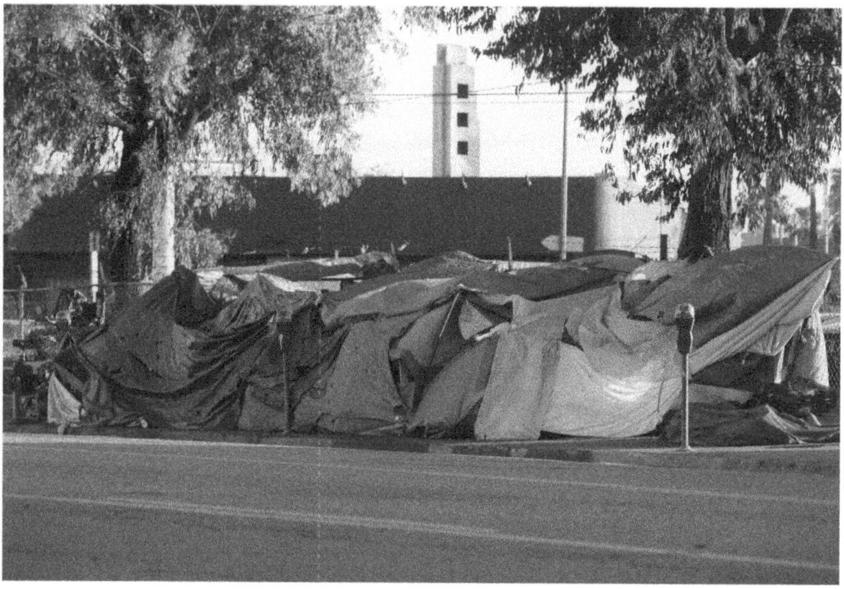

Figure 5.2 How does our definition of social class change the way we think about the concept of "home"? iSTOCK BY GETTY IMAGES

An example of classism is the existence of food deserts. A **food desert** is a residential area where most people don't have access to a supermarket or transportation to other communities' food resources. About 23.5 million Americans live in food deserts (Jones et al., 2019). Low-income areas are less likely to draw supermarket businesses that sell fresh produce, dairy, and meats. Rather, convenience stores and fast-food restaurants are most likely to populate these neighborhoods. These food sources sell ultra-processed food items that hold very little nutritional value. Consumption of ultra-processed foods is linked to higher rates of heart disease, diabetes, and obesity (Jones et al. 2019).

Memphis, Tennessee, is a food desert and has been called the "hunger capital" of the United States (Jones et al. 2019). High-income, mostly white north Memphis residents have access to multiple national chain grocery stores within a mile radius. In contrast, low-income, mostly Black south Memphis residents use public transportation, traveling for over an hour, to access a supermarket. If you look closely at the maps in figures 5.3 and 5.4, you can see the connection between poverty and race. Unsurprisingly, the residents of the wealthiest parts of Memphis have lived thirteen years longer, on average, than those living in the poorest (Jones et al. 2019).

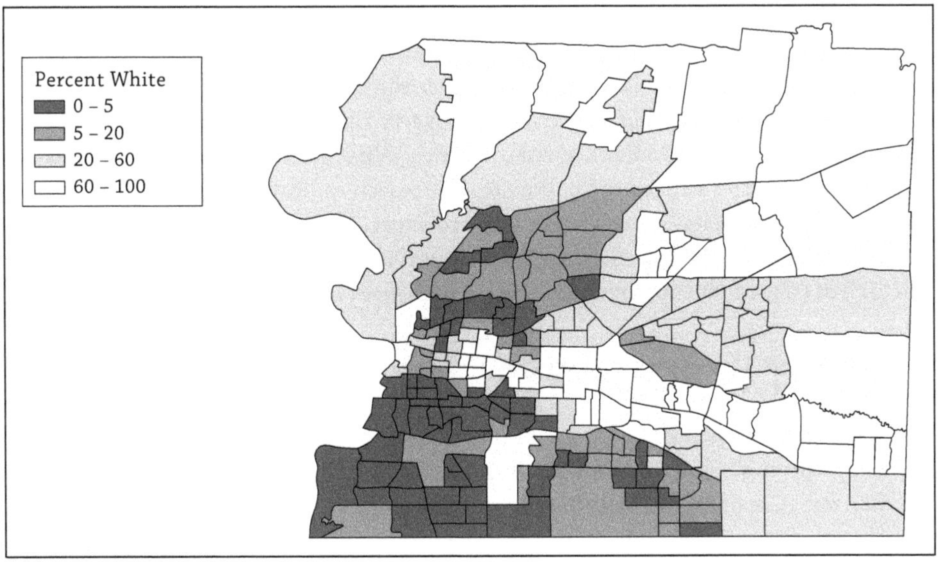

Figure 5.4 This map illustrates the racial makeup of Memphis, Tennessee, by depicting the percentage of white residents. DATA FROM OPPORTUNITY INSIGHTS: TRACK THE RECOVERY

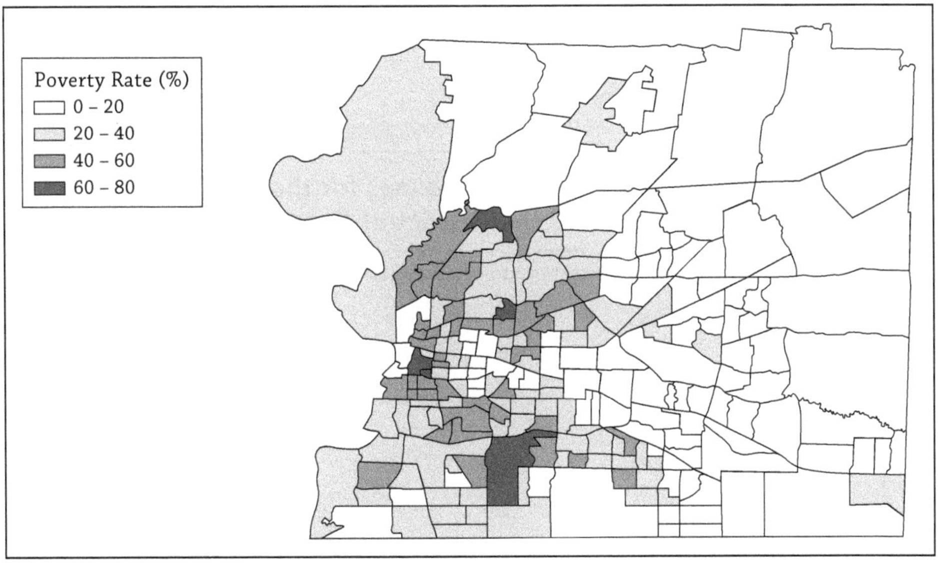

Figure 5.3 This map illustrates the pervasiveness of poverty in Memphis, Tennessee. The darker the color, the higher the incidences of poverty. DATA FROM OPPORTUNITY INSIGHTS: TRACK THE RECOVERY

Like Memphis, many cities in the United States experience persistent poverty. **Persistent poverty** refers to sustained poverty rates (generally 20% or more) in a geographic location for the past thirty years (Benson, Bishaw, and Glassman 2023). Measuring persistent poverty allows for a societal analysis of systemic deficits in individual communities. What are the common shortfalls of communities experiencing poverty? Research indicates that people living in areas of persistent poverty are likely to experience more pervasive systemic inequalities, such as inadequate medical services, food source insecurity, and lack of educational opportunities (Benson, Bishaw, and Glassman 2023).

WHAT IS POVERTY?

Well, it depends on who you ask. The official **poverty rate,** or the ratio of people living below the poverty line, in the United States in 2021 was 11.6 percent (Creamer, Shrider, Burns, and Chen 2022). The **poverty guideline** is a measure of need, which includes the minimum annual household income allowable to be considered in poverty. The minimum household income is adjusted based on number of people in the household. The more people in the house, the higher the allowable income. The poverty guideline is annually defined by the US Department of Health and Human Services to determine eligibility for government safety net and aid programs (US Department of Health and Human Services 2024). To be eligible for most government support, a person's household must have an annual household income calculated at or below the poverty line (see table 5.1).

TABLE 5.1 2023 Poverty Guidelines for the 48 Contiguous States and the District of Columbia

Persons in Family/Household	Poverty Guidelines
1	$14,580
2	$19,720
3	$24,860
4	$30,000
5	$35,140
6	$40,280
7	$45,420
8	$50,560

For families/households with more than 8 persons, add $5,140 for each additional person.

Source: US Department of Health and Human Services, 2023

The US Census Bureau measures poverty status by comparing annual household income to poverty threshold values. The **poverty threshold** is a dollar value for annual income that varies based on family size, number of children, age, and geographic location (Creamer et al. 2022). If a family's annual income before taxes is more than the threshold associated with their household composition, then they are not labeled as in poverty. However, if a family's annual income is *less than* the threshold for their family composition, every person in that family is in poverty (Benson et al. 2022).

Both the poverty threshold and poverty guideline are attempts at calculating absolute poverty. **Absolute poverty** refers to a household income that is considered too low to purchase food for all its members (Conly 2020). However, critics argue there are many flaws with this definition. First, why focus on food? People have varying food preferences and dietary restrictions. Which types of foods are considered "adequate?" What about organic produce, gluten-free bread, or dairy-free yogurt? Many other necessities are required to live—like central heating and water. Do we consider having a phone a necessity? What about a computer or internet access? Focusing only on food expenses diminishes the lived impact of other needs.

To address these concerns, some theorists advocate the implementation of relative poverty measurements. **Relative poverty** refers to the median income in a particular location to determine the definition of poverty. The most common definition used internationally is that anyone with one-half the median income of their location is poor (Conly 2020). While not perfect, this measure accounts for the cost-of-living differences, which can dramatically change the amount of income needed to sustain a family. Finally, relative poverty focuses on the *median income*—or the bottom half—of household incomes. For example, the median household income in Detroit, Michigan, is approximately $36,000, making the relative poverty threshold $18,000. In Fremont, California, however, the median household income is approximately $156,000, making the relative poverty threshold $78,000 (Ainsworth 2023).

POVERTY PREVALENCE

In the United States, women experience higher poverty rates than men. This phenomenon—the higher incidence of poverty among cisgender women, trans women, and girls versus cisgender men, trans men, and boys—is called the **feminization of poverty**. In 2018, the poverty rate for women was 12.9 percent while the poverty rate for men was 10.6 percent. The median annual income for households headed by women was $45,128, which is lower than households headed by men ($61,518) (Semega 2019). Over 30 percent of children living in poverty lived in a female-headed household (National Women's Law Center [NWLC] 2022).

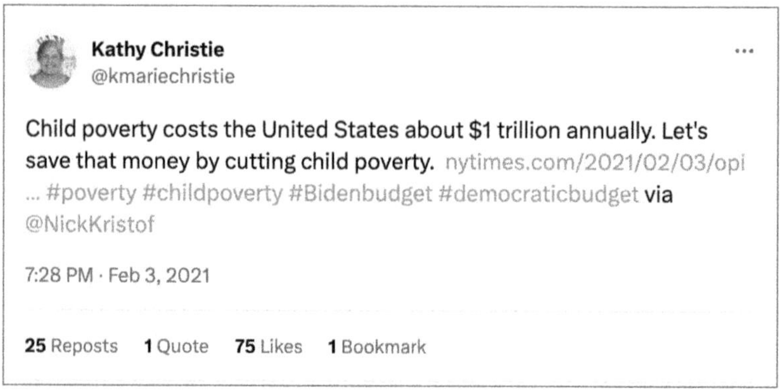

Figure 5.5 The correlation is clear: when women experience poverty, so do children. POSTED ON X

Unmarried mothers with children account for the largest household segment living in poverty, while dual-earner, married couple families are the least (IWPR 2016). Almost 25 percent of unmarried mothers live below the poverty line (Bleiweis, Boesch, and Cawthorne Gaines 2020). This should anecdotally make sense: more workers mean more potential income. It follows that this group is less likely to live in poverty. As the number of earners decreases, the number of dependents increase. With the exacerbating factors of unequal pay and discrimination, poverty is more likely.

LGBTQIA+ and gender nonconforming women experience higher rates of poverty, mostly because of the intersection of oppression experiences based on gender identity and sexual orientation (Bleiweis, Boesch, and Cawthorne Gaines 2020). According to a UCLA study, 17.9 percent of lesbian cisgender women and 29.4 percent of bisexual cisgender women live in poverty. This is compared to 17.8 percent of straight cisgender women and 13.4 percent of straight cisgender men living in poverty (Badgett, Choi, and Wilson 2019). The data suggests similar poverty rates for gender nonconforming and transgender people. Since federal surveys do not collect data on sexual orientation and gender identity, these numbers are not sufficiently measured.

Women of nearly all racial and ethnic groups have higher rates of poverty than men of the same group (Bleiweis, Boesch, and Cawthorne Gaines 2020). Black and Native American women and girls have the highest rates of poverty (approximately 18%) (NWLC 2022; IWPR 2016). Latina women experienced a 17 percent poverty rate in 2021 (NWLC 2022).

Starting at age five, women experience higher rates of poverty across the life course than men (Bleiweis, Boesch, and Cawthorne Gaines 2020). When 2021 poverty data was analyzed by demographic group, the findings showed no significant changes in poverty rates for most groups, except for one measure: age. The data shows that the child poverty rate was 4.6 percent higher than the national average, while poverty rates for those sixty-five and older were 2.5 percent less than the average rate (Creamer et al. 2022). The poverty rate for senior women was 11.6 percent, which is more than 60 percent of all seniors living in poverty (NWLC 2022). Over 11.1 million children (approximately 14%) lived in poverty in 2021. These numbers are exacerbated by racism, with children of color experiencing higher rates of poverty: 27.3 percent of Black children and 22 percent of Latinx children (NWLC 2022).

Women with disabilities are more likely to live in poverty than both men with disabilities and individuals without disabilities. Approximately 23 percent of women with disabilities live below the poverty line, compared to about 18 percent of men with disabilities, and 11.4 percent of women without disabilities (Bleiweis, Boesch, and Cawthorne Gaines 2020).

As educational attainment increases, so do the increased assumptions of high-earning employment. Following this trend, those obtaining less than a high school diploma are the largest demographic group living in poverty, while those earning a graduate degree are the lowest demographic group living in poverty (IWPR 2016). According to the Bureau of Labor Statistics, the median weekly earnings for someone with a bachelor's degree is $1,432, but only $682 for those earning less than a high school diploma (Bureau of Labor Statistics 2022). Let's be careful, however, not to confuse correlation with causation. Many people have advanced degrees yet have not secured high-paying careers.

Causes of the Gender Wealth Gap

Women earn less money than men. Why? The gender wage gap is created through a host of factors, such as gendered job segregation (women pushed into lower-wage, lower-prestige jobs), hours worked, and years of experience (women are often penalized for years out of the workforce due to care labor). No other factors, including educational attainment or differences within an occupation, explain this inequality (Bleiweis, Boesch, and Cawthorne Gaines 2020). Researchers cite the inability to work, discrimination from employers, and insufficient supplementary income benefits as contributing factors (American Psychological Association 2023).

Because women earn less money, they are also accumulating less wealth. This is called the **gender wealth gap**. Discrimination in banking leads to predatory loans and more loan denials for women (McCulloch 2017). The wealth gap is considerably higher for women of color, who experience both sexism and racism. We'll discuss these concepts in depth in chapter 11.

The United States does not universally provide supportive policies for mothers in the workforce, policies such as guaranteed paid family and medical leave, funding support, or childcare subsidies (the Family and Medical Leave Act guarantees unpaid leave). As we discuss in chapter 11, women complete the majority of unpaid care work, including childcare and elder care. Without the ability to complete both unpaid care work and paid labor, women are often forced to reduce their work hours, forgo career opportunities, or leave the workforce altogether.

As we discuss in depth in chapter 7, domestic violence has real effects on survivors' finances. Financial abuse can leave a victim without established credit or with intentionally ruined credit scores. Financial costs associated with divorce proceedings, child custody disputes, and civil protection proceedings can add up quickly. Additionally, missed days of work, lost wages, or job termination can result from abuse. It's not surprising that multiple studies found that among mothers with children who are homeless, more than 80 percent of them were survivors of domestic violence (Office of Family Violence Prevention 2016). Eleven percent of all emergency shelter beds in homeless service systems were used by survivors of domestic violence and their families (National Alliance to End Homelessness 2023).

Affordable housing is defined as housing that costs the occupant no more than 30 percent of their income on housing costs, including utilities (US Department of Housing and Urban Development 2023). There is a shortage of 7.3 million affordable and available rental homes for people with low incomes, an increase of 8 percent from 2019 (Yentel 2023). Women are more likely to be single parents than men (Lu et al. 2019). This distinction is critical to understanding the complex considerations women must face when negotiating housing. Because mothers are making housing decisions for a family, not just an individual, their housing options—particularly affordable housing options—are limited.

Low-wage workers are mostly likely to be **cost-burdened**—or spending more than 30 percent of their income on rent. Another way to measure cost burden is by evaluating the **residual-income** approach. Using this model, the cost burden is determined by evaluating whether a household has enough income to pay for all household expenses after paying for housing (National Low Income Housing Coalition [NLIHC] 2022). Research indicates that 100 percent of households earning $30,000 annually are cost-burdened (Airgood-Obrycki 2022).

Communities of color experience the greatest impact of a lack of affordable housing. The well-documented racial wage gap not only leaves people of color with less income but also concentrates people of color into low-wage jobs. The increased cost of rentals disproportionately affects Black and Latino renters, because they are more likely to be renters at all income levels (NLIHC 2022). Due to income inequality and pervasive systemic racism and sexism, women of color are impacted the most by unaffordable housing.

POVERTY AND PUBLIC POLICY

Data show that when we invest in public policy initiatives that support families, people experience more financial stability and are protected from poverty (NWLC 2022). However, the political divide on these policies continues to threaten the longevity of these programs. Let's review some of the public policies and social supports that help women (and others) in poverty.

Unemployment Insurance. In 2021, unemployment insurance raised 2.3 million people out of poverty (NWLC 2022). This public support program pays unemployed workers a part of their lost wages as they search for a new job. However, many of the requirements to maintain unemployment insurance make some women ineligible. For example, women are more likely to work part-time or leave jobs to support caregiving tasks (NWLC 2019b). Each of these circumstances would render a person ineligible.

Refundable Tax Credits. In 2021, refundable tax credits raised 9.6 million people out of poverty (NWLC 2022). These include the Earned Income Tax Credit (EITC) and the Child Tax Credit (CTC). Researchers argue that these tax credits are the most directly effective income supplements for low-income families (Gallagher-Robbins and Vallas 2019). The EITC is a federal tax credit for people with low incomes. The maximum credit was $530 in 2020. While this money helps, it is not enough to substantially benefit low-income families. The CTC grants families with up to a $2000 tax credit per child under seventeen years old. Again, while this tax credit is a help, the increased cost of living, particularly for young children, makes this credit insufficient (Bleiweis, Boesch, and Cawthorne Gaines 2020). Finally, each of these tax credits is offered just once a year, so their impact is short-lived.

Supplemental Nutrition Assistance Program (SNAP). SNAP benefits, or food stamps, kept 2.8 million people above the poverty line in 2021 (NWLC 2022). These benefits are one of the largest federal social welfare initiatives, operating in some capacity for over sixty years (Desilver 2023b). In 2023, 22.4 percent of American households received SNAP benefits. The national average SNAP benefit in April 2023 was $182.72 per person monthly, but this varies from state to state (Desilver 2023b). However, over 50 percent of SNAP benefit users exhaust their monthly stipend in the first two weeks of the month (Carlson, Llobrera, Keith-Jennings 2021). The money provided is often too low to truly meet a family's food needs.

In the News . . .

The cost of attending college has dramatically increased over the past thirty years. Average tuition costs at a public university in the United States grew from $4,160 to $10,740 (Hahn 2023). In 2023, about half of all students leave their college with student debt used to offset these costs. In the United States, this has led to $1.75 trillion in student loan debt in the form of both federal and private loans (Hahn 2023). Data show that student loan debt is disproportionately affecting students of color, with 86 percent of Black students taking on student loan debt to attend college (Wright 2023). This significantly adds to the already well-documented racial wealth gap in the United States.

In 2023, US President Biden proposed a $400 billion plan to cancel or reduce federal student loans for millions of borrowers. However, in a 6–3 decision, the Supreme Court stated that the president overstepped his authority, forcing student loan repayment to continue (Sherman 2023). Despite this setback, the Biden administration vowed to reduce student loan debt. In 2024, the administration implemented several policies promising to relieve $132 billion in student loan debt, including federal loan forgiveness for low-income borrowers, those employed in the public service sector, borrowers with serious medical issues, and those attending colleges that engaged in misconduct (Minsky 2024).

Special Supplemental Nutrition Program for Women, Infants, and Children (WIC). WIC provides food assistance and other support services for low-income pregnant and postpartum women (Bleiweis, Boesch, and Cawthorne Gaines 2020). These resources could include breastfeeding counseling, substance abuse referrals, and health screenings (US Department of Agriculture [USDA] 2022). WIC benefits are utilized by over 1.5 million women each year; however, only about 50 percent of eligible mothers receive WIC benefits (USDA 2022).

Social Security. In 2021, social security lifted 26.3 million people above the poverty line (NWLC 2022). Social security helps replace lost earnings due to disability, retirement, or death (Bleiweis, Boesch, and Cawthorne Gaines 2020). Women who are sixty-five or older utilize social security income more than men do. Approximately two-thirds of social security beneficiaries are women (NWLC 2019b). Because social security is collectively funded by payroll taxes, federal tax policies, specifically those that reduce income taxes for the wealthy, threaten the ability of elderly and disabled women to achieve economic security (Bleiweis, Boesch, and Cawthorne Gaines 2020).

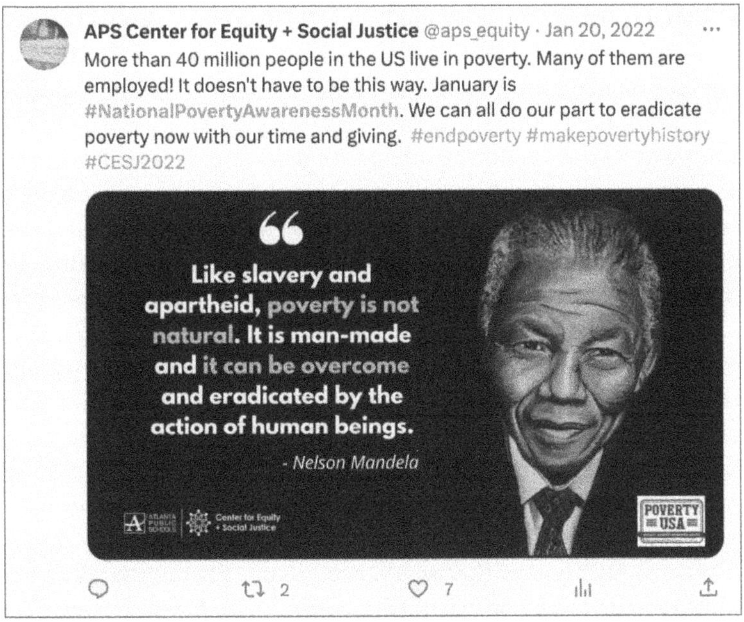

Figure 5.6 Public awareness campaigns are one way to encourage people to make social change. Posted on X

Medicaid. Medicaid is federally funded healthcare coverage for low-income people. Women and girls make up the majority of people who access Medicaid benefits (Kaiser Family Foundation 2019). In 2020, thirty-six states and the District of Columbia expanded eligibility for Medicaid to include people within 138 percent of the poverty line, which offered healthcare benefits to an expanded group of people. This specifically benefited low-income women of color.

MOVING FORWARD

How do we address poverty in the United States? Individual-level interventions seek to ease the burden of poverty in the short term. For example, we might stock our local food pantry, donate blankets to the emergency housing shelter, or give money to a person requesting help. Indeed, these actions will provide immediate relief to some individuals, but they do not address the social structures that produce and reproduce classism and poverty. To create long-term solutions, we need large-scale change. Many scholars advocate increasing wages and decreasing housing and other living costs as a path to ending poverty.

Housing subsidies, such as public low-income housing and the Housing Choice Voucher Program (Section 8) continue to help low-income families (US Dept of Housing 2023b). In 2021, 2.4 million people were raised out of poverty with the support of housing subsidies (NWLC 2022). Affordable housing options are at historic lows. For renters, 49 percent of households are considered cost-burdened (spending more than 30% of income on housing) (Joint Center for Housing Studies 2023). To address this concern, the National Low Income Housing Coalition (NLIHC) advocates for the use of a **housing wage**—the estimated full-time wage for workers to rent a modest home, while spending no more than 30 percent of their income on housing (NLIHC 2022). The 2022 national housing wage was $21.25 per hour to afford a one-bedroom home. At the same time, rental costs have increased significantly—more than 4.5 times greater than previous increases. This is largely due to increased demand, investor purchases, and inflation (NLIHC 2022).

Access to affordable housing is critical, but so is earning an income to pay for living necessities. Some scholars advocate for a **living wage**, or the amount of money one full-time worker would need to pay for their family's necessities while remaining self-sufficient (Glasmeier 2023). Massachusetts Institute of Technology scholar Amy Glasmeier created a tool to determine the living wage value for specific states and counties (see livingwage.mit.edu). The calculation determines the specific hourly wage a worker must make to cover basic expenses. In many locations, the federal minimum wage is much lower than the living wage needed to survive.

Finally, we know that women, children, and trans women are most likely to live in poverty. Public policies that address gendered social problems will ultimately have an impact on low-income women specifically. These policies include providing child tax credits and ensures access to child-friendly work policies and unemployment insurance. Local, state, and federal governments can pass laws to address unequal pay, domestic violence protections, and racial wealth inequality. These changes appear straightforward; however, as with most social welfare issues, the actual advocacy around these issues is much more complex. Social support and social justice measures remain a consistent source of political division which makes actual change challenging to legislate.

Key Takeaways

- Social class is a key sorting mechanism in society where some experience unearned class privilege and others experience classism.
- The feminization of poverty refers to the societal condition of women, girls, and trans women experiencing higher rates of poverty than other social groups.
- Women experience higher incidences of poverty because of many other gendered social problems, like domestic violence, the gender wage gap, and unpaid care work.
- Public social welfare policies such as tax credits and supplementary income support those in poverty in the short term.
- Long-term social change to end poverty requires societal changes to living wages and affordable housing.

6

MEN AND MASCULINITIES
#TOXICMASCULINITY

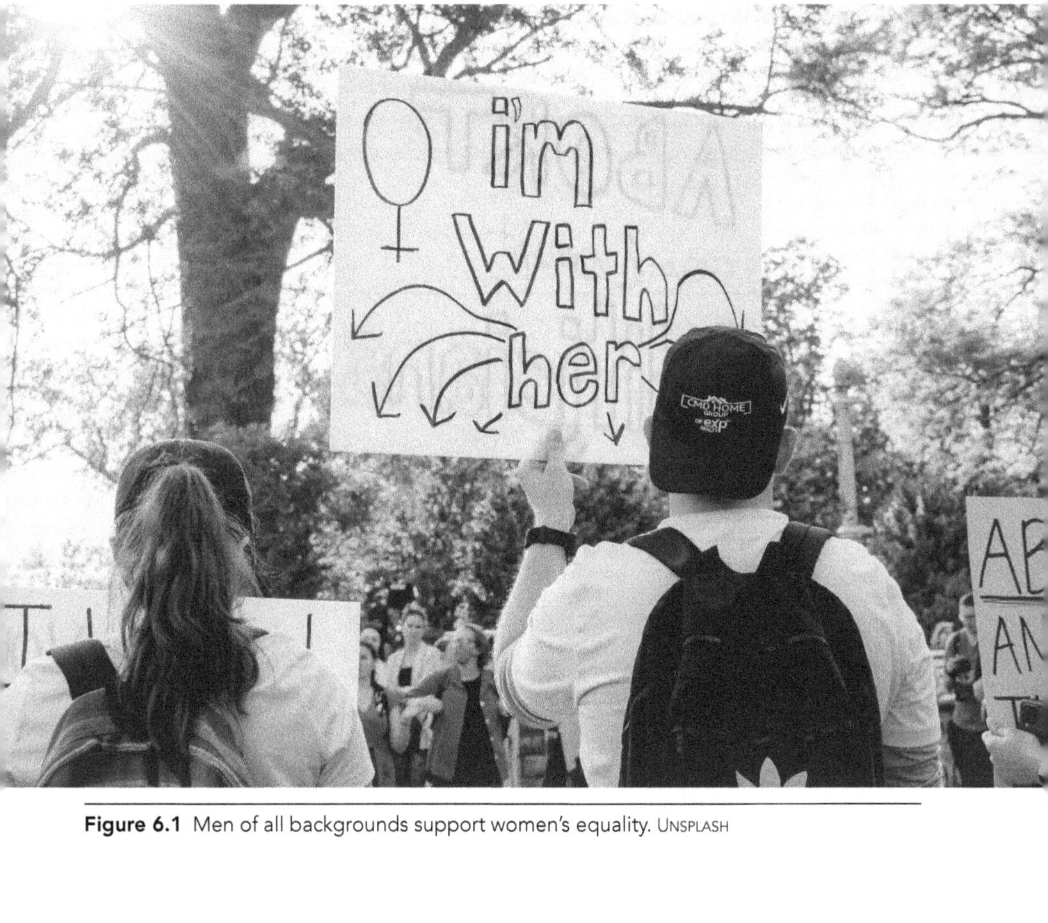

Figure 6.1 Men of all backgrounds support women's equality. UNSPLASH

IN JULY 2023, filmmaker Greta Gerwig's movie *Barbie* hit the box office by storm. Earning $155 million in its opening weekend, the film boasts the highest US opening of a movie directed by a woman (Weatherbed 2023). The film drew rave reviews, many of which highlight *Barbie*'s unmistakable feminist themes (Murray 2023).

However, the response was not entirely positive. The antifeminist backlash was swift and searing. Ben Shapiro, a well-known conservative commentator, released a 43-minute YouTube video claiming the message of the film is to "hate men" (Murray 2023). Elon Musk, billionaire and CEO of X, tweeted, "If you take a shot every time Barbie says the word 'patriarchy,' you will pass out before the movie ends."

Specifically, critics attack the presentation of Ken as "not masculine," and the (debatable) portrayal of men in the real world as useless, stupid, predatory, and violent (Jerkovich 2023).

Despite these varied responses, the movie provides a clear explanation of **toxic masculinity**, or the performance of manhood that is harmful to both the men who embody it and to society at large. Does this mean that all men are toxic? Are all forms of masculinity harmful? *What does it mean to be a "real man" in our society? Let's dig in.*

LEARNING GOALS

By the end of this chapter, you should be able to

1. Define masculinities, including toxic masculinity
2. Explain the benefits of male privilege
3. Assess the consequences of toxic masculinity on individual men and society

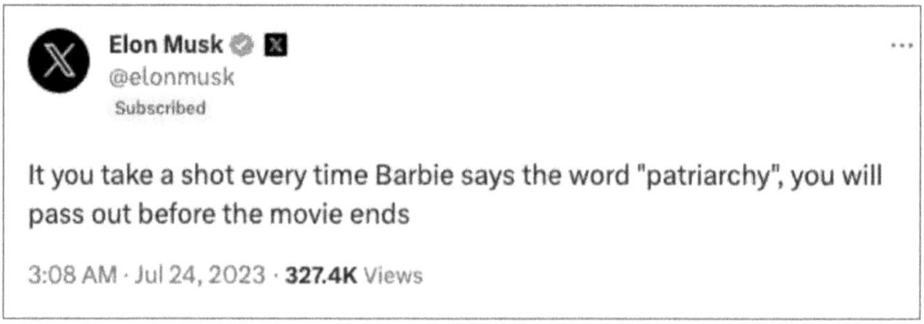

Figure 6.2 Billionaire Elon Musk reacts to *Barbie*'s critique of patriarchy. POSTED ON X

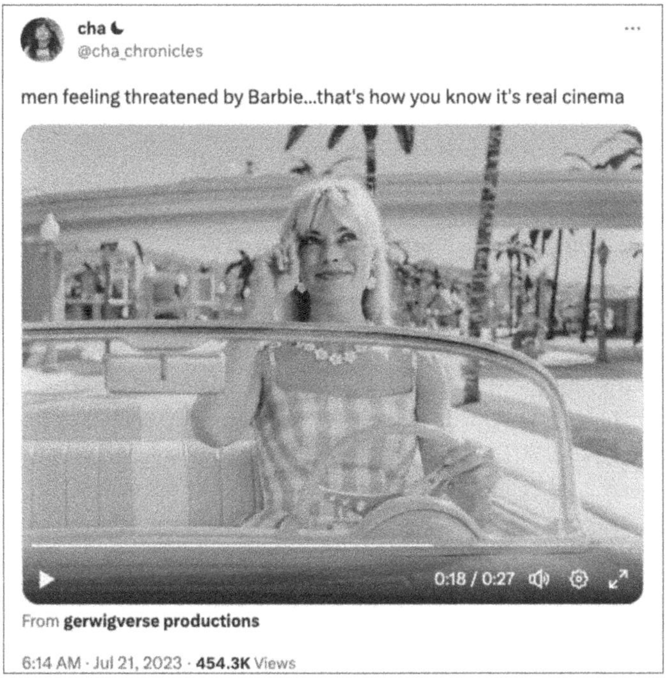

Figure 6.3 Women react to some men's criticism of *Barbie*. POSTED ON X

THE GENDER HIERARCHY

Many argue that traits like aggression and competitiveness are biologically predetermined characteristics of men. This argument is easily refuted based on our understanding of the social construction of gender (see chapter 2 for a review). As we've already discussed, gender definitions are not biological, but rather created by society. We know that many types of men display a wide array of characteristics. However, regardless of individual personality traits or preferences, men are pressured to "do gender" in a way that is harmful to both them and society at large.

Doing gender explains that gender isn't something we just *are* but is an act that we *perform* to the world. Think of it as a costume mask worn to act in a play. The mask helps us to perform a believable character. Theorists argue that problematic forms of gender require people to perform a gender expression that meets the narrow definitions created by society (Butler 1999).

Male Privilege

Gender inequality affects all people, but those effects are not equally distributed. In the United States, our society is a type of **patriarchy**, or a society that is ruled by men. Patriarchies privilege men's experiences, ideas, and ways of being (Johnson 2005). While much progress has been made toward equality, we still live in a modified patriarchy where women are granted formal gender equality, but male power and privilege are still alive and well (Wade and Ferree 2019). By virtue of being male-bodied with a masculine gender expression, men receive societal privilege. **Male privilege** is the unearned societal benefits of being a part of a social group at the top of the hierarchy. One aspect of male privilege is the ability to dismiss inequality and sexism. Even men who acknowledge the presence of inequality are likely to underestimate its impact.

According to a 2019 US survey, men have a skewed understanding of the pervasive effect of gender inequality on women. When asked about a variety of gendered topics, such as the gender pay gap, representation in government, and unpaid labor, men were much less likely to admit the impact of sexism. When asked the question "How serious a problem is sexism today?", 45 percent of respondents indicated "extremely or very serious." However, when those responses are analyzed by sex, 35 percent of those respondents are male versus 54 percent female (Barone 2019).

Male privilege looks like a world that is **male-identified** (Johnson 2005). Our cultural ideas of what is considered good, desirable, preferable, and even "normal" are associated with men and masculinity. Our very language illustrates this for us. Have you ever said, "Hey guys!" to a group of friends that includes both male *and* female-bodied people? Have you heard "mankind" or "man" to describe people? "Guys," "mankind," and "man" are gendered words—they're masculine; however, we use the male-identified words to work as a proxy for *all* people, including all genders.

Our patriarchy is **male-centered**, which means that men's experiences often operate as a proxy for all people's experiences (Johnson 2005). This male-centered perspective has led to a sharp lag in women's health research, as historically, white heterosexual male bodies were used as the "universal model" for all (Plataforma 2008). It is only since the mid-1980s that medical research started to diversify using gender and sex, race, and ethnicity as factors (Glezerman 2016).

Remember your high school American history classes? Many textbooks explain the major timelines of events, but this analysis is only tracking what men (often only white men) were doing. Of course, this is not presented as "men's history," but rather "American history." To learn about what women were

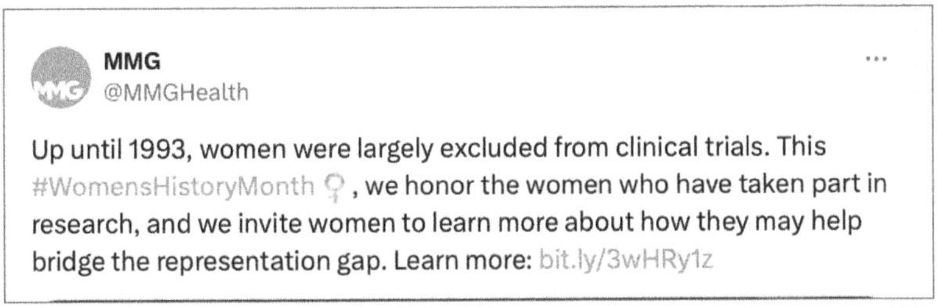

Figure 6.4 Early medical research used men's bodies as a proxy for all bodies.
POSTED ON X

doing historically, sidebars or FAQs are included as *additional* information to the main (male) events.

Our patriarchy is **male-dominated** with positions of power reserved for men (Johnson, 2005). Sometimes these positions of power are explicitly set aside for men as are many positions of authority within organized religion. Conversely, other powerful positions are open to all people *in theory*, but our social imagination only accepts men as the "correct" or "normal" people for the job. Think about the presidency of the United States. In 2016, Secretary of State Hillary Clinton was the first major woman US party nominee for president. Throughout her campaign, her clothing, speaking style, and marriage relationship were consistently compared to those of previous male candidates (Dittmar 2017).

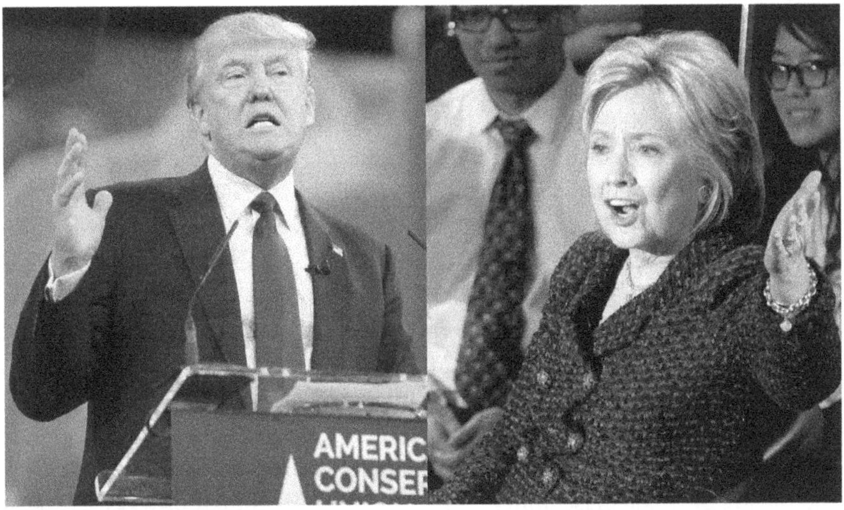

Figure 6.5 In a male-dominated society, positions of power are reserved for men.
GAGE SKIDMORE, WIKIMEDIA COMMONS

In the News . . .

Us Weekly is usually known for reporting on celebrity breakups and feuds, but in 2023, the magazine offered a different type of report: men celebrities as proud feminists. While the entire list is quite long, some of the self-described celebrities include Regé-Jean Page. He openly responded to harassing comments about actress Florence Pugh on social media, asking men to "step up." He further stated, "When the boys are out of line, have a word." Some of the other celebrity feminists listed include Ryan Gosling, Harry Styles, Chris Hemsworth, and Daniel Radcliffe (Us Weekly Staff 2023).

The long-lasting legacy of patriarchy in our society is of **androcentrism**. In an androcentric society (like ours), higher power, prestige, and respect are offered to anyone who conveys traditionally masculine traits (Johnson 2005). The research is clear: we value masculinity more than femininity. This is a result of the men's positioning on our society's hierarchy.

The Harm of Toxic Masculinity

Former NFL player Joe Ehrmann once stated, "'Be a man' is one of the most destructive phrases in our culture" (Newsom 2015). While the impact of gender inequality disproportionately affects women, men are still negatively impacted by patriarchy. A 2018 national survey of ten- to nineteen-year-olds found that young women believed there are many ways to "be a girl"; for example, they could enjoy math, sports, or music and still have the title of a "girl." However, young men are culturally allowed only one narrow route which includes dominance, rugged good looks, wealth, and athleticism (Orenstein 2019). Some men acknowledge the need to end "toxic" masculinity but are unclear about what healthy masculinity should look like (Emba 2023).

The "manning-up" of boys begins in infancy. Research indicates that mothers use less emotionally rich language with their toddler boys, and fathers are less likely to sing to soothe their young sons (Reiner 2023). And this parental modeling matters. Data show that sons model their version of masculinity after their paternal figure. Men who scored highly on traditional masculinity scales are likely to have fathers who exhibit traditional masculinity (Perales et al. 2023).

The American Psychological Association (APA) published the first report on boys and men in 2018. The report reinforces what we've already deduced: the culture of "toxic masculinity" is harming men in numerous ways. The APA lists harsh discipline, academic challenges, mental health issues, and physical health concerns as just some of the ways that traditional masculinity harms men (APA 2018).

The results show that although boys and men are disproportionately represented in most social problems' populations (i.e., school-age learning disabilities and behavioral problems, violent crimes), men are also less likely to receive services and support for these problems (APA 2018). This is largely due to boys' and men's socialization to not show weakness or need help from others, as men are not societally allowed to show sadness or experience pain (Booker, Rothman, and Kargbo 2019). Research conducted by the Harvard School of Public Health found that boys who withhold their emotions are a third more likely to die prematurely (Hagan 2013). Men commit suicide at a rate four times that of women (National Institute of Mental Health 2019).

Across all violent crimes, men are more likely than women to be the offender (77%) but also shoulder almost half of the victimizations (46.6%) (Morgan and Oudekerk 2019). This means that while men commit most of the violence against women, they also inflict the majority of violence against men. These consequences are more nuanced for men of color. Black and Latino men are overrepresented at every point in the criminal justice system from juvenile arrest to prison incarcerations (National Council on Crime and Delinquency 2019). Some argue that engaging in criminal activity is a form of "doing gender" for men of color (Rios 2020). This creates a double bind: not only do young men of color experience masculinity as violence against other men (and women), but the criminal justice system also uses this racialized and gendered definition to justify the disproportionate incarceration of those men (Rios 2020).

The expression of toxic masculinity is also harmful to society as a whole. Men commit the majority of all violent offenses, including murder (88.7%), forcible rape (99.1%), and aggravated assault (77.2%) (FBI 2012). This culture of violence seeps into college campuses, where sexual assault of university women in fraternity houses has become a cultural norm (Armstrong, Hamilton, and Sweeney 2006). One X user posed the question to women: "What would you do if there were no men on earth for 24 hours?" Responses included "feel safe," and "walk outside at night without fearing for my life." Most mass shootings are

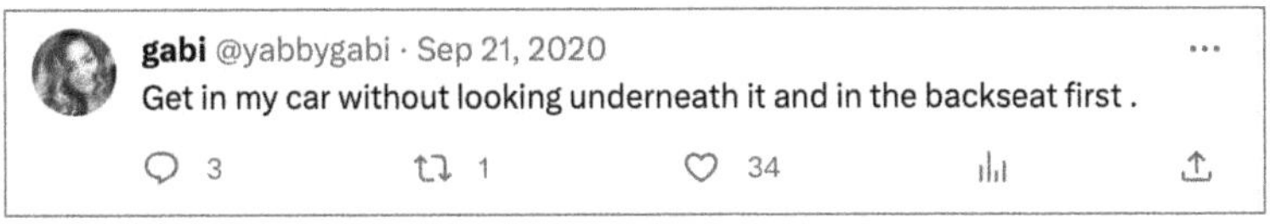

Figure 6.6 Women were asked to respond to the question, "What would you do if men didn't exist for a day?" The answers are chilling. POSTED ON X

In the News . . .

In 2021, a twenty-one-year-old Ohio man and self-proclaimed incel (involuntarily celibate) was charged with attempting to commit a hate crime. Prosecutors outlined his plan to acquire automatic weapons to "slaughter women out of hatred, jealousy and revenge" (Diaz 2021). Thankfully, local police were able to prevent this mass shooting from occurring, but the impact of men's violence on women's lives cannot be understated.

committed by men. Between January 2013 and August 2019, there were fifty-three mass shootings, and fifty of those involved male suspects (Reese 2019).

This same cultural definition of masculinity has encouraged white power organizations to recruit using the language of traditional manhood (Kimmel 2018). Hate groups appeal to men who feel as if their "rights as men" are being disrupted by women and immigrant minorities. Using language like "join your brothers!" or "feel like a real man!", violent white supremacist groups appeal to the sense of male societal entitlement. Interestingly, what do most members of white power groups have in common? They are men (Gilson 2018).

MOVING FORWARD

When people discuss this topic, many assume that since masculinity can be toxic, *all* masculinity is toxic. This reasoning is the classic correlation and causation myth. Just because most violence is conducted by men, it does not mean that all men are violent. Men are not naturally devoid of emotion or biologically violent. These traits are part of the gender socialization taught beginning in childhood. Understanding this gender socialization is empowering because this means that men can unlearn these harmful societal messages. Gender socialization begins at an early age, most commonly within the primary family. Young men base their definitions of manhood on the lessons observed or taught by their fathers. In the absence of this relationship, society at large will fill the void (Newsom 2015). Parents, especially fathers, have the unique opportunity to create social change in their sons by teaching healthy forms of masculinity.

We have numerous examples of men stepping up to show society that a healthy form of masculinity is possible. Joe Talbot, the lead singer and lyricist for the British band Idles, is using the band's songs to promote a healthier form of masculinity. The lyrics, like "they laugh at me when I run / I waste away for fun," and "I am my father's son / his shadow weighs a ton," all speak to the vulnerabilities that men face (Booker, Rothman, and Kargbo 2019).

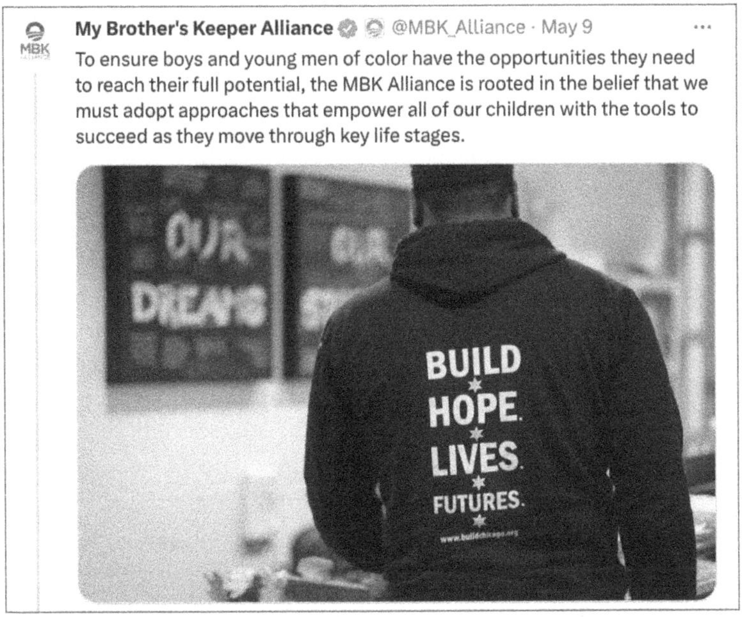

Figure 6.7 My Brother's Keeper Alliance works to support the healthy development of young men and boys of color. POSTED ON X

Because law and public policymakers are eager to secure and defend the long-fought rights of women, it is often viewed as contradictory to also advocate for support for men (Emba 2023). However, former President Obama created My Brother's Keeper Alliance. This group of intersectional community, religious, and public policy partners works to provide resources for success for young men and boys of color (My Brother's Keeper 2022). The organization fosters positive outcomes for men of color including high school graduation, freedom from violence, and postgraduation employment.

The organization A Call To Men suggests that men commit to six principles of healthy, respectful manhood, which include "embrace and express a full range of emotion; do not conform to the pressure to always be fearless and in control; value a woman's life, treat all people equally, and promote the betterment of humanity; do not use language that denigrates women and girls; develop an interest in the experience of women and girls, outside of sexual conquest; model a healthy, respectful manhood to other men and boys" (A Call To Men 2019). This organization is challenging men to make personal changes to impact individual men, but also disrupt the messaging conveyed to young men to create long-term social change. The Center for Disease Control and Prevention is funding primary violence prevention work with young men, as well as public awareness campaigns and clubs for high school young men to encourage healthy expressions of manhood. As many men have noted, there is no blueprint to unravel the patriarchal lessons deeply embedded within us. Making social change requires the hard work of purging sexist socialization and relearning healthy ways of embodying manhood (Powell 2020).

Finally, Salma Hayek has announced a new initiative called the Global Boyhood Initiative, which conducted an extensive study on masculinity and the stereotypes about manhood that are portrayed in television and film (Kapralau 2020). Their research found television supports the masculine stereotypes of being self-sufficient, acting tough, engaging in risky behavior, and aggression (Global Boyhood Initiative 2024). This organization continues to provide educational resources, public policy advocacy, and research to support men and boys.

Key Takeaways

- Toxic masculinity is an expression of manhood that hurts individual men and society; however, it does not mean that all men or manhood is toxic.
- Male privilege exists as an outcome of social hierarchy, which creates our patriarchy that is male-centered, male-identified, and male-dominated.
- Men experience the harmful effects of gender socialization that defines masculinity as being unemotional, disconnected, and violent.
- As a result, men commit the majority of violence in our society. This violence is against women, but also against other men.
- Many men exhibit healthy masculinity and are working on initiatives to create lasting social change to end toxic masculinity.

7

INTIMATE PARTNER VIOLENCE
#SURVIVOR

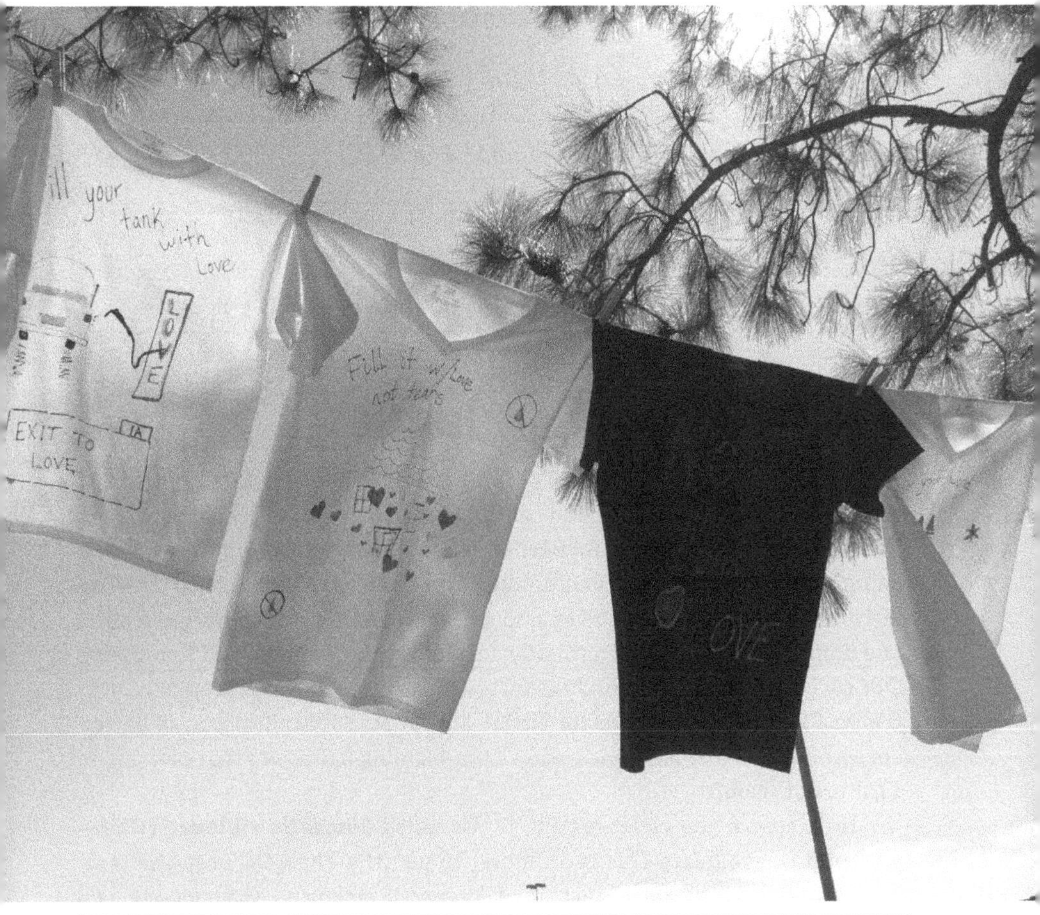

Figure 7.1 The Clothesline Project is a public awareness campaign for domestic violence awareness month (October). PHOTO BY AIRMAN 1ST CLASS TY-RICO LEA, US AIR FORCE

IN 2021, the United Nations published a report citing domestic violence as a global "shadow pandemic," with intimate partner violence incidents increasing 25–30 percent globally (Mineo 2022). Worldwide, domestic violence is the number one cause of homicide for women (Vagianos 2018). The COVID-19 pandemic exponentially increased the number of domestic violence hotline calls with mass isolation creating escalating conditions (Bocanegra 2020; Boserup et al. 2020).

In the United States, the Centers for Disease Control and Prevention (CDC) agree with the UN's assessment. This government agency—the federal department that addresses public health concerns like smoking—considers intimate partner violence as a public health dilemma. Why? Because violence at the hand of an intimate partner is an overwhelming cause of harm for women (CDC 2020a). *Why does intimate partner violence continue? Are women the only victims? What about men? Let's dive in.*

LEARNING GOALS

By the end of this chapter, you should be able to

1. Explain intimate partner violence as a function of power and control
2. Evaluate causes of intimate partner violence
3. Assess strategies for supporting victims and preventing violence

A NOTE ABOUT LANGUAGE

Intimate partner violence (IPV) is a pattern of coercive tactics meant to establish and maintain power and control of a current or past intimate partner. These tactics include physical violence, psychological abuse, emotional harm, and stalking. These tactics are culturally learned and socially condoned (DeWard 2010). Culturally, we continue to associate masculinity with control, strength, and dominance, while systematically devaluing girls, women, and femininity. Our society continues to condone intimate partner violence through limited criminal and civil protections for victims, the popularity and success of batterers without social consequence, and victim-blaming narratives that perpetuate a culture of shame.

Intimate partner violence (IPV) is also called **domestic violence (DV)**—you might have heard this term more frequently. The CDC uses the term "intimate partner violence" instead of "domestic violence." Although you will see both terms in this chapter, there are several reasons why victim advocates prefer using IPV. Since the advent of the modern antiviolence against women movement in the 1970s, advocates used the term "domestic" because it referred to the home. The trailblazers of the antiviolence movement wanted to distinguish between violence that happens between strangers in public places and violence happening between those living in the same residence. Since so-called domestic violence was not a topic discussed at that time—both by the public and the justice system—this term provided a voice to a commonplace social problem usually shrouded by silence.

However, as victim advocates continued their important work, several flaws in this terminology emerged. From a legal perspective, domestic violence includes any violence happening between household members, which includes child abuse (FindLaw 2020). Child abuse is a harrowing social problem that requires different tools and strategies to address. It is not the same as violence between intimate partners. Second, advocates discovered that the term was leading police officers, judges, and the public to think of domestic violence as a private matter best left untouched by public interference. Police officers often refused to arrest batterers, judges neglected to convict perpetrators, and families blamed the victim for the dispute.

As research continued to grow about the nature and dynamics of violence, we learned that not just married, heterosexual partners living in a single household experience domestic violence. Same-sex couples, dating couples, teens in relationships—all of these are examples of groups who were excluded from the traditional domestic violence framework. Using the term "intimate partner violence" more clearly defines the social problem and allows for the inclusion of all affected.

Victim versus Survivor

Language has the power to define a social problem, as well as provide the mental scaffolding necessary to understand and address the issue. When discussing IPV, advocates prefer to use the term "**survivor**" for those affected by abuse to honor the courage and strength of those who experience IPV (DeWard 2010). However, not everyone who experiences abuse prefers that language. Some argue that using the term "survivor" doesn't adequately recognize their victimization. On an individual level, it is better to use **people-first language** to honor the unique lived experiences of each person. People-first language makes the person the subject, and all other descriptions are secondary. Regardless of preferred terminology, intimate partner violence need not define an individual—it happens to the person; it is *not* the only aspect of their lives. As always, we should empower individuals and use the language they prefer (DeWard 2010).

In addition, this chapter will use the feminine pronouns "she" and "her" to refer to survivors of IPV. This choice is not meant to demean or exclude men or nonbinary people who are survivors—we do know that they exist. However, overwhelming empirical data coupled with clear anecdotal evidence from the antiviolence against women movement leads to one conclusion: most victims of IPV are women (DeWard 2010).

POWER AND CONTROL

Power and control are the core foundational concepts from which to understand the perpetration of intimate partner violence. The Power and Control Wheel was created by advocates at the Domestic Abuse Intervention Project in Duluth, Minnesota, to provide a visual representation of how IPV happens. The image looks like an old-timey wagon wheel. On the outside rim, we see physical and sexual violence—the aspect of IPV that is most known. At the center of the wheel, we see "Power and Control."

The exertion of power and control over an intimate partner is the "cog" that holds the wheel together—it is the key problem at the core of IPV. How does this desire for power and control connect to physical and sexual violence? That's where the wagon spokes come in. Listed here are some examples of power and control "tactics." They are unhealthy, controlling behaviors that establish and maintain power and control in intimate relationships.

For example, economic abuse often plays a key role in IPV, as it allows the batterer to maintain control over money, financial decisions, employment, and credit scoring. To safely exit an abusive household, survivors need a car, money for food and rent, and employable skills. Knowing this, perpetrators remove access to resources that could provide economic independence (Powers 2019). Perpetrators may use substance abuse addiction (either the victim's or batterer's) to keep the victim scared of arrest. Indeed, many domestic violence shelters do not allow victims under the influence of any substance to obtain residential services (Tron 2020).

While there is no single timeline or narrative that suits all IPV dynamics, many advocates cite these tactics as warning signs or precursors to physical violence. In the 1970s, psychologist Lenore Walker developed the theory of the "cycle of abuse." The cycle of abuse theory posits that intimate partner violence follows three distinct phases: the tension-building stage, the incident or crisis stage, and the calm or honeymoon stage (Gillette 2022). For years this framework was used to help understand the senseless violence by a loved one, and for many, this theory did describe the pattern they experienced. However, many

POWER AND CONTROL WHEEL

Physical and sexual assaults, or threats to commit them, are the most apparent forms of domestic violence and are usually the actions that allow others to become aware of the problem. However, regular use of other abusive behaviors by the batterer, when reinforced by one or more acts of physical violence, make up a larger system of abuse. Although physical assaults may occur only once or occasionally, they instill threat of future violent attacks and allow the abuser to take control of the woman's life and circumstances.

The Power & Control diagram is a particularly helpful tool in understanding the overall pattern of abusive and violent behaviors, which are used by a batterer to establish and maintain control over his partner. Very often, one or more violent incidents are accompanied by an array of these other types of abuse. They are less easily identified, yet firmly establish a pattern of intimidation and control in the relationship.

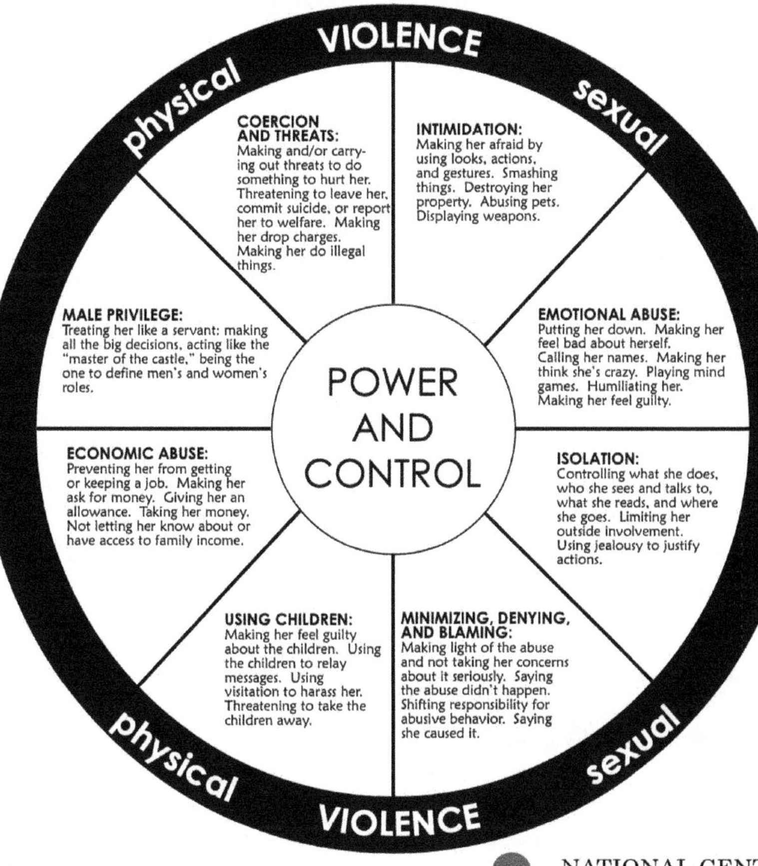

Developed by:
Domestic Abuse Intervention Project
202 East Superior Street
Duluth, MN 55802
218.722.4134

Produced and distributed by:

NATIONAL CENTER
on Domestic and Sexual Violence
training • consulting • advocacy
4612 Shoal Creek Blvd. • Austin, Texas 78756
512.407.9020 (phone and fax) • www.ncdsv.org

Figure 7.2 The Power and Control Wheel illustrates the dynamics of intimate partner violence. DOMESTIC ABUSE INTERVENTION PROGRAMS, HOME OF THE DULUTH MODEL victim experiences did not follow this mold. Sometimes the different phases were present, but in a different order, sometimes the violence escalated at different paces, and some victims never experienced the reprieve of the honeymoon and calm phase. Because of this, many victim advocates discourage the use of this model to explain violence. Every intimate partner violence victim is unique, and that unique experience should be heard and honored.

The scope and magnitude of power and control tactics vary. In each situation, however, using intimidation, emotional abuse, and isolation are common. Pay particular attention to the "using male privilege" tactic in the wheel's lower left. We must remember that the societal perpetuation of sexism and patriarchy teaches and condones toxic masculinity.

INTIMATE PARTNER VIOLENCE PREVALENCE

According to the National Intimate Partner Survey on Domestic and Sexual Violence Survey (NISVS) conducted by the CDC, approximately 41 percent of US women experience a form of IPV which causes a negative impact, compared to approximately 11 percent of US men (Leemis et al. 2022). During the 2020 COVID-19 pandemic, domestic violence service providers saw an average of 25 percent increase in hotline calls (Tolan 2020). Teens in the LGBTQIA+ community and racial and ethnic minority teens are disproportionately represented in these statistics (CDC 2022).

Approximately 44 percent of lesbian women and 26 percent of gay men experience some form of intimate partner violence in their lifetime (CDC 2010). Bisexual persons experienced domestic violence at eight times the rate

In the News . . .

In the summer of 2022, the news broke of the disappearance of twenty-two-year-old Gabby Petito. Petito was a van-life blogger with her fiancé Brian Laundrie. While Gabby was still missing, Brian returned home to Florida. Her body was later found in a Wyoming campground. Brian admits to killing Gabby in a notebook found near her body. Brian was later found dead in a Florida nature reserve (Clark 2023). Later, police body camera footage was released. The police were called to intervene after a stranger saw Brian slap and hit Gabby. Her parents have publicly stated that they believe that Gabby would still be alive if the police had acknowledged the seriousness of the violence and followed protocols (Clark 2023).

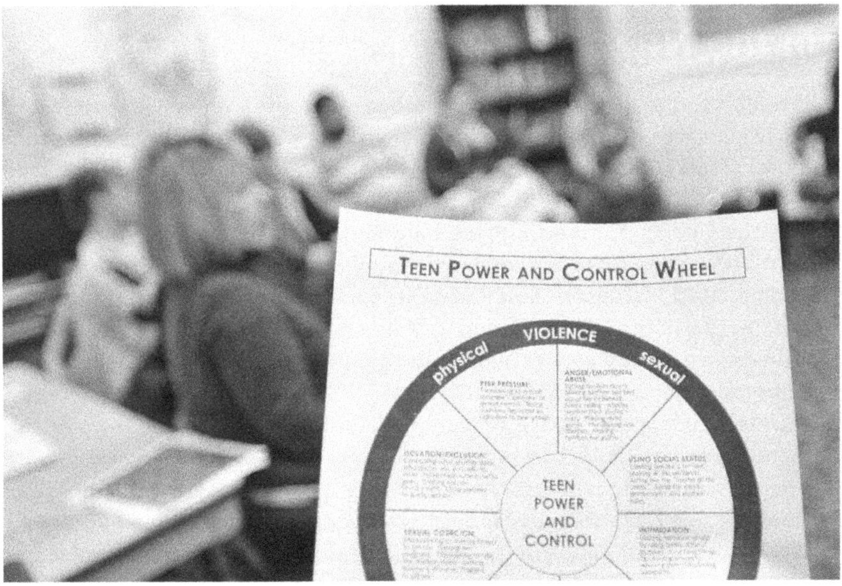

Figure 7.3 Perpetrators of teen dating violence often use unique tactics of power and control. PHOTO BY SGT. VERONICA MONTES, US AIR FORCE

(43.5 victimizations per 1,000) experienced by straight persons (4.2 victimizations per 1,000). Gay or lesbian persons experienced a rate of domestic violence two times greater (10.3 victimizations per 1,000) than straight people (Truman and Morgan 2022). A recent study found that 57 percent of transgender adults experienced IPV in their lifetime (Hillman 2022).

Teen dating violence is a subtype of IPV that happens in close relationships during teen years (CDC 2020a). Teen dating violence often presents as extreme jealousy or possessiveness, isolation from friends, and controlling demands (Hope Shores Alliance 2020). Dating violence can happen in person, but the use of technology (i.e., social media, texting) is also quite common. Approximately one in eleven teen girls and one in fifteen teen boys experienced physical dating violence in 2015 (CDC 2020a).

Domestic homicides, or being murdered by an intimate partner, are on the rise. Researchers at Northeastern University found that domestic homicides increased by 26 percent between 2010 to 2017 (Fridal and Fox 2019). Researchers from John Hopkins University found that the primary predictor of intimate partner homicide is the presence of strangulation. The research indicates that perpetrators who strangle their victims are seven times more likely to attempt or complete murder (Johnston 2019). On a macro level, domestic violence is often a predictor of other societal violence. A study of 749 mass shootings

In the News . . .

Research suggests that domestic violence increases whenever time with family increases, so what happens when you are trapped at home with your abuser (Taub 2020)? During the COVID-19 pandemic in 2020, people were ordered to shelter in place. While this order was difficult for many, domestic violence victims endured intense hardship. Abusers may have used the COVID-19 pandemic to further exert control over the victim (Dastagir 2020). Victims cited increased isolation from social support networks and the inability to exit the residence during violence (due to fear of COVID-19). In addition, many survivors experienced the economic impact of layoffs and increased violence due to stress (Goodman 2020). Domestic violence service providers report that police officers were hesitant to detain low-violence offenders due to COVID-19 outbreaks in jails and prisons (Goodman 2020). Providers worked to help survivors create a safety plan for this unique situation. Shelters, hotlines, and other advocacy services remained open despite the risk of exposure to the virus to provide safety and support to survivors (Dastagir 2020).

found that 60 percent of the perpetrators were men with histories of domestic violence (Gu 2020).

Men and Nonbinary People as Victims of IPV

Yes, people of all gender identities and biological sexes can be victims of IPV. However, these statistics have become controversial since the theory of gender symmetry was developed in the early 2000s. **Gender symmetry theory** states that men and women are victims of intimate partner violence at the same rate. Advocates rushed to make sense of these claims, as current data and anecdotal experiences did not reflect this conclusion. In fact, the majority of victims were overwhelmingly women. How was this data measured, collected, and disseminated?

The data from the National Intimate Partner and Sexual Violence Survey (NISVS) can help us to be critical consumers of these claims. In 2015, NISVS researchers reported that approximately one in three women (36.4 %) and one in three men (33.6%) have experienced physical violence, sexual violence, or stalking by an intimate partner (Smith et al. 2018). If we stop our analysis here, we might conclude that IPV is experienced equally between men and women. However, the NISVS measured another variable that helps make sense of these numbers: IPV-related impact. Intimate partner violence–related impacts include needing help from law enforcement, missing at least one day of school or work, and needing medical care, all due to IPV. When including this variable, the data change: one in four women (25.1%) and one in ten men (10.9%) have experienced physical violence, sexual violence, or stalking *and* reported an IPV-related impact (Smith et al. 2018). While men and women do experience IPV, the overall severity and lifetime impact on women is much higher.

A 2023 study analyzed the experiences with intimate partner violence at the population level. Twenty-three tactics of IPV were analyzed across types (e.g., psychological, sexual, moderate physical, severe physical, controlling behaviors) (Fanslow et al. 2023). Significant differences were found among these variables, with women experiencing a higher prevalence of IPV with a greater severity overall. The study provides evidence that IPV exhibits gender asymmetry (Fanslow et al. 2023). While it is true that anyone can be a victim of IPV, the data is clear that women experience domestic violence at greater rates and severity. The gender symmetry theory is a myth.

Why Doesn't She Just Leave?

A common question among those who have not experienced IPV is why doesn't the victim simply leave the abuser? On its face, this does seem like a straightforward answer to the problem. However, we know that a complex web of personal and institutional factors keeps survivors trapped in violent relationships. Before we dive into this topic, let's first analyze the assumptions behind the question. When social commentary or media outlets discuss IPV, it is often in the context of the victim: What did she do to provoke the abuser? Why does she stay with the batterer? Why does she return to the violent home? These questions amount to **victim-blaming**, or the assumption that the reason for the abuse falls solely on the one most affected. While these questions can be asked, they do little to help us understand and prevent violence. Why not ask why the batterer abuses?

Leaving Does Not Equal Safety

A common misconception about domestic violence is that if a victim leaves her abusive partner, then the violence will end. From a short-term perspective, leaving the violent home may stop immediate battering. However, since we know that power and control are at the core of abusive behavior, the threat of violence increases after the victim flees. Why? The batterer's authority and control over the victim is challenged, and this challenge is often met with vehement backlash. The most dangerous time for victims of IPV is when they're leaving. Two-thirds of domestic homicides happen upon separation, and there is a 75 percent increase in violence for the first two years after separation (Center for Relationship Abuse Awareness 2023).

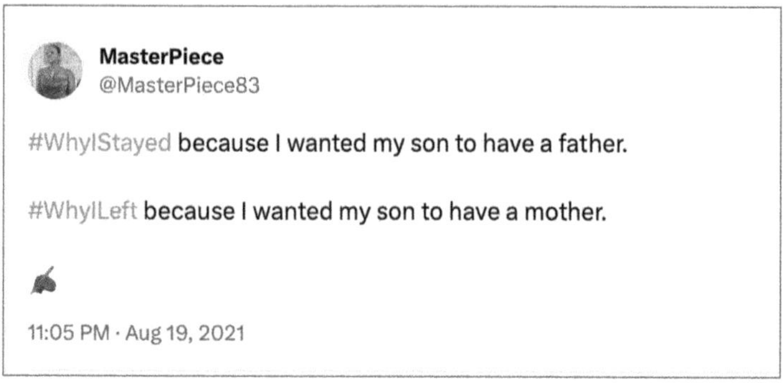

Figure 7.4 In 2021, #WhyIStayed and #WhyILeft were trending on social media. MASTERPIECE POSTED ON X

In addition, survivors may deal with unsupportive family or friends, clergy members encouraging return, and a lack of financial resources. If the victim has children with the batterer, she must navigate court proceedings and a legal system that does not have the resources to offer protection. What does the victim risk if she stays in the violent home? Well, most of the difficulties listed above; however, the violence may be less. We must remember that leaving does *not* equal safety, and quick, easy answers are often not the solution to this multifaceted problem. The complexity of individual experiences with IPV is illustrated in the viral hashtags #WhyIStayed and #WhyILeft.

Why Do Perpetrators Abuse?

Perpetrators of intimate partner violence use this power and control to get what they want on their terms. Batterers have learned that when they use power and control tactics, physical or sexual violence, they get what they want. They have the opportunity and self-interest to meet their desires by any means necessary.

Finally, batterers abuse because they can. As we will discuss in the forthcoming legislation and public policy section, there is little accountability for intimate partner violence. Violence continues to be correlated with toxic forms of manhood, and very few formal consequences are enacted against batterers.

INTIMATE PARTNER VIOLENCE AND PUBLIC POLICY

The most prominent piece of federal legislation addressing intimate partner violence is the **Violence Against Women Act (VAWA)**. First championed by

Senator (now President) Joe Biden in 1994, VAWA financially supports state and local responses to domestic violence, sexual assault, stalking, and dating violence (National Network to End Domestic Violence 2019). This legislation is up for renewal every five years with each subsequent renewal seeking to better address the nuanced needs of survivors. For example, the 2013 reauthorization included protections for LGBTQ and Native American survivors (National Network to End Domestic Violence [NNEDV] 2020).

In 2022, the VAWA Reauthorization Act passed and was signed into law by President Biden on March 22. This bipartisan act made great strides in modernizing and updating the provisions of the legislation. This law provides thousands of victims/survivors and state and local domestic violence programs with the funding necessary to access safety. It also strengthens nondiscrimination policies, providing funding for nonbinary and LBGTQIA+ victim services. VAWA 2022 also provides dedicated funding streams for providing culturally responsive services to communities of color and indigenous peoples (NNEDV 2022).

Mandatory Arrest Laws

Mandatory arrest laws became prevalent in the 1980s in local and state legislation as a response to the hands-off policies regarding domestic violence. However, including law enforcement in every IPV situation is not always ideal. **Mandatory arrest laws** require an arrest of the perpetrator as a result of every domestic violence complaint. Sixteen states (Alaska, Arizona, Colorado, Connecticut, Kansas, Louisiana, Maine, Mississippi, Nevada, New Jersey, Ohio, Oregon, Rhode Island, South Dakota, Utah, and Washington) have mandatory arrest laws (Summers 2022). However, states that enact mandatory arrest policies see a disproportionate number of victim arrests and dual arrests (Hirschel 2008). A **dual arrest** refers to situations where law enforcement is unsure of the primary aggressor during a domestic violence investigation and therefore arrests both people (victim and perpetrator). Mandatory arrest laws often create unintended consequences for survivors. Law enforcement involvement can exacerbate structural inequality experienced by communities of color. A survivor-centered approach supports varied options for survivors to maintain safety and justice (Garcia 2019).

At the state and local level, many domestic violence cases are not prosecuted due to lack of evidence or refusal of the victim to testify. In New Jersey, 80 percent of domestic violence cases are dismissed (Lowe 2017). Some politicians are speaking out against the lack of prosecution of domestic violence offenders. Governor Gretchen Whitmer of Michigan signed a bill into law that requires deferred domestic violence charges to count as prior convictions (Dado 2019). This is a step forward in closing a sentencing loophole often found in

IPV cases. If a batterer is not convicted or accepts a plea deal for a lesser charge, the sentencing guidelines are altered. Upon the next offense, the perpetrator's record does not list prior domestic violence convictions, even though prior violence did occur.

MOVING FORWARD

Despite the grim prevalence of intimate partner violence, amazing work is being done to raise public awareness, support survivors, and prevent violence. For example, artist and activist Alexandro Palombo created a public awareness campaign about the prevalence of violence against women by depicting women leaders (like Hillary Clinton, Angela Merkel, and Michelle Obama as victims of physical assault (Joseph 2020).

Prevention is key to ending violence. The CDC (2019) developed IPV prevention strategies that include

- teaching safe and healthy relationship skills
- engaging influential adults and peers
- disrupting developmental pathways toward partner violence
- creating protective environments
- strengthening economic support for families
- supporting survivors to increase safety and lessen harm

To implement these strategies, the CDC funds state and local programs to provide social-emotional programs for youth, bystander empowerment and education, and engagement of men and boys as allies in prevention (2019).

Technological advancements support survivors in their journey to justice. For example, the application Victims Voice (https://victimsvoice.app/) provides a secure location for victims of IPV to record and track instances of abuse for use in future legal actions. All submissions are geolocated and time-stamped so that details can be presented to lawyers and prosecutors in an organized, chronological way. Using this application helps victims to remember key events to support the application of protection orders, criminal proceedings, and child custody agreements.

Local victim advocacy programs engage in community education events to raise awareness about intimate partner violence. One popular community event is called Walk a Mile in Her Shoes. This event asks men to literally "walk in her shoes" by completing the community awareness march in high heels. The march asks men to sign a pledge agreeing to work to overcome personal and community gender bias and end violence against women.

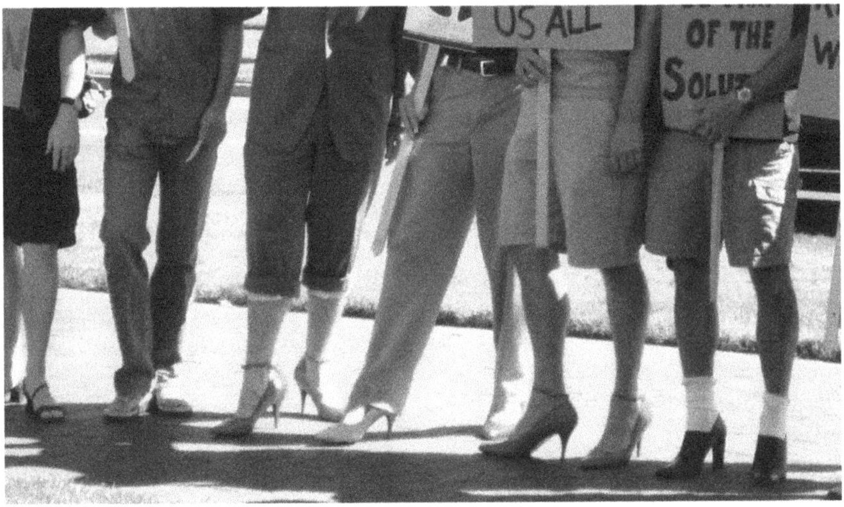

Figure 7.5 Walk a Mile in Her Shoes is a domestic violence public awareness event that asks men to walk a mile wearing red high heels. POSTED ON INSTAGRAM

Key Takeaways

- Intimate partner violence is a pattern of coercive tactics meant to establish and maintain power and control over an intimate partner.
- Tactics of power and control include economic control, using male privilege, and psychological abuse, but the tactics vary based on the situation.
- Teen dating violence is coercive tactics used by a romantic teen couple, often using stalking behaviors and technology.
- The Violence Against Women Act (VAWA) is the key federal legislation that provides funding for victim services and prevention work.
- The Centers for Disease Control and Prevention engages in prevention education to raise awareness and stop intimate partner violence.

National Domestic Violence Hotline

If you or someone you know is a victim of Intimate Partner Violence, consider reaching out to the National Domestic Violence Hotline at 800-799-7233 or thehotline.org.

8

GENDER AND EDUCATION
#EDUCATIONEQUITY

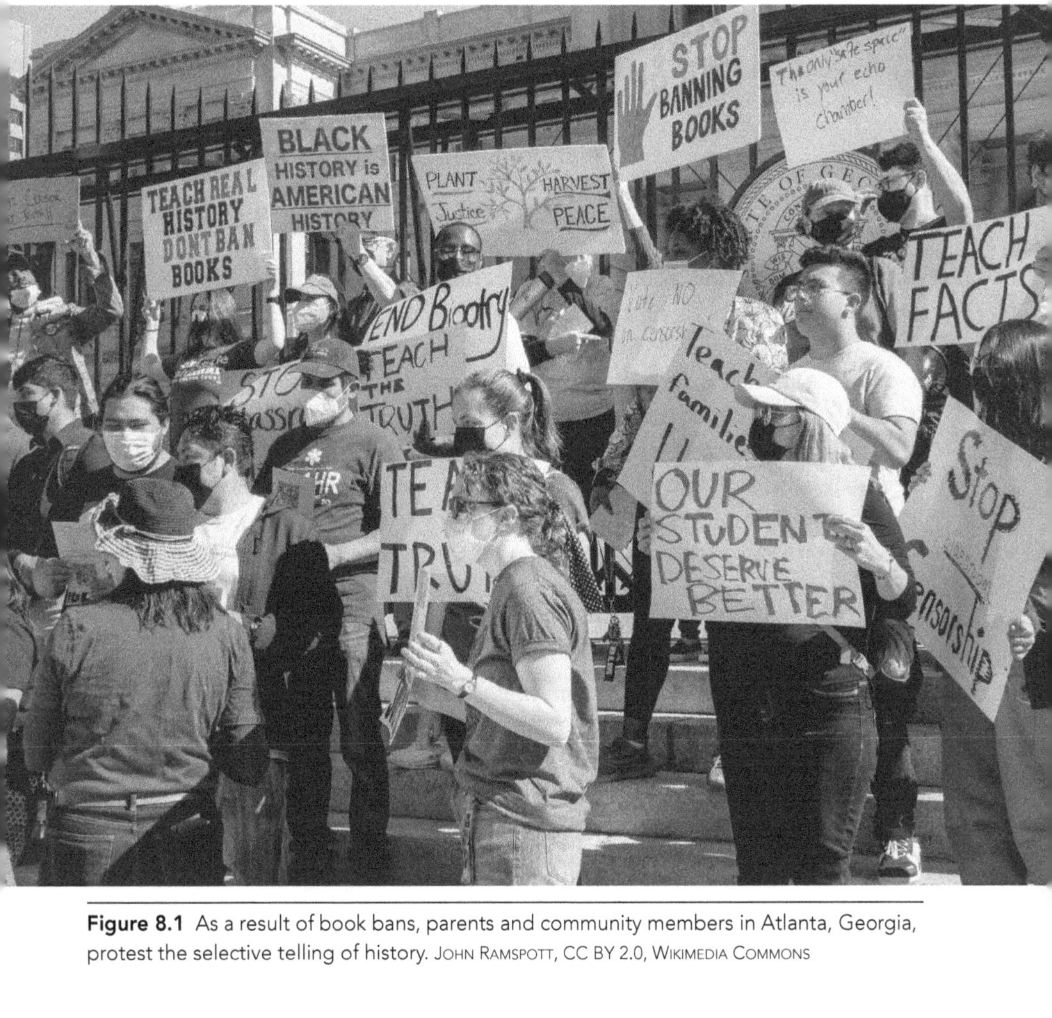

Figure 8.1 As a result of book bans, parents and community members in Atlanta, Georgia, protest the selective telling of history. John Ramspott, CC BY 2.0, Wikimedia Commons

Some researchers contend that boys are lagging in school performance, graduation rates, and university degree completion. Others cite the significant lack of girls in science, technology, engineering, and math in both secondary and higher education. This entire debate leaves nonbinary students ignored and invisible. *So who is actually getting the short end in our educational system?*

LEARNING GOALS

By the end of this chapter, you should be able to

1. Summarize the major inequities found in the institution of education
2. Analyze how boys, girls, and nonbinary students experience bias in schooling
3. Evaluate the effects of bias in education on women's long-term career aspirations

EDUCATION AS A SOCIAL INSTITUTION

In the field of sociology, education is defined as a social institution. A **social institution** refers to a structure that's organized to meet specific societal needs. They are the way that society allocates meaning, maintains order, and reinforces shared beliefs and ideologies. In the United States, formal education began as haphazard, individualized, and reserved for people who were wealthy and white. Access to education was a way to reinforce that inequality. People who were enslaved were prohibited from learning to read. Indigenous children were forced into religious schools to strip them of their culture and indoctrinate European, white ideology. Poor children could not afford access to private schooling. Education for girls was considered a waste and outside of the "natural order."

As the need for an informed citizenry became more apparent, advocates called for a public schooling system that would be available to all children without cost. Reformers argued for "common schools," advocating for universal education that might eliminate some of society's inequalities. Gradually, the idea of free public education took hold, with 78 percent of children aged five to fourteen enrolled in public schools in 1870 (Kober and Rentner 2020). Schools developed as centers of community engagement.

Educational Hierarchies

Despite the desire to diminish social inequality, the institution of education often worked to further discriminate against students of color, poor children, and girls. Seeking to maintain racially segregated schools, the Supreme Court ruled in ***Plessy v. Ferguson*** (1896) that states could operate "separate but equal" schools for Black and white students. However, separate never equated to equal. Schools for Black students were underfunded, lacking in books, trained teachers, and safe buildings (National Archives 2024a).

In 1954, the Supreme Court ruled on the groundbreaking civil rights case ***Brown v. Board of Education of Topeka, Kansas***. This ruling stated that state-sanctioned segregation was a violation of the Fourteenth Amendment, and therefore illegal (National Archives 2024b). Thus began the process of integrating public schools, which was met with violence and hatred by many white people. In November 1960, Ruby Bridges was the first Black student to attend an integrated elementary school in the South. Each day, Ruby and her mother were escorted by four federal marshals past screaming crowds (Michals 2015).

While this black and white photo conveys that Bridges's police escort to school was long ago, social media tells us otherwise. Ruby Bridges is an active advocate and author and is well-known in her community today.

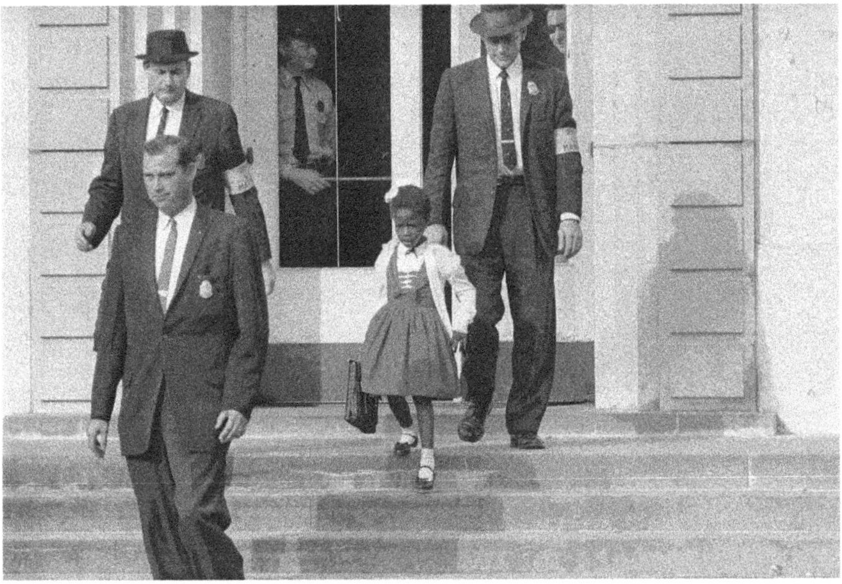

Figure 8.2 After a federal court ruling ended segregation in public schools, Ruby Bridges was the first Black student to attend a formerly all-white elementary school (November 1960). Uncredited Department of Justice photographer, Wikimedia Commons

In-Depth: The Fourteenth Amendment

The Fourteenth Amendment to the Constitution was one of three major pieces of legislation proposed after the Civil War to guarantee equal civil and legal rights to Black citizens. The amendment grants citizenship rights to formerly enslaved people with the statement "all persons born or naturalized in the United States." In addition, the amendment includes the right to liberty and due process for all citizens: "nor shall any State deprive any personal of life, liberty, or property, without due process of law; nor deny to any person . . . the equal protection of laws."

The Fourteenth Amendment was the focus of the debate surrounding segregation in public schools. In *Plessy v. Ferguson*, the Supreme Court ruled that the legislation did not grant Congress the right to prevent discrimination committed by private citizens. States, therefore, were left to make their own determination, leaving many to pass Jim Crow laws requiring separate schools based on race. Sixty years later, the Supreme Court ruled in *Brown v. Board of Education* that state-sanctioned school segregation was a fundamental violation of the Fourteenth Amendment (National Archives 2021).

Schools were slow to provide full educational access to girls. When allowed to attend, girls were often taught a different curriculum than boys and encountered limited access to high school and higher education. The **Elementary and Secondary Education Act of 1965** worked to ensure equal access to education for students of color, low-income children, and girls (Kober and Rentner 2020). Despite these advancements in educational equity, inequality in education continues to pervade American schools.

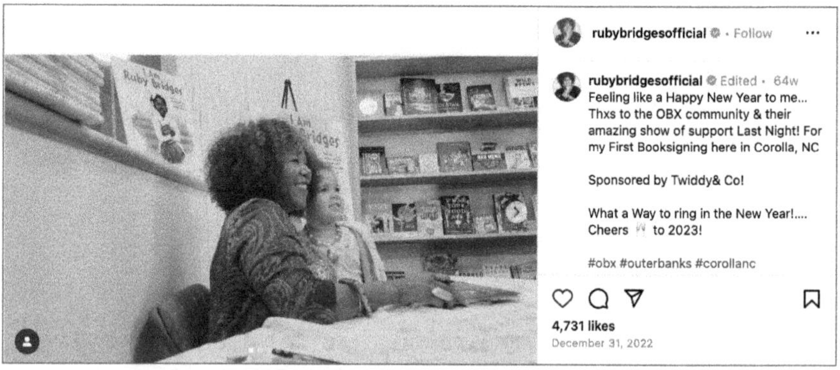

Figure 8.3 Ruby Bridges at a book signing of *I Am Ruby Bridges.* Posted on Instagram

GENDER BIAS IN K–12

Gender expectations limit boys and girls and render nonbinary children invisible. While nonbinary gender identities are increasingly recognized, many teachers don't feel confident in their knowledge about gender or their ability to accurately explain these concepts to their students (Ehrenhalt 2019). Thus, teachers often avoid discussions of nonbinary identities altogether, leaving nonbinary students' experiences unheard (2019).

Gender stereotypes are reinforced by teachers, with more than 75 percent of public school teachers being female and 80 percent of teachers being white (Cimpian 2018). The number of male teachers has dropped significantly for middle school (Whitmire and Baily 2023). Gendered job segregation in teaching is apparent, as teaching continues to be considered a "woman's job" (Wong 2019). Data on K–12 teachers show that pay scales increase when the number of male teachers increases (Whitmire and Baily 2023).

Gender Tracking

Teachers play a central role in school-aged children's lives. While they teach the fundamentals of math, science, and reading, they also contribute to the gender socialization of their students. **Gender tracking** refers to the stereotypes and assumptions regarding students' academic abilities based on gender (American Association of University Women [AAUW] 2023a).

As children enter their preschool classrooms at age four or five, socialization about gender expectations begins. As they begin exploring their classrooms, many students find highly gender-segregated toys which leads to gender-segregated play (Quinlan 2016). Research suggests that play is essential to young children's learning and development. Indeed, the data show that different types of play support different kinds of development. For example, building with blocks supports spatial skills, while dramatic play in a kitchen supports social skills (Quinlan 2016). Lack of engagement with all types of play can leave developmental holes for both boys and girls.

Upon entering kindergarten, boys and girls display no gender gap in math test scores. By the time those same children advance to third grade, a significant gap in favor of boys emerges (Cimpian 2018). Researchers argue that teacher beliefs about student ability significantly contribute to this gender achievement gap. Teachers consistently rate girls' math abilities lower than boys, even when their test scores are equivalent (Cimpian et al. 2016).

Numerous studies show that teachers are more likely to attribute boys' failures at math to lack of effort, but girls' failures at math to lack of ability

(Cimpian et al. 2016). These teacher assumptions about math ability are applied to female students regardless of observed academic performance (2016). Teacher impressions of girls' math abilities contribute to the gender gap in math, accounting for about half of the gap (Cimpian 2018). While math test scores confirm that girls and boys are essentially even in abilities, girls are still guided away from STEM fields as early as elementary school (AAUW 2023a).

In the News . . .

In 2022, Governor Ron DeSantis signed legislation that restricted how Florida teachers could teach sexism and racism in Florida schools. The Stop the Wrongs to Our Kids and Employees (WOKE) Act prohibits instruction that teaches that people are inherently biased, that people can be privileged or oppressed based on race, gender, or national origin, and that people bear personal responsibility for the actions of their ancestors. The legislation prohibits the teaching of critical race theory, which explores how societal institutions perpetuate racism. Both teachers and advocates are outraged by this restriction of content, which has included the cancelation of civil rights presentations and the rejection of math textbooks because of graphical depictions of racial data (Reilly 2022).

Measuring math proficiency continues to be a struggle. State standardized tests show little, if any, gender differences in math performance. However, the cumulative effect of a consistent underestimation of girls' math abilities can be tracked to perceived career aptitude and college majors (Cimpian 2018). Research shows that gender differences in high school students' future career plans have the largest effect on pursuing STEM majors in college, much more than test scores, perceived math abilities, or family expectations (Weeden, Gelbgiser, and Morgan 2020). The perceived gender segregation in the workforce persists in college major choices, so scientists insist that normalizing women in STEM careers while students are in high school is key (Weeden, Gelbgiser, and Morgan 2020).

Gendered Behavior and Expectation Bias

While classroom participation is relatively even in elementary schools, that equality diminishes within higher grades. Observations in middle and high school classrooms show male students dominating classroom discussions. They tend to raise their hands and volunteer to read aloud more often than other students (Alber 2017). Because male students are so eager, teachers often rely on male students to be their responders and volunteers, while female students are called on less frequently. Research shows an uneven distribution of teacher attention in favor of male students (Sadker and Zittleman 2009).

Research shows that teachers tend to punish boys' behavior more severely, but they also give them more praise and specific feedback on assignments. Girls, however, are rarely praised for their work product but rather for their physical appearance, neatness, or cleanliness (Nduagbo 2020). Consider the subtle messaging of the saying "be a good girl," reinforcing compliance, versus "boys will be boys," reinforcing inappropriate behavior (AAUW 2023a). Nonbinary students are often relegated to virtual invisibility. Some teachers avoid classroom discussions or substantive content on gender identity, fearing community backlash.

An example of unequal expectations and reactions to student behavior is the school-to-prison pipeline. The **school-to-prison pipeline** refers to the connection between severe, zero-tolerance school discipline policies that funnel students into the criminal justice system. The students most affected by this pipeline are low-income male students of color. School resource officers (SROs) stationed inside schools increase arrests for low-level offenses. Particularly in low-income schools, students with developmentally appropriate behavioral issues are sent to the school resource officer rather than supported by counselors or mental health professionals. Indeed, 1.7 million students are in schools with embedded police officers but no counselors or social workers. Despite the overwhelming evidence of negative outcomes, schools over-rely on suspensions and expulsions to address misbehavior. Schools report a 22 percent increase in suspensions and/or expulsions after the inclusion of a school resource officer (American Bar Association 2023). The data is clear that children of color and those with disabilities are most likely to be arrested at school (Mendel 2021). Black students are 2.2 times more likely to be referred to law enforcement compared to their white peers (American Bar Association 2023).

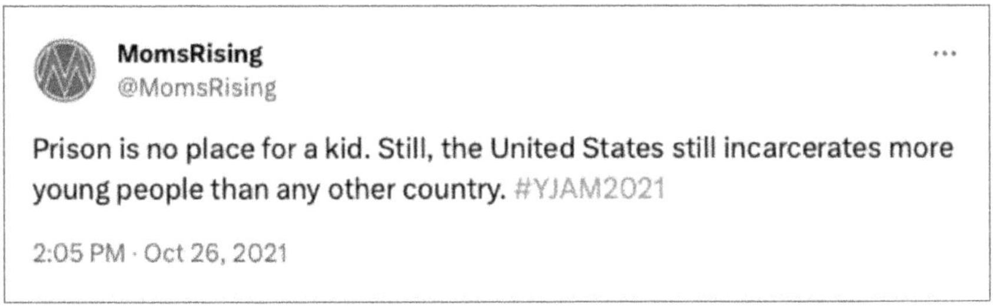

Figure 8.4 The school-to-prison pipeline significantly contributes to the mass incarceration of men of color. Posted by Girls Inc. on X

Gender Bias in Higher Education

A growing gender gap in higher education enrollment and graduation rates has become a hot topic of debate. Women are more likely than men to be enrolled in college and complete their degrees (Parker 2021). However, research suggests that male students are more commonly admitted to selective private colleges due to the bias of admissions officers. For female students to be admitted, they must display higher academic achievement than their male peers (Whitmire and Baily 2023).

Why is there a gender gap in higher education degree completion? When asked about why they did not complete their college degree, men discussed personal choice as the main factor: 29 percent said they just didn't want to, and 23 percent stated they didn't need the degree to get the job they wanted (Parker 2021). Women (44 %) were most likely to cite financial barriers as a reason to not obtain a degree. Of college graduates, approximately half of men and women state that their college education was very useful to them in the job market (Parker 2021).

Students also participate in classes differently based on gender. Research suggests that masculinity and androgyny are associated with increased in-class participation, while femininity is associated with more student-professor interactions after class (Leraas, Kippen, Larson 2018). Law schools show similar outcomes, with research demonstrating that women are less likely to speak in law school classrooms than men (Shadel, Trawalter, and Verkerke 2022). Similar findings exist in engineering (Sharlach 2022), biology (Aguillon et al. 2020), and medicine (Cromer, D'Silva, and Phadke 2022) classrooms.

Gender in Science, Technology, Engineering, and Math (STEM)

Research shows that transgender and gender-diverse students are more likely to select majors in the arts and humanities as compared to their cisgender peers. Conversely, transgender and gender-diverse students are less likely to choose business, science, and technology majors than their cisgender peers (White 2023). Cisgender male students tend to choose majors that lead to high-paying jobs, such as technology and engineering, while female students are concentrated in majors with lower-paying jobs, like liberal arts and the social sciences (Carmichael 2017).

Women earning bachelor's degrees in STEM continue to be the minority. Women earn 42 percent of mathematics and statistics degrees, 25 percent of

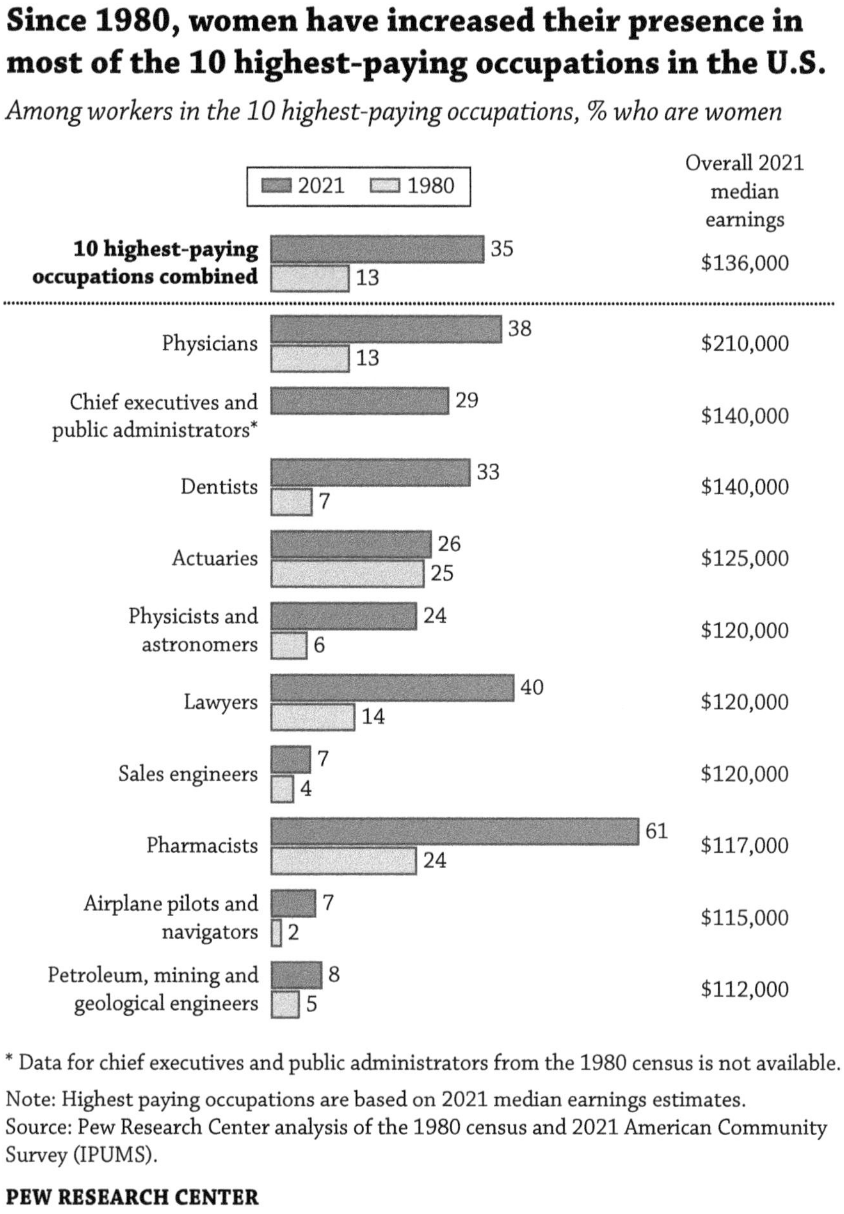

Figure 8.5 Women's employment in the highest-paying careers has significantly increased in the past forty years. DATA FROM THE PEW RESEARCH CENTER, AMERICAN COMMUNITY SURVEY (2021)

physics degrees, and 23 percent of engineering degrees (Hurst and Fry 2023). Women are underrepresented not only in STEM majors but in other fields of study such as criminal justice and philosophy (Ganley et al. 2017). The factor most predictive of whether a female student chooses a specific major is the degree of perceived gender discrimination in the field. Women are not "math-phobic" or "science-phobic"—they just prefer to avoid gender discrimination (Ganley et al. 2017).

Even when women do complete STEM majors, they are more likely than their male peers to access lower-paying jobs in that field. For example, the data show that women biology graduates are most likely to find a job as a lab or pharmacy technician, which are low-paying and low prestige. However, men biology graduates are more likely to work as a managers or data analysts, which are higher paying jobs with higher prestige (Carmichael 2017).

As most of the highest-paying jobs require advanced training, women are completing more specialized graduate degrees. Women now earn approximately half of all juris doctor (JD), doctor of dental surgery or doctor of dental medicine (DDS or DMD), and doctor of medicine (MD) degrees (Hurst and Fry 2023).

In 2023, women comprised over 35 percent of the workforce in the ten highest-paying careers, an increase from only 13 percent in 1980 (Hurst and Fry 2023). Women's overall labor force participation is 47 percent, so their inclusion in these careers is still well below their share of the workforce. There is one outlier to this data: women make up 61 percent of pharmacists. However, women still make up only about 7 percent of the employees in the top-earning engineering careers (Hurst and Fry 2023).

EDUCATION AND PUBLIC POLICY

The most well-known piece of federal legislation about gender and education is Title IX. **Title IX** prohibits federally funded high schools and colleges from discriminating based on sex. Sixty-three percent of Americans have heard about this law and believe that it has a positive impact (Igielnik 2022). However, as a deeper understanding of gender continues to grow in the United States, debates have emerged asking us to further define "sex" and clearly define "discrimination."

Gender and Sexuality Curriculum

Local school districts have taken center stage as gender in the curriculum is debated. For example, in Washington, DC, parents can select "nonbinary" as a third gender option (Stein 2018). However, other states have adopted more restricted laws and policies. In 2022, Florida's Board of Education expanded the

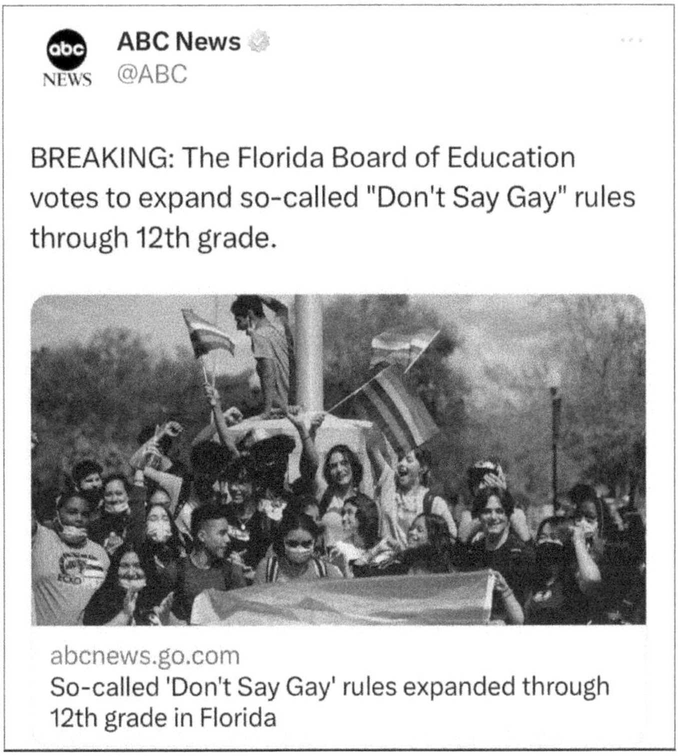

Figure 8.6 Florida's "Don't Say Gay" bill originally prohibited teachers from teaching about sexuality or gender to students through third grade. The 2023 update expanded that prohibition to students through twelfth grade. POSTED ON INSTAGRAM

Parental Rights Education bill (commonly called the "Don't Say Gay" law) which bans public schools from teaching about gender or sexual orientation to students through the twelfth grade (Burga 2023b). These policies further restrict teachers from engaging authentically with their students and render nonbinary students invisible.

In 2023, approximately two thousand books were banned from American schools. According to the American Library Association, this represents a 20 percent increase in book censorship, the most since the organization began tracking book censorship in the early 2000s (Archie 2023). Most of the books were written by or topically about people of color or members of the LGBTQIA+ community (Archie 2023). The United States Department of Education deems this increase as evidence of discrimination against LGBTQIA+ Americans. In response, President Biden appointed a book ban coordinator at the Education

Department whose role includes informing local school districts how book bans can violate civil rights laws (Ordoñez 2023).

Parental Rights versus Student Privacy

Another controversial topic involves student privacy rights versus parental notification policies. In school districts across the United States, students can change their official gender identity and subsequent pronouns without parental consent. This also allows the student access to facilities that reflect their gender identity.

Some parents insist that they should have access to all aspects of their child's education, from the specifics of curriculum to the bathroom used. Other parents have objected, claiming that parental notification is "forced outing" of gender identity, which may dissuade nonbinary and transgender students from revealing their identities. Parental notification may also put students in danger from their parents if they are unsupportive (Cowen 2023).

In this battle, some school districts favor student rights and protection. Approximately 168 public school districts, or 6,000 schools in the United States have policies that block parents from being told their child's gender identity. These districts include Chicago Public Schools, Los Angeles Unified School District, and Seattle Public Schools (Christenson 2023). The school districts included rural, suburban, and urban areas found in politically conservative and politically liberal leaning states.

However, opponents argue that parents have the legal right to know any information about their child. Many school districts have adopted parental notification policies which require teachers to notify parents if their child asks to be identified by a different name or pronouns. Currently, these policies can

In the News . . .

In 2024, students attending college in Florida's state university system, including the University of Florida and Florida State, may no longer take sociology to meet general education or core requirements. The board of governors, in conjunction with Governor Ron DeSantis, claims that sociology has become too "woke" and does not provide general knowledge to students. Florida sociology professors and the American Sociological Association disagree, stating that sociology is the scientific study of social facts and is critical to civic literacy (Hartocollis 2024).

be found in school districts throughout five states, including Alabama, California, Florida, Indiana, and North Carolina (Burga 2023a). Another six states have widespread policies that protect parental access to all school records, including sessions with a school counselor or psychologist.

MOVING FORWARD

Creating a learning environment where academic achievement by all students is considered popular by peers is essential to closing any gender gap (Whitmire and Baily 2023). The research is clear that schools that set high standards for all students and involve parents and the community can overcome achievement gaps based on race and gender. Research suggests that mentoring and role-modeling programs, including men engaging in non-traditionally masculine careers, are helpful. Encouraging fathers to read to children, thereby normalizes literacy in men and boys (Whitmire and Baily 2023).

The research is clear that curriculums that include respect for others regarding gender and sexual orientation are effective (Meckler 2022). Activists continue to encourage teachers to learn and use correct gender vocabulary, model inclusive language, and acknowledge mistakes (Ehrenhalt 2019). For example, the organization Advocates for Youth developed a lesson plan entitled "Pink, Blue and Purple," which guides first-grade teachers to explain gender, gender identity, and gender role stereotypes (Advocates for Youth 2021). In addition, students explore gender role stereotypes and discuss how they can be limiting.

Education Equity is an organization seeking to bring awareness and solutions to educational inequities. Their work highlights the inequities in schools due to a lack of funding, school environment (e.g., class sizes, relationship with teachers, building safety), and lack of diversity of teachers. The organization also engages in public awareness around the school-to-prison pipeline in "Finger-paint to Fingerprints."

Finally, the **Gender Equity in Education Act** is meant to provide educational institutions with the resources they need to fully comply with Title IX. If passed, this bill would provide training and technical assistance to support Title IX compliance for schools and Title IX coordinators, create an Office of Gender Equity in the US Department of Education, and provide funding for grants supporting gender equity work (AAUW 2023b). This bill was introduced to Congress in 2021 and reintroduced in June 2023. Publicly, there is support for enhancements to Title IX.

Key Takeaways

- Education is an institution that has both contributed to social equality and reinforced institutional discrimination against low-income students, female and gender-nonconforming students, and students of color.
- Teachers engage in gender tracking, assuming boys are more capable of math and science, while girls are more capable of reading and writing.
- Female students' negative experiences in STEM classes in high school affect college majors and career aspirations.
- Local school districts debate the application of Title IX protections, including parental notifications, gender curriculum, and book bans.
- Organizations continue to advocate for clear education of students, teachers, and the public about gender identity and sexuality.

9

MARRIAGE AND FAMILY
#GOODMOM

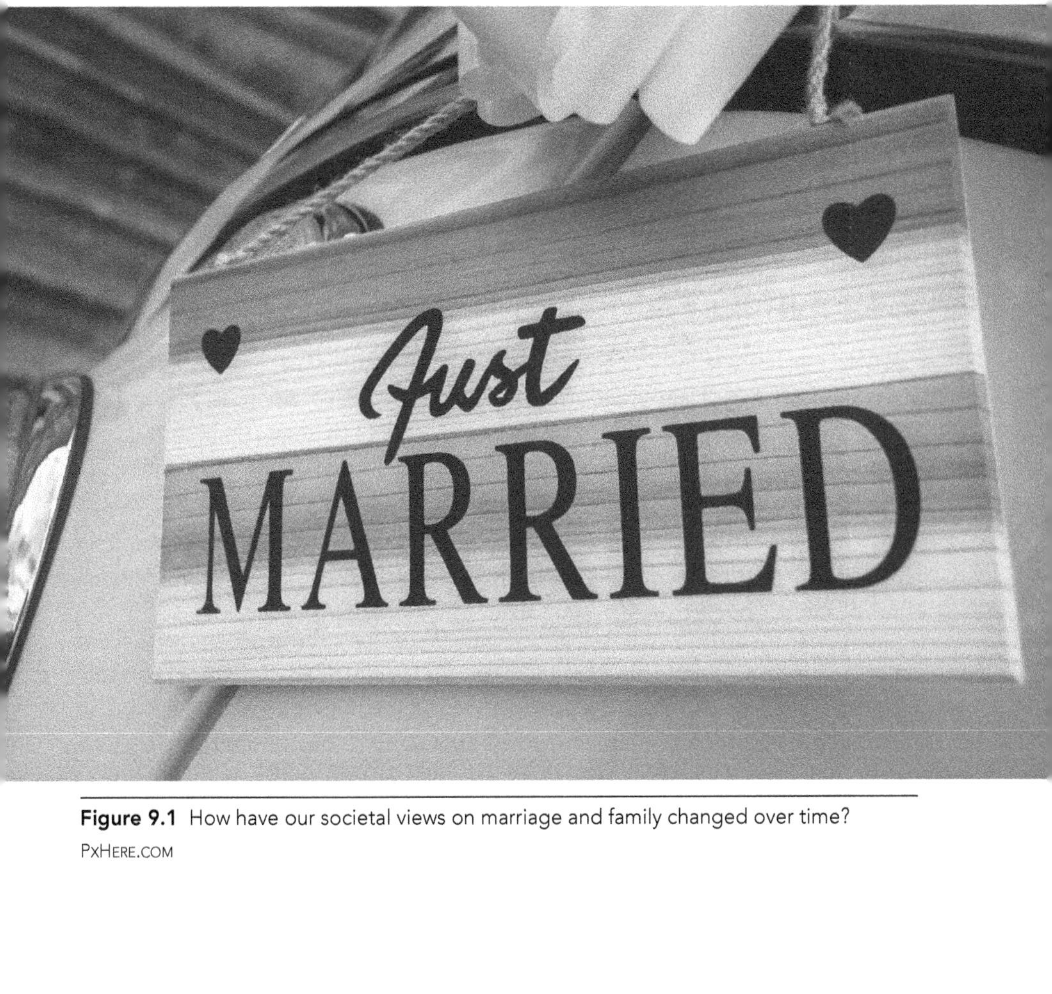

Figure 9.1 How have our societal views on marriage and family changed over time?
PxHere.com

TAKE A MOMENT to google the search term "good mom." What types of descriptions and images are most prominent? In my search, common traits include being hardworking, nurturing, and always available. Oh, and funny, a good role model, and fun (Lange 2022)! Now, do the same search, but change the term to "good dad." Consider the search results. A "good dad" is a disciplinarian, controls his anger, and is a role model (Onu 2022). These differences are pronounced and leave mothers with a high bar to achieve "good mom" status. *How do these gendered expectations affect marriage and family relationships? How does inequality affect parenting?*

LEARNING GOALS

1. Summarize the gendered differences in experiences with dating, marriage, and parenthood.
2. Analyze the impact of gendered household labor and the care economy.
3. Evaluate the effectiveness of public policy and social change efforts around marriage and family.

DEFINING FAMILY

How do we define a family? Social scientists, policy officials, legal scholars, and the public tend to disagree about its definition. Generally, we think of **family** as a group of people living together who have legal ties (like marriage) or biological ties (like parents and children). The label of "family" includes an expectation of care and commitment, as well as authority and responsibility (Cohen 2021). However, some argue that a **chosen family**, people with whom there are no legal or biological ties, yet experience love and commitment by choice, are just as important and valid.

In the 1970s, 67 percent of Americans (ages 25–49) were living with their spouse and minor children (Aragáo et al. 2023). Fifty years later, that same demographic has dropped to 37 percent. What family structures have become more popular? Married couples with no kids remain the close second (21 percent). However, new family structures have also become more popular, such as cohabiting with no kids (7 percent) and cohabiting with kids (5 percent). There are many contributing factors to these changes, including marrying later in life, remaining unmarried, and reduced fertility rates. While marriage overall has declined, there has been an increase in interracial and same-sex marriages (Aragáo et al. 2023).

Americans' views on marriage and family have changed, too. Marriage and family are seen as less important aspects of a fulfilling life. Having a job or career they enjoy (71 percent) and having close friends (61 percent) were seen as most important while having children (26 percent) and being married (23 percent) were seen as less important (Parker and Minkin 2023).

In a recent survey, 31 percent of Americans agree that marriage is old-fashioned, while 67 percent feel otherwise (Cox 2023). Yet commenters have long proclaimed the necessity of two-parent marriages as the most stable for children, calling the nuclear (heterosexual) family "indispensable" (Wilcox and Boyd 2020). However, admonishments to heterosexual women to marry can miss the lived experiences of women attempting to date (Sussman 2023).

A (BRIEF) HISTORY OF MARRIAGE AND FAMILY

Nearly everything about marriage, including its very purpose in society, is socially constructed (Gendler 2014). Historian and gender scholar Stephanie Coontz outlines the history of marriage, debunking the myth of the "traditional family." For most of recorded history, marriage was used as a political or financial contract to obtain land, power, and/or in-laws (Coontz 2015). These marriages followed the **patriarch/property model**, which acknowledges the husband as the head of the household and owner of their wives and children (Wade and Ferree 2019). A woman was the property of her father until "given away" to her husband upon their marriage. Heterosexual marriages were the only unions recognized, as the primary purpose was to produce heirs to maintain the husband's name and wealth.

The industrial revolution forced people into the workforce to be employed by other men. Employers under capitalism sought increases in profit, often at the expense of husbands' ability to financially support their families. White men unionized under the issue of a **family wage**, or an income sufficient to support a husband, wife, and children (Wade and Ferree 2019). The focus on the family wage forced women and people of color out of these jobs, relegating them to low-paying jobs or unemployment. For white middle-class families, the family wage led to the breadwinner/housewife model of marriage.

The **breadwinner/housewife model** included a husband employed for money and a wife working in the home (Wade and Ferree 2019). Despite some

Americans decrying the need for the return of the traditional family, Coontz reminds us that the traditional breadwinner/homemaker marriage is a relatively new phenomenon—one that gained prominence in the 1920s, and was accessible to mostly middle- and upper-class, heterosexual, white families (Coontz 2015). The breadwinner/housewife model also established the **doctrine of separate spheres**: women's domain was the home, and men's domain was their paid employment.

However, this model became unsustainable as white, middle-class women increasingly branched outside of the home into higher education and the paid workforce. As the family model changed, and two incomes became a cultural norm and financial necessity, so did the traditional gender roles associated with heterosexual marriages. Currently, the most common form of marriage is the **partnership model**, which is based on love and companionship between two equals. This model also includes same-sex marriages by deemphasizing gender roles.

However, there continues to be a backlash to these changes. In 2023, the **trad wife (or traditional wife) movement** gained momentum on social media. Young (mostly white middle- and upper-class) women express their love of caring for men through cooking, cleaning, and homemaking. These posts often openly criticize feminists for "man-hating" and lack of home-care abilities; however, feminists reject this premise, reminding us that personal choice and shared support are foundational premises of the feminist movement.

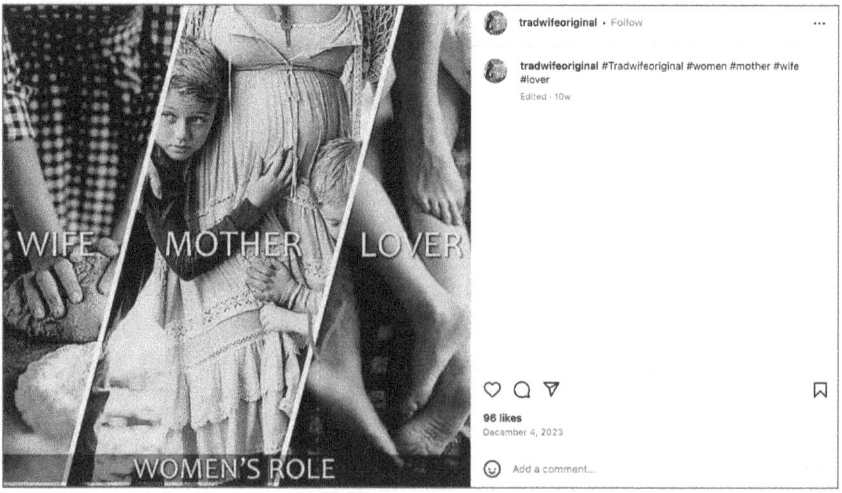

Figure 9.2 The trad wife movement positions itself as the revolution against the #GirlBoss.
POSTED ON INSTAGRAM

GENDERED DATING

Since arranged marriages for political gain or traditional matches based on homemaking capabilities are no longer the norm, how do couples meet? Increasingly, online dating has become the primary method for relationship connections. The first online dating site was Match.com, which made rudimentary online connections for couples in 1995. In 2023, one in ten partnered adults in the United States met on an online dating site or app (Vogels and McClain 2023). Online dating provides new avenues to dating, but only 23 percent of Americans report having used online dating apps or websites (Cox 2023).

Of US adults, 30 percent say they have used an online dating site or app. Young adults (age 18–29) are the largest group to use online dating, with Tinder being the most used dating app (Vogels and McClain 2023). Gay and lesbian Americans are also among the most frequent users of online dating sites (58 percent) (Cox 2023). No statistically significant differences in online dating use exist regarding race or ethnicity (Vogels and McClain 2023).

Online dating site users have mixed reviews about experiences with survey data indicating 53 percent describing their experience as positive, and 46 percent describing their experience as negative (Vogels and McClain 2023). One new phenomenon in the online dating sphere is called ghosting. **Ghosting** is the experience of someone who is a romantic interest suddenly cutting off contact (Cox 2023). Of American adults ages 18 to 29, 42 percent say they've been ghosted (A. Brown 2020).

Ghosting has become so ubiquitous that MTV launched a reality show named *Ghosted* (2019) where the hosts track down absent exes, friends, and family members. Similarly, the dating app Hinge hosts the podcast *Ghost Stories* with a similar goal: to uncover the reasons for the communication stoppage and reveal the negative consequences of the behaviors (Bonos 2020). But is ghosting universally considered "bad?" Some feminist authors have made the case that it is permissible for women to ghost men and is a necessary self-protective measure in response to men's violence against women (Dular 2020).

While we continue to see a cultural shift in our societal beliefs about gender, the traditional roles related to dating have remained surprisingly stable. Research about heterosexual relationships shows that both men and women express a preference for egalitarian, equitable relationships. However, they still desire traditional dating rituals, including the man planning and paying for dates. While these traditions seem harmless, research shows that gender inequality gets disguised as romance, which lays a foundation of inequality in relationships (Lamont 2020).

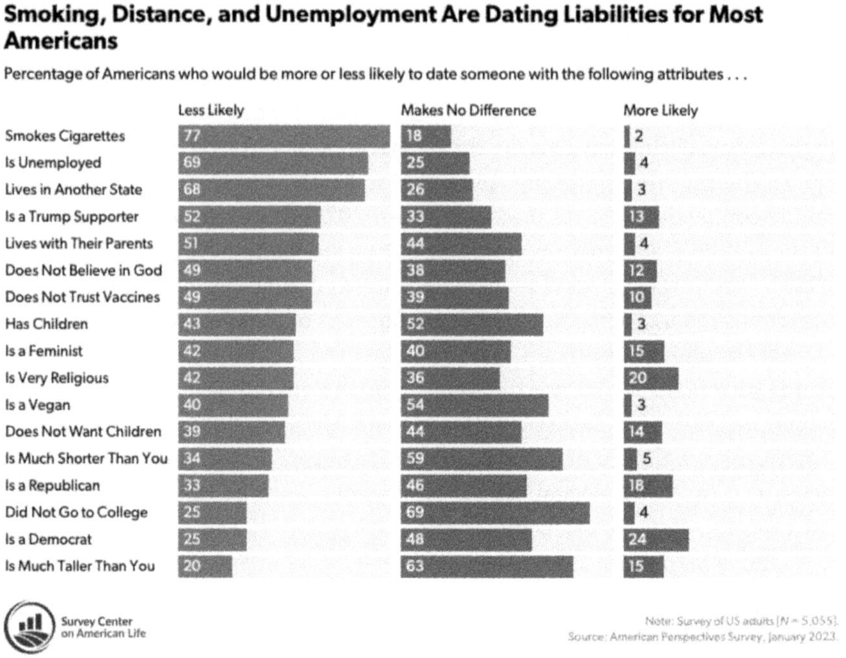

Figure 9.3 Our societal views on marriage and family have substantively changed over time.
DATA FROM THE SURVEY CENTER ON AMERICAN LIFE, AMERICAN PERSPECTIVES SURVEY, JANUARY 2023

Women report more negative experiences with online dating platforms compared to men. Almost half (47 percent) of single men report being interested in dating, while only 36 percent of single women report the same (Cox 2023). Thirty-eight percent of single women state that they aren't dating because they can't find someone who meets their expectations. For men, 23 percent reported the same. This is especially true for college-educated single Americans, with both men (33 percent) and women (45 percent) reporting they cannot find a partner who meets their expectations. In a recent survey, almost half of adult women stated that their partner had cheated (Cox 2023).

Gendered expectations continue to evolve in relationships, and research indicates that men are less likely to convey the emotional intelligence and sensitivity that women now require. Women report trying to find a partner without success. As a result, they change their online dating profiles—for example, removing their PhD from their educational status to be less "intimidating" (Sussman 2023). Finding a meaningful relationship is clearly hard to find.

Continuing gendered traditions, approximately 80 percent of women in heterosexual marriages report taking their husband's last name compared to 5 percent of men taking their wives' last name (Lin 2023). Women who keep their last names are likely to be older when married (C. Miller 2023a).

In the News . . .

In July 2022, performer Jennifer Lopez married Ben Affleck after years of separation. For fans of the couple, this was a fairy tale ending. However, Jennifer decided to take Ben's last name, making her Jennifer Affleck, and fans did not approve. When asked about the backlash received by this name change, Mrs. Affleck responded with shock. She explained that everyone would still call her "Jennifer Lopez," but that taking her husband's name was romantic and conveyed that they are "joined together" (Walsh 2022). What do you think?

GENDERED PARENTING

Americans are not only reconsidering the family's composition but also the gender role expectations within them. Jennifer Siebel Newsom, "first partner" to Governor Gavin Newsom (D-CA) and a film writer and director, described parenting as "women's burden and men's adorable hobby" in a *Glamour* magazine article (Newsom 2019). Fathers who actively engage with their children are usually praised for "helping" take care of their children (Toalson 2017). Fathers playing with their children at the park are put on a pedestal for "babysitting."

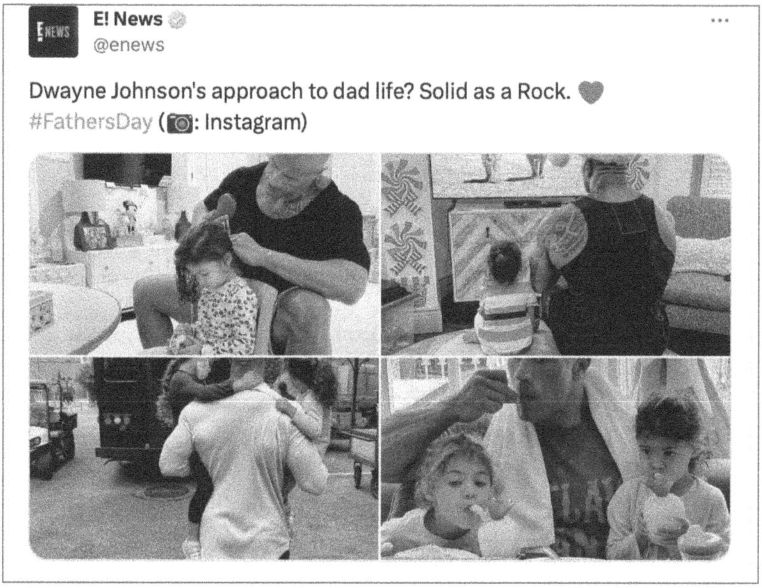

Figure 9.4 Actor Dwayne Johnson (aka The Rock) shows his hands-on approach to fathering his daughters. POSTED ON INSTAGRAM

However, mothers and researchers alike posit that these tasks are the basic requirements of *parenting*, and each parent should equally shoulder the load of care tasks for their shared children. As Toalson explains, "Friends and babysitters and full-time nannies help. Dad's [*sic*] parent" (2017).

The **default parent** refers to the parent in a relationship who is the automatic go-to for anything related to their child (Clancy 2022). In cisgender, heterosexual (cishet) relationships, the default parent tends to be the woman (Zapata 2021). A viral video on TikTok in 2022 illustrates the concept of helpful hurting. **Helpful hurting** describes when a parent attempts to help in parenting tasks but makes more work for the default parent (Clancy 2022). In the TikTok, an exhausted stay-at-home mother describes the feeling of being overwhelmed when caring for her crying ten-month-old. She responsibly placed the baby in his crib so she could eat lunch and regain composure. The father, who worked from home, said that he would help with the baby. Within a couple of minutes, however, he brought the baby back down to the mother. She was not yet calm and had not finished her lunch. The response on TikTok was instantaneous, eliciting thousands of comments from mothers sharing their similar experiences. The reactions were clear: everyone deserves a break, and a rested parent is a good parent (Clancy 2022).

The **parental happiness gap** is a researched phenomenon where adults without children show greater measures of happiness than adults with children (Preisner et al. 2019). Researchers found that indicators of happiness did not change from white fathers to nonfathers, but happiness significantly decreased for white mothers compared to nonmothers. Black fathers and mothers experience no difference in happiness compared to their nonparent peers (M. Miller 2023). Regardless of race, women report experiencing motherhood imposter syndrome. **Motherhood imposter syndrome** is an experience described by mothers in which everything wrong is their fault as a mom and everything right is despite their parenting mistakes (Wilson 2022).

Gendered Inequality in Household Labor

In 1989, sociologist Arlie Russell Hochschild published her groundbreaking book *The Second Shift*. In the book, she outlines the in-depth qualitative analysis she undertook by observing families and reviewing time logs. In her findings, she reports that women in heterosexual marriages engage in what she called a **"second shift"**—or the unpaid work of household tasks and childcare that happens after completing their first shift at their paid job (Hochschild 1989). The research from this book has been updated throughout the years, but the presence of the second shift remains. Many women report that the invisible

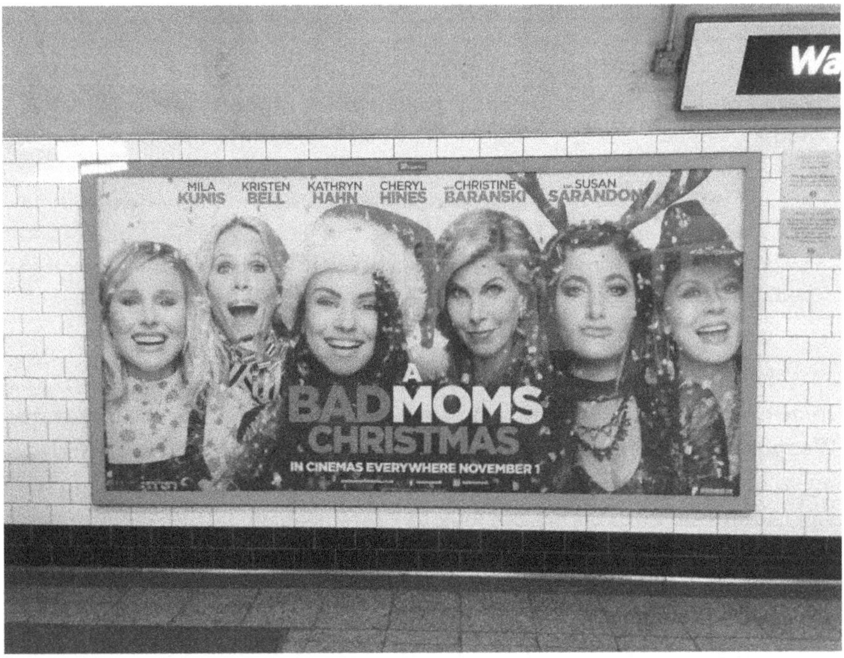

Figure 9.5 The movie series *Bad Moms* showcases the unattainable societal definition of being a "good mom." FLICKR

work of the second shift for mothers became unavoidably visible during the COVID-19 pandemic. Working mothers, who previously managed a work persona of being "masculine and childless" were unable to maintain this ruse while working with their children during quarantine (Malone 2022).

Data suggest that mothers still complete over 65 percent of household labor (Lockman 2019). Researchers argue that the "culture of fatherhood" has changed at a rate much faster than the actual behavior of fathers. Sociologists discuss a consistent resistance of men to fully engage in true household parity, which some argue is rooted in the belief that household labor, at its core, is "women's work" (Lockman 2019).

The first explanation for paternal negligence is the **"maternal gatekeeping" theory**. While an easy answer is that women take over routines like children's bedtime, meal preparation, and homework supervision, research suggests that women step in to provide consistent routines. The second theory is that of the father's forgetfulness or obliviousness. Fathers state that child-related tasks are not as important as other work or that their attention to detail and follow-through is lacking (Lockman 2019).

Fair Play

Based on the *New York Times* bestselling book of the same name by Eve Rodsky, *Fair Play* (2022) is a documentary that tries to make invisible care work visible. The movie discusses inequality in the home, which historically leaves women with the care of children and home. The documentary follows three families as they try to find balance in household labor and asks us to envision a world where we normalize care work for men. The documentary was written and directed by Jennifer Siebel Newsom (Representation Project 2023).

The gender socialization around home and care tasks is so significant that some men engage in weaponized incompetence to maintain the status quo. **Weaponized incompetence** or strategic incompetence refers to pretending to be incapable or insufficient at a task so that someone else will do it for you (Abramson 2023). This can look like intentionally letting delicate clothing shrink in the dryer or refusing to load the dishwasher because you'll do it "incorrectly." While anyone in a relationship can engage in this behavior, it is more likely to be exhibited by men in heterosexual relationships. This manipulation has the goal of frustrating one's partner into doing the task themselves, which can take a significant toll on the relationship (Abramson 2023).

Some men blame their wives' personalities, stating that the wife did more tasks because she is "uptight," "anxious," or "overbearing" (Lockman 2019). Mothers disagree, explaining that a household pattern consistently emerges where the father neglects a task while the mother completes it. Despite trying to change this dynamic, mothers state that this pattern, which clearly privileges paternal time and preferences, is unlikely to change (Lockman 2019).

The cultural norm that expects women to be the primary caretaker benefits men in committed relationships. While men and women in heterosexual marriages tend to live longer than their unmarried counterparts, this advantage benefits men more. Studies suggest that wives tend to influence the health decisions of their husbands for the better—eating healthier, attending doctor appointments, and exercising more frequently (Richards, Franks, and Shrout 2023). Husbands do not influence wives' behaviors in the same way. Marital support also influences engagement in healthy behaviors for men; however, this association is much less for married women (Richards, Franks, and Shrout 2023). Inequity in household labor affects women's well-being, as they have less leisure time, sleep, and fewer career opportunities (Lockman 2019).

Middle-aged women experience dual caretaking of young children and aging parents, referred to as the **sandwich generation** (Richards, Franks, and Shrout 2023). The term refers to people who are "sandwiched" between a parent who is sixty-five years or older, and at least one child under the age of eighteen. In the United States, 23 percent of adults are part of this so-called generation, with most of them in their forties (Horowitz 2022). The research is clear that the chronic stress associated with caregiving negatively affects immunity and stress hormones (Whittaker and Gallagher 2019). In addition, women are socialized to do more of the emotional labor around relationship health, which adds continued strain (Richards, Franks, and Shrout 2023).

The Census Bureau estimates that 1.2 percent of marriages in the United States are between same-sex couples. Of those, 52.6 percent are between two women and 47.4 percent are between two men (Desilver 2023a). In same-sex marriages, gay and lesbian couples experience the health benefits of marriage, reporting a 36 percent increase in reports of good health after marriage (Hsieh and Liu 2019). Among bisexual adults, good health reports increased more with a same-sex partner than with an opposite-sex partner. Bisexual people often experience higher rates of relationship stigma, thus reducing the protective impact of marriage (Hsieh and Liu 2019). Research indicates that the division of household labor and economic contribution in same-sex relationships is closer to equal than in heterosexual couples (Lazarus and Mandel 2023).

MARRIAGE, FAMILY, AND PUBLIC POLICY

The Defense of Marriage Act (DOMA) was passed in 1996 and defined marriage as between one man and one woman. This federal legislation prohibited the legal recognition of same-sex marriage. However, the Supreme Court overturned this ruling in 2013, allowing individual states to recognize marriages as they choose. In June 2015, the Supreme Court issued a watershed ruling (***Obergefell v. Hodges***) legalizing same-sex marriage nationwide (Fitzsimons 2019).

However, this hard-earned right to marriage was still under threat. After Supreme Court Justice Clarence Thomas stated that he supported the overturn of *Obergefell*, Congress acted (Edelman 2022). The **Respect for Marriage Act** was passed in December 2022, which provides federal protection and recognition of same-sex marriage (Warburton 2022).

If the Supreme Court were to overturn *Obergefell*, the legality of same-sex marriages would now be left to individual states. Unfortunately, most states would prohibit same-sex marriages under these circumstances. The Respect of Marriage Act does not change this outcome but does require that states recognize the legality of same-sex marriages performed in other states (Radde 2022).

Parental Leave

Globally, the United States is one of seven countries that provide no national paid maternity leave. Of the other countries that provide guaranteed leave, the average length of maternity leave is twenty-nine weeks (C. Miller 2023b). The **Family Medical Leave Act (FMLA)** provides up to twelve weeks of unpaid leave to care for a newborn, adopted child, foster child, or other family member (Williamson 2023).

According to the Bureau of Labor Statistics, 27 percent of civilian workers had access to paid paternity or maternity leave and 90 percent had access to unpaid family leave. These statistics are similar for private-sector and governmental employees (BLS 2023). Most Americans must cobble together paid vacation and sick time, coupled with unpaid leave (Rosalsky 2023).

Only 13 percent of private-sector fathers can access paid paternity leave (Rosalsky 2023). Many Americans support this lack of access, with one in seven indicating that men should not have paternity leave. However, 71 percent of Americans think that new babies should have equal time to bond with both the mother and father (Horowitz 2017). To encourage dads to take family leave, some employers have introduced a daddy quota. The **daddy quota** is leave that is only allowed to be taken by the dad, and if it's not used, the whole family loses the benefit (Rosalsky 2023). Employers have found this incentive encourages dads to take leave.

Of the fathers who do take paternity leave, 70 percent return to work full-time after two weeks of paid leave (Rosalsky 2023). One study found that the average American mom takes three times the amount of parental leave as the average American father (Herr, Roy, and Klerman 2020). As mothers need to recover from the birth, this difference in leave makes sense. Economically, women often earn less than men (see chapter 11, "Gender and Work"). However, evidence suggests that this pattern of mothers taking more time with new babies is one of the contributing factors to the gender pay gap.

Maternal leave is taken because it makes financial sense, which reinforces the lack of gender pay parity. For example, approximately one million women are missing from the labor force after the pandemic, a full 1 percent less than before the pandemic (Ferguson and Lucy 2022). This impact disproportionately affected women of color who are most likely to engage in care work (Berger 2023). Some of these losses are because women are more likely to be in jobs susceptible to layoffs during pandemic lockdowns. However, the data show that most women left the workforce due to a lack of childcare. Nearly 60 percent of parents state a lack of childcare as the reason for leaving the workforce (Ferguson and Lucy 2022). When childcare is required, the parent most likely to stay home is the one making less money.

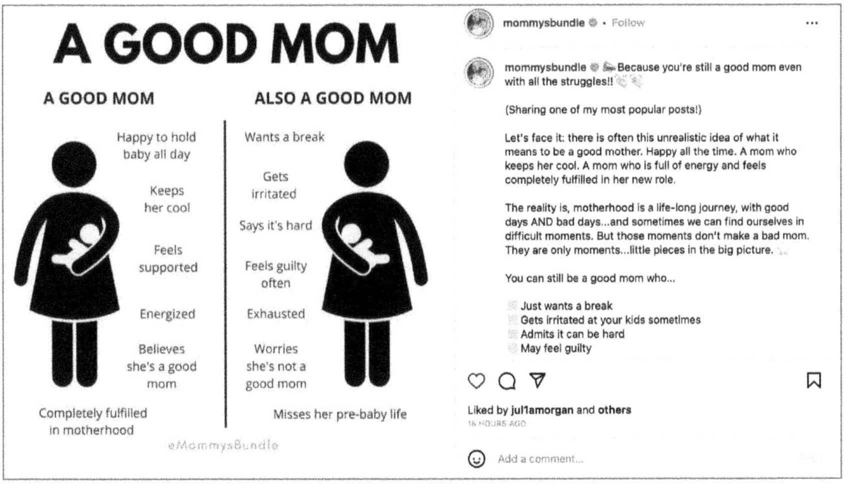

Figure 9.6 What makes a "good mom?" This blogger seeks to normalize the hard parts of motherhood through social media. POSTED ON INSTAGRAM

Policymakers and academics agree that parental leave is important due to its perceived benefits of promoting gender equality (Petts and Carlson 2019). Paid leave for fathers promotes the sharing of parental tasks that would traditionally be left to mothers. Couples who report equal division of household labor report greater satisfaction in their relationships. New mothers are more likely to report relationship satisfaction if the father takes paternity leave (Petts and Carlson 2019).

Access to Childcare

In 2021, President Joe Biden revealed his American Rescue Plan, which focused on the need to invest in the economy of care work. The **care economy** refers to both the paid and unpaid labor associated with meeting the needs of children and the elderly. Indeed, research suggests that mothers of young children are laid off at higher rates than mothers of school-aged children (Berger 2023).

As a part of this legislation, $24 billion was allocated to the childcare industry (White House 2023a). This money was used to stabilize childcare costs for parents, delaying a predicted 10 percent increase annually (approximately $1,250 per child). Other states used the federal funds to retain childcare workers with bonuses and higher pay. This increase made childcare worker wages comparable to K–12 workers. The impact on working mothers of young children was significant. Their labor force participation increased by approximately 3 percent due to these interventions (White House 2023a). In

In the News . . .

The impact of social media influence cannot be understated. Research indicates that women make 70 percent of household purchasing decisions, and influencers endeavor to capitalize on that market. Mom influencers share their experiences with pregnancy, childbirth, and childcare, while also sharing advice and insights about motherhood in general. Also known as "mommy bloggers" or "mompreneurs," this group of women can share experiences with a wide range of products—from children's toys to fashion. In 2023, the Top 3 Mom Influencers were (1) Tammy Hembrow (@ tammyhembrow) with 11.9 million followers, (2) Savannah Labrant (@sav. labrant) with 6.6 million followers, and (3) Katie Stauffer (@kcstauffer) with 3.6 million followers (Arma & Elma 2023).

2023, the Biden administration requested an additional year of childcare stabilization funding to prevent childcare costs from increasing and the number of childcare employees from decreasing (White House 2023b).

MOVING FORWARD

Americans are increasingly cynical about the future of the family. When asked about the future of marriage and family, 40 percent of US adults indicated that they were pessimistic (Parker and Minkin 2023). While Americans indicate general acceptance of multiple family structures, a heterosexual married couple with children garnered the most support (90 percent). A single parent raising children on their own had only 60 percent acceptance, while an unmarried same-sex couple raising children had only 41 percent acceptance. Some Americans consider these family arrangements as harmful to society, with 49 percent saying that single parents or unmarried couples raising children will have a negative impact (Parker and Minkin 2023).

Current research efforts have shifted from the risk factors associated with absent fathers to the protective outcomes for children with an engaged, present father (Institute for Research on Poverty 2020). The **involved fatherhood model** categorizes the essential functions of fatherhood. These include positive engagement, accessibility, and responsibility. Other researchers have added additional dimensions, such as providing financial support, direct care, and play. Generally, children who have active fathers tend to have higher school achievement, better behavior, and more positive social interactions than those without active fathers (Institute for Research on Poverty 2020).

Many organizations exist to support fathers. Globally, the organization MenCare is an international campaign promoting men's equitable involvement in the family. Their fundamental goals include men contributing 50 percent of caregiving work and widespread adherence to equitable and nonviolent fatherhood. With gender equality at its core, MenCare seeks to normalize nurturing behavior and care work tasks as fundamental to masculinity (MenCare 2023).

In the United States, the National Responsible Fatherhood Clearinghouse (fatherhood.gov) is a nationally funded resource for individual fathers and public organizations. The goal of this office is to disseminate current research-supported strategies to encourage and strengthen fathers. Their activities include social media campaigns, outreach training, publications, and research (National Responsible Fatherhood Clearinghouse 2023).

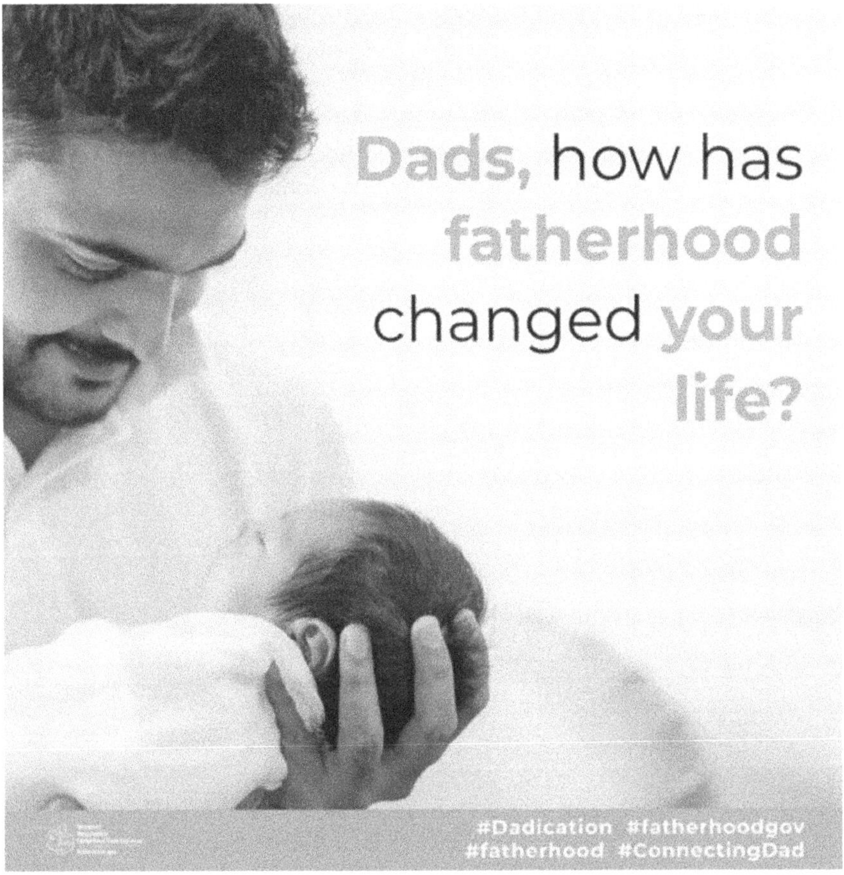

Figure 9.7 Fatherhood.gov is a federally funded resource meant to support dads.
POSTED ON INSTAGRAM

Finally, Moms F1rst (momsfirst.us) is an organization making visible the unpaid care work completed by women. The organization acknowledges that the United States does not provide a social safety net for families but instead asks women to bear the burden themselves. Moms F1rst strives to empower employees and executives to transform policies to work better for mothers. Their efforts include public awareness campaigns and political advocacy.

Key Takeaways

- The definition of family, while continuing to change, refers to a group of people connected by biological and emotional ties.
- Mothers are more likely to be the default parent, experiencing weaponized incompetence from their partners.
- The unpaid labor of household tasks and parenting cause millions of women to leave the workforce. Significant public policy changes must take place to support mothers' return to work postpandemic.
- The data is clear that equitable sharing of household tasks and childcare leads to happier partnerships and supports gender equality.

10

SEXUAL VIOLENCE
#METOO

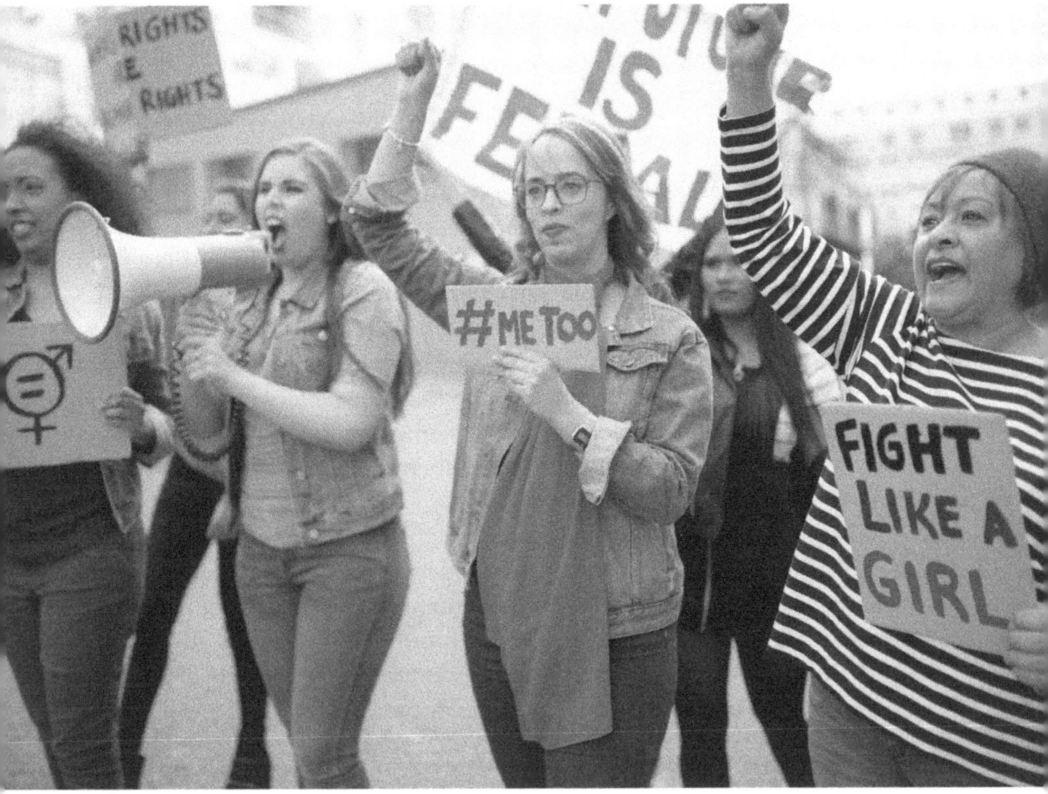

Figure 10.1 The #MeToo movement continues to raise awareness about the pervasiveness of sexual violence. iStock by Getty Images

THE **#METOO MOVEMENT** began in 2006 by founder Tarana Burke in response to increasing sexual violence against women (Jenkins 2019). Her goal was to spread the message to sexual assault survivors that "you're heard, you're understood" (North 2017). The #MeToo movement saw its highest momentum with the hashtag going viral in the fall of 2017 (Fang 2019). In October 2017, the *New York Times* published a report recounting three decades of sexual harassment against women in Hollywood (Framke and Grady 2017). The floodgates opened with dozens of actresses describing inappropriate behavior from film producer Harvey Weinstein—from sexually explicit requests to forced sexual violence. Rose McGowan, an actress best known for the series *Charmed*, continues to be vocal in her pursuit against Weinstein as well as other Hollywood gatekeepers who abuse women (Grady 2017). Within the first year, nineteen million people tweeted about #MeToo (Jenkins 2019), and the term has been Google-searched in 196 countries (Langone 2018).

In 2019, Weinstein pleaded not guilty to two counts of sexual assault (Queally and Winton 2019). In February 2020, Weinstein was convicted of first-degree criminal sexual act and third-degree rape. He was sentenced to twenty-three years in prison (Levenson, Valle, and Moghe 2020). This investigation into Weinstein's perpetration of sexual assault is recounted in the feature-length film *She Said* (2022). Five years after the hashtag went viral, research shows that 49 percent of Americans fully support the #MeToo movement (A. Brown 2022b). Seventy percent of Americans believe that, compared to five years ago, people who perpetrate sexual harassment and sexual assault were more likely to be held accountable because of the #MeToo movement. Additionally, 62 percent of respondents indicated that victims of sexual harassment and assault are more likely to be believed currently (A. Brown 2022b).

The impact of this social media campaign cannot be overstated. Awareness of sexual harassment and sexual violence has increased considerably; however, support for the #MeToo movement has become widely partisan with increasing gaps between parties (A. Brown 2022b; Conroy 2019). *What is #MeToo all about? Let's get started by discussing the aspects of our society which allow and perpetuate sexual violence.*

LEARNING GOALS

By the end of this chapter, you should be able to:

1. Define rape culture and victim-blaming
2. Explain the unique impact sexual assault has on college campuses
3. Assess the cultural impact of the #MeToo movement and other social change efforts

RAPE CULTURE

Rape culture refers to an environment that promotes, accepts, and justifies sexual violence against women. These contexts facilitate the normalizing and inevitability of sexual assault. One institution that perpetuates rape culture is the media. Readily available network television shows glamorize sexual force, ambiguity of sexual consent, and jokes about victimization (Wade and Ferree 2019). A study of college men found that those who consumed men's magazines, reality TV, and pornography increasingly sexually objectified women and held stronger attitudes of support for violence against women (Wright and Tokunaga 2016).

Advertising routinely features women in sexualized clothing being grabbed by a man; these images are often ambiguous, so it is hard to discern if the woman is being ravished or raped (Jhally 2010). Music videos capitalize on this trope, often showing images of women as sexual property or demeaned servants in sexualized attire (Killoy et al. 2007). While sexualized images are not inherently inappropriate, they create the social norm of the willing, compliant, hypersexualized female body. Likewise, the media normalizes a "boys will be boys" mentality—that being sexually aggressive is part of behaving as a "real man" (Katz 2006).

Pornography culture plays a critical role in the maintenance of rape culture. As pornographic images and videos become more readily available, the mainstream media continue to pull their storylines and images from those narratives. A content analysis of the fifty most downloaded or watched pornographic videos found that 88 percent of scenes portrayed physical violence, and of those, 87 percent were perpetrated against women (Powell 2019). Women were portrayed as being stoic or neutral about this physical violence 95 percent of the time (Bridges et al. 2010). Not all pornography has this effect, as current research suggests that some pornography can support healthy sexual development. Pornography that is known to be ethically produced, practices safe sex,

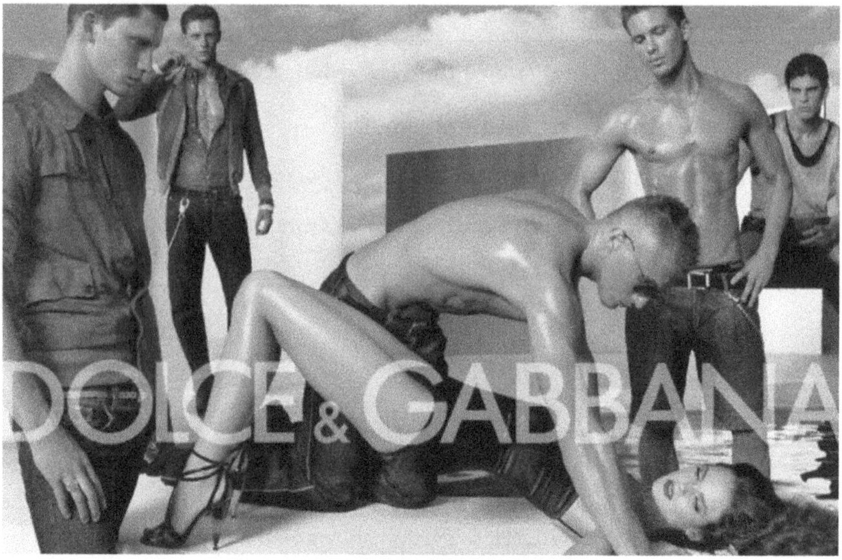

Figure 10.2 Dolce & Gabbana received significant backlash for this advertisement. Critics argue that the image depicts male aggression (at best) and sexual violence (at worst).

includes diversity in body types, genders, and races, and focuses on pleasure for all participants meets these criteria (McKee, Dawson, and Kang 2023).

Researchers argue that street harassment (such as whistling and sexually aggressive comments) reflects the desire to impose masculine power over women in public spaces. Indeed, even as the COVID-19 pandemic raged through cities, men continued harassing women with the same frequency (Felix 2020).

Rape Myths

Rape culture is bolstered by the pervasive presence of **rape myths**, or stereotypes, prejudices, and misinformation about sexual assault victims and perpetrators. In 1975, a legal scholar published "The Rape of Mr. Smith" to discuss the double standard imposed upon female victims of sexual violence but not on other victims of assault. In this dramatic retelling, a police officer asks a victim of a mugging to account for the expensive suit he wears ("Doesn't it advertise that you have money?"), his lack of resisting the armed mugging ("Why didn't you scream? Did you consent to give away your money?"), and his previous history of philanthropy ("You mean you've given away money in the past?") (Borkenhagen 1975). This article highlights common rape myths,

In the News . . .

In 2019, the docuseries *Surviving R. Kelly* premiered on the Lifetime Network. This series allowed victims and peers to describe approximately twenty years of sexual assault of underaged girls by Kelly. In response to the announcement of the series, Oronike Odeleye and Kenyette Barnes started the #MuteRKelly movement, seeking to bring media attention to the cause and halt the streaming or playing of any R. Kelly content (Garcia-Navarro 2018). Performers Lady Gaga, Celine Dion, and the Pussycat Dolls have asked that their collaborations with Kelly be removed from streaming services (Tsioulcas 2019a).

In 2019 Kelly was indicted on eighteen criminal charges in both Chicago and New York. Kelly pleaded not guilty (Tsioulcas 2019b; Savage 2020). In April 2020, a judge denied a request for Kelly to be released due to fear of COVID-19 exposure (Hill and Hutchinson 2020). In August 2020, associates of Kelly were charged with harassment and intimidation of Kelly's accusers (Mustian 2020).

In September 2021, a Brooklyn jury deliberated for nine hours and ultimately found Kelly guilty of all charges including sex trafficking and racketeering. He still faces charges in Illinois and Michigan (Vagianos and Finley 2022). The final season of the documentary aired in January 2023 and outlines the thirty years of tireless work by victims' families and women of color activists that led to Kelly's conviction.

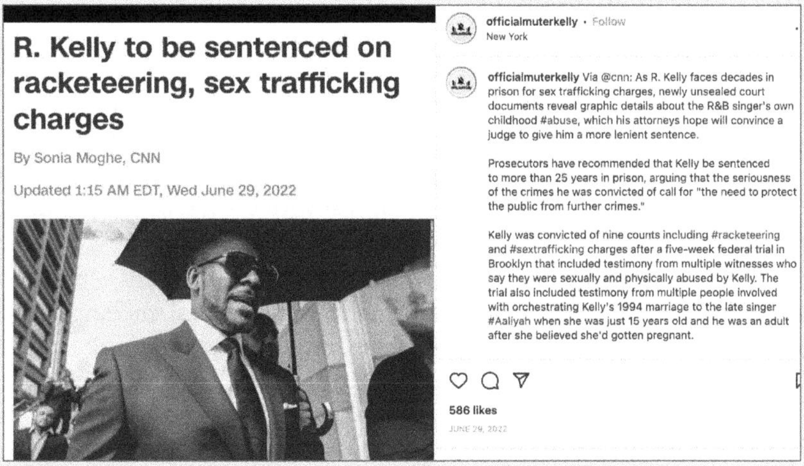

R. Kelly to be sentenced on racketeering, sex trafficking charges

By Sonia Moghe, CNN

Updated 1:15 AM EDT, Wed June 29, 2022

officialmuterkelly • Follow
New York

officialmuterkelly Via @cnn: As R. Kelly faces decades in prison for sex trafficking charges, newly unsealed court documents reveal graphic details about the R&B singer's own childhood #abuse, which his attorneys hope will convince a judge to give him a more lenient sentence.

Prosecutors have recommended that Kelly be sentenced to more than 25 years in prison, arguing that the seriousness of the crimes he was convicted of call for "the need to protect the public from further crimes."

Kelly was convicted of nine counts including #racketeering and #sextrafficking charges after a five-week federal trial in Brooklyn that included testimony from multiple witnesses who say they were sexually and physically abused by Kelly. The trial also included testimony from multiple people involved with orchestrating Kelly's 1994 marriage to the late singer #Aaliyah when she was just 15 years old and he was an adult after she believed she'd gotten pregnant.

586 likes

JUNE 29, 2022

Figure 10.3 Singer R. Kelly was sentenced in 2021. POSTED ON INSTAGRAM such as "victims provoke rape by dressing provocatively," "previous consent implies present consent," and "rape victims will be hysterical" (Illinois Coalition against Sexual Assault 2019).

Rape myths involve victim-blaming. **Victim-blaming** is the belief that the victim is the cause of the crime instead of the perpetrator. By definition, nothing that a victim can do or say can cause the assault (Illinois Coalition Against Sexual Assault 2019). One way this operates in our society is the policing of women's clothing in the form of modesty culture. For example, in 2019 a mother wrote a letter to the University of Notre Dame newspaper expressing her dismay at women wearing leggings. She states, "Leggings are so naked, so form-fitting, so exposing. Could you think of the mothers of sons the next time you go shopping and consider choosing jeans instead?" (White 2019). The response was swift, challenging the mother to teach her sons not to ogle women, rather than to tell women to dress for their sons (Ganesh 2019).

SEXUAL ASSAULT PREVALENCE

Just how pervasive is sexual assault? When studying sexual assault, understanding methodology is important. The Uniform Crime Report (UCR) is conducted by the Federal Bureau of Investigation (FBI) and measures crimes reported to the police. According to this data, over half of all women and one out of three men experience some form of sexual violence involving physical contact in their lifetime (Basile et al. 2016/2017).

However, we know that many sexual assaults are not reported. When victims were asked in an earlier survey why they did not report the assault, 20 percent cited fear of retaliation and 13 percent believed the police would not help (Bureau of Justice Statistics 2013). To get a more comprehensive picture of sexual assault, the Bureau of Justice Statistics administers the National Crime Victimization Survey (NCVS) each year with the intent to hear directly from individuals about their experiences including those not reported to police. The NCVS measures both rape and sexual assault. Sexual assault is measured, separately from rape or attempted rape, as unwanted sexual fondling or groping. Between 2016 and 2018, violent crimes, including sexual assault and rape, steadily increased (Morgan and Oudekerk 2019).

While sexual assault can affect anyone, some groups of people are at an increased risk. One in four women in the United States report experiencing attempted or completed rape in their lifetime; one in twenty-six men report the same (Basile et al. 2016/2017). Women of color are more likely to be victims of sexual assault. According to the most recent National Intimate Partner and

Sexual Violence Survey (2016/2017), 43.7 percent of Indigenous/Alaska Native women and 48 percent of multiracial women are raped in their lifetime (Basile et al. 2016/2017). Rates of sexual violence are also higher for bisexual women (46% reported sexual victimization) and gay and bisexual men (40% and 47% reported sexual victimization) (CDC 2010).

People who are in particularly vulnerable societal positions are more likely to be victimized. For example, a 2011 study found that 12 percent of transgender youth report being sexually assaulted by school staff or peers before the age of eighteen and 20 percent of Black transgender people were sexually assaulted at work (Grant et al. 2011).

False Reporting?

Public perception of false reporting is inflated and problematic. A review of the research finds the prevalence of false reporting is between 2 and 10 percent, which is comparable to false reports with other crimes (National Sexual Violence Resource Center [NSVRC] 2012). The variability is attributed to many measurement factors, for example, how does the researcher define a "false" report? What type of evidence is required to deem an allegation "false"?

As a result of this myth of false reporting, many sexual assault and rape victims choose not to report to the police out of fear of not being believed (NSVRC 2012). Current data support these concerns. Out of 1,000 sexual assaults, only 236 will be reported (Bureau of Justice Statistics 2017), and of those, only 46 will lead to an arrest (Federal Bureau of Investigation 2017). In the end, only 5 of those arrests will lead to convictions and incarceration. To put this in context, out of 1,000 robberies, 20 robbers will be incarcerated; of 1,000 assaults, 33 criminals will be incarcerated (FBI 2017). Unfortunately, even those who do report their assault are often unsupported (Loofbourow 2019). An estimated hundreds of thousands of rape kits are sitting untested in American police departments (Vagianos 2018). This backlog allows perpetrators to go free, which is particularly disturbing since we know many are serial rapists.

Recent research indicates that public opinion on false reporting is changing, in part due to the success of the #MeToo movement. A recent Pew Research Center survey found that many Americans agree that false reporting is a rare occurrence (48 percent). Forty-six percent of respondents indicated they believe it is extremely common for people to experience sexual harassment or sexual assault and not report it to authorities (A. Brown 2022b). However, this does not translate to actual services for victims. A recent study published in the *Journal of the American Medical Association* found that emergency department visits for sexual assault increased by 1533 percent from 2006 to 2019.

This increase far outpaced the growth in reporting to law enforcement during the same period (Vogt et al. 2022).

SEXUAL ASSAULT ON COLLEGE CAMPUSES

In 2015, *The Hunting Ground*, a documentary about campus sexual assault, was released. This award-winning documentary follows college students Annie Clark and Andrea Pino through their journey of college acceptance, sexual victimization on campus, and filing of a Title IX complaint against their university (Dick and Ziering 2019). Title IX is part of the Education Amendments of 1972, which prohibits discrimination based on sex in education. Title IX is best known for its application to women's university sports, which has increased girls' participation in high school sports by almost 900 percent since it was passed (National Women's Law Center 2012).

However, questions have remained about how to interpret those anti-discrimination protections further to include sexual harassment and sexual assault (North 2019). In 2011, the Obama administration published the "Dear Colleague" letter, which outlined new guidelines for schools when adjudicating sexual assault or harassment claims (Ali 2011).

With these new protections, college students began speaking out regarding their experiences. In January 2015, Stanford University student Brock Turner sexually assaulted an unconscious woman, known as Emily Doe in court documents. Turner was caught assaulting the unconscious victim by two bystanders, who held Turner until the police arrived (Fuller 2016). In 2016, a jury convicted Turner of three felonies, including intent to rape an intoxicated or unconscious person. Social media erupted as Turner was sentenced to just six months in jail, although he was eligible for fourteen years in prison. Turner was released after serving only three months of that sentence (Fang 2019). After years of being known as only as Emily Doe, Chantal Miller published her personal memoir *Know My Name* (2019) in which she reclaims her identity after this harrowing event and provides support to other survivors.

Columbia University student Emma Sulkowicz began carrying a twin-size mattress across campus every day until her rapist was expelled. This art project, called "Mattress Performance (Carry That Weight)" has been replicated in campuses all over the United States to bring awareness to campus sexual assault (North 2019). In August 2021, protesters on almost twenty college campuses demanded the suspension of fraternities on campus or the elimination of Greek life altogether (S. Brown 2021b).

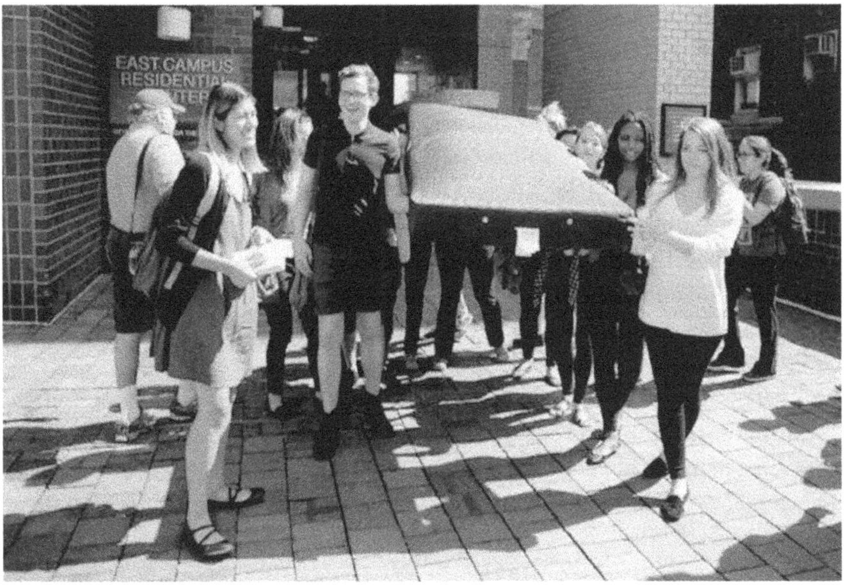

Figure 10.4 Mattress Performance: Carry That Weight. WIKIMEDIA COMMONS

In the News . . .

In 2019, Swarthmore College students engaged in a sit-in to protest a pattern of sexual assault. Wesleyan University was sued for refusing to intervene against a fraternity house called the "Rape Factory" (Read 2012). Activists say that the house is the location of a myriad of rapes on campus (Bauer-Wolf 2019). A Georgia Tech fraternity was disbanded by university leadership after an email circulated which called women "rape bait" and instructed younger frat brothers on how to lure women at parties (Ryan 2014). In 2010, fraternity members at Yale University marched through campus chanting "no means yes! yes means anal!" (Clark-Flory 2010).

Recently, protests continued in other universities, including Auburn University, University of Nebraska–Lincoln, and University of Massachusetts Amherst. Social media apps like GroupMe, TikTok, and YikYak were used to engage in digital activism and organizing (Hidalgo Bellows 2021). While there are calls to end the Greek life system altogether, they are met with steadfast resistance (S. Brown 2021b).

Despite this increase in empowerment and activism, the Trump administration rolled back the 2011 protections in September 2017, placing a greater burden on accusers by changing the investigative requirements of universities (North 2017; North 2019). On May 6, 2020, the Department of Education led by Secretary Betsy DeVos rolled out a new set of guidelines on how universities are to interpret Title IX in sexual assault cases (Bedera 2020). The new guidelines significantly reduced the types of sexual misdeeds that the university must investigate and narrowed the definition of sexual harassment (Fung 2020). Survivors were required to endure cross-examination in a live hearing, and perpetrators were allowed to deny formal hearings and instead participate in informal resolution (Bedera 2020).

Responses to these new guidelines were mixed. Some applauded the requirements as "due process" while others believed these rules would be retraumatizing to survivors (Slagter 2020). In the context of the COVID-19 pandemic, victim advocates argued that requiring students to read, understand, and advocate for their rights is unsettling in a time of upset (Fung 2020).

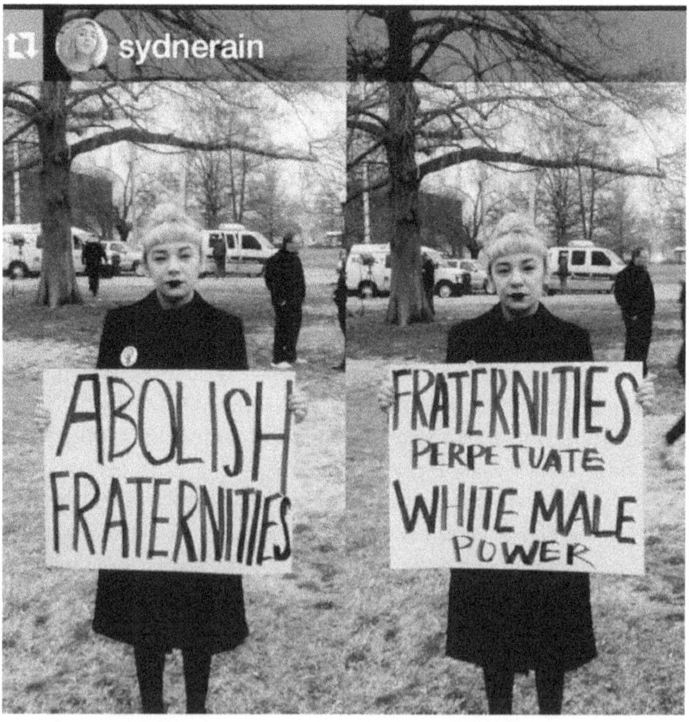

Figure 10.5 Protests to end Greek life were organized under #Abolish Fraternities. Posted on Instagram

In 2022, the Department of Education under President Biden has reversed many of these changes, removing the live hearing requirement and broadening the definition of sexual harassment. The implications of how the Biden administration will interpret Title IX provisions are still under scrutiny (Balingit and Anderson 2022).

The Association of American Universities states that 23.1 percent of female undergraduates and 5.4 percent of male undergraduates will experience sexual assault while in college (Cantor et al. 2015). In one study, fraternity men who watched pornography were compared to men who did not. Researchers found that fraternity men who viewed mainstream pornography expressed increased intent to commit rape if they knew they would not be caught. Fraternity men who consumed more violent, sadomasochistic pornography reported stronger beliefs in rape myths and less willingness to intervene as a bystander (Foubert, Brosi, and Bannon 2011). Another recent study found that the majority of alcohol-involved sexual assaults (87%) are committed by so-called serial rapists. In addition, student-athletes and fraternity members were significantly more likely to perpetrate alcohol-involved sexual assault than other college males (Foubert, Clark-Taylor, and Wall 2020).

A recent campus climate survey at the University of Michigan reflects this data. According to the survey, undergraduate women or gender nonconforming people are most at risk for experiencing unwanted sexual behaviors, including harassment and rape (Cantor et al. 2017). In addition, when students were asked if the campus administration would provide a fair and honest investigation of sexual misconduct allegations, 60.6 percent of undergraduate male-identified respondents answered "very or extremely likely" compared to only 40.4 percent of female-identified undergraduate respondents (Cantor et al. 2017). Therefore, it's unsurprising that another lawsuit is pending against a University of Michigan fraternity brother for allegedly drugging and raping an eighteen-year-old female freshman during orientation week in 2019 (Marowski 2020).

MOVING FORWARD

According to Tarana Burke, the founder of #MeToo, the movement is just getting started. Burke states, "For every Harvey Weinstein, there's a hundred more men in the neighborhood who are doing the exact same thing." She intends to increase the number of healing circles offered to survivors by offering leader training institutes around the country. In addition, she created a digital platform where all survivors, regardless of race, ethnicity, or religion, can be heard and validated in their experiences (see metoomvmt.org) (Jenkins 2019). Burke is clear that awareness needs to lead to activism. Burke also spoke out about the connection between the #MeToo movement and the Black Lives Matter movement. Burke argues that after excessive force, sexual assault is the second most reported form of police misconduct (Connellan 2020).

In 2021, Burke launched a new organization, We, As Ourselves, to center the experiences of Black survivors of sexual violence and reshape the often coercive narrative around Black victims (We, As Ourselves 2021). Their website provides resources and action-focused suggestions on how to support women of color survivors of violence.

Some universities are also making changes to college climate and enacting policies to reduce sexual assault and support survivors. As reporting sexual assault becomes increasingly difficult, some universities have chosen to follow a restorative justice approach to lesser offenses which focuses on healing the victim instead of punishing the assailant (North 2019). At the university level, sexual assault survivors can choose to forego the criminal justice system and pursue a Title IX investigation. During this civil proceeding, the university holds a hearing to determine if the respondent (accused) should incur suspension or expulsion. At the College of New Jersey, for example, a prevention education specialist oversees this process, which includes educating the accused about healthy masculinity and sexuality (North 2019).

Social media plays an important role in this activism and organizing on college campuses. First, victims of sexual violence use social media as a form of digital archive that not only names and acknowledges the lived experience of college victims of sexual assault, but also documents the failure of the university administration to make actionable changes to protect students (Hidalgo Bellows 2021). This form of **digital activism**—the use of social media and technology to engage in social justice organizing and social change work—has been successful. University officials do not want to be seen as ineffective in protecting tuition-paying students or as uncaring toward victims of sexual violence on their campus. University responses to these social media campaigns vary; however, the ever-present nature of social media provides protesters with immediate information about the administration's handling of violence. For many universities, this amounts to nothing less than a PR nightmare.

In addition, the organization It's On Us was founded in 2014 as a recommendation from the White House Task Force to Prevent Sexual Assault. The goal of the organization is to encourage male college students to take the It's On Us pledge committing to change campus culture. Students are asked to engage in **bystander intervention** or the practice of interrupting words or behaviors that perpetuate rape culture.

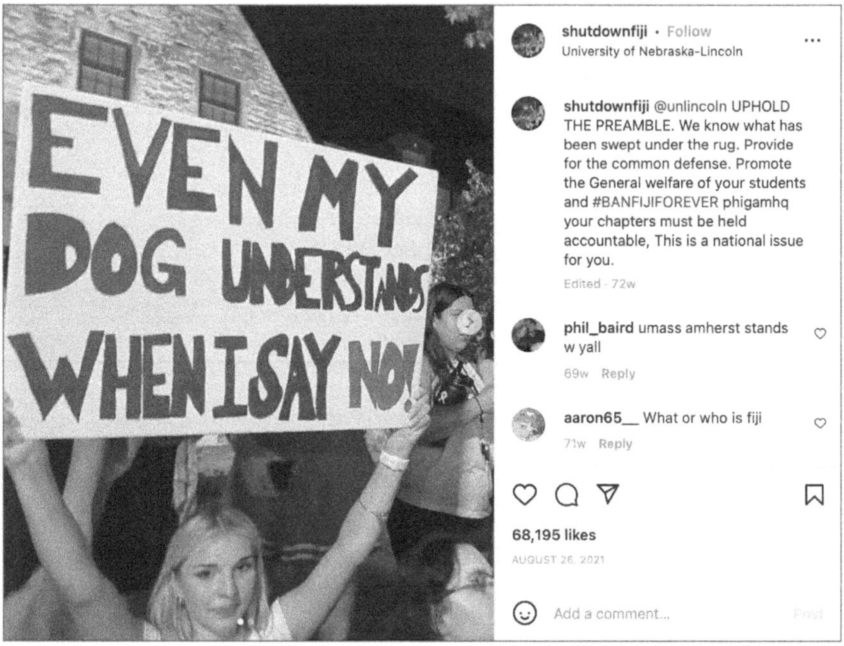

Figure 10.6 Social media posts, including this post from the University of Nebraska–Lincoln, create digital archives for sexual assault survivors. Posted on Instagram

California and New York have both passed legislation that increases the consent standard on university campuses. This new standard is based on **affirmative consent**, that consent is a "voluntary, conscious agreement to engage in sexual activity" (End Rape On Campus 2019). This definition also refutes popular rape myths by specifically stating that consent can be removed at any time, that previous consent does not imply future consent, and consent cannot be obtained by coercion or threat. At this time, only two states have adopted this legislation, but individual universities can adopt this model. At the time of publication, only nine US universities have adopted affirmative consent policies, including Yale University, University of Virginia, and University of Minnesota (End Rape On Campus 2019).

Politicians continue to play an important role in changing sexual assault policy. In 2021, a California law went into effect that changed the distinction between "spousal rape" and "rape." Under previous definitions, spouses who sexually assaulted their partners were often spared greater criminal penalties. Now, all perpetrators of sexual assault are subject to the same mandatory minimum penalties (Baker 2021).

Getting Help

If you or someone you know is a victim of sexual violence, the following resources are available to help you:

National Sexual Assault Hotline: rainn.org, 1-800-656-4673
National Sexual Violence Resource Center: nsvrc.org
Love Is Respect: loveisrespect.org, 1.866.331.9474

Key Takeaways

- The #MeToo movement is meant to provide solidarity and support for victims of sexual assault. #MeToo has influenced the creation of #TimesUp and #MuteRKelly.
- Rape myths are commonly held ideas and misinformation about sexual assault. These include victim-blaming or believing that the victim of sexual assault somehow causes the victimization.
- Sexual assault is a gendered crime with over 90 percent of victims being female.
- Sexual assault is pervasive on college campuses as undergraduate females have a one in five chance of being victimized.
- Bystander intervention encourages all people to challenge rape culture.

11

GENDER AND WORK
#EQUALPAY

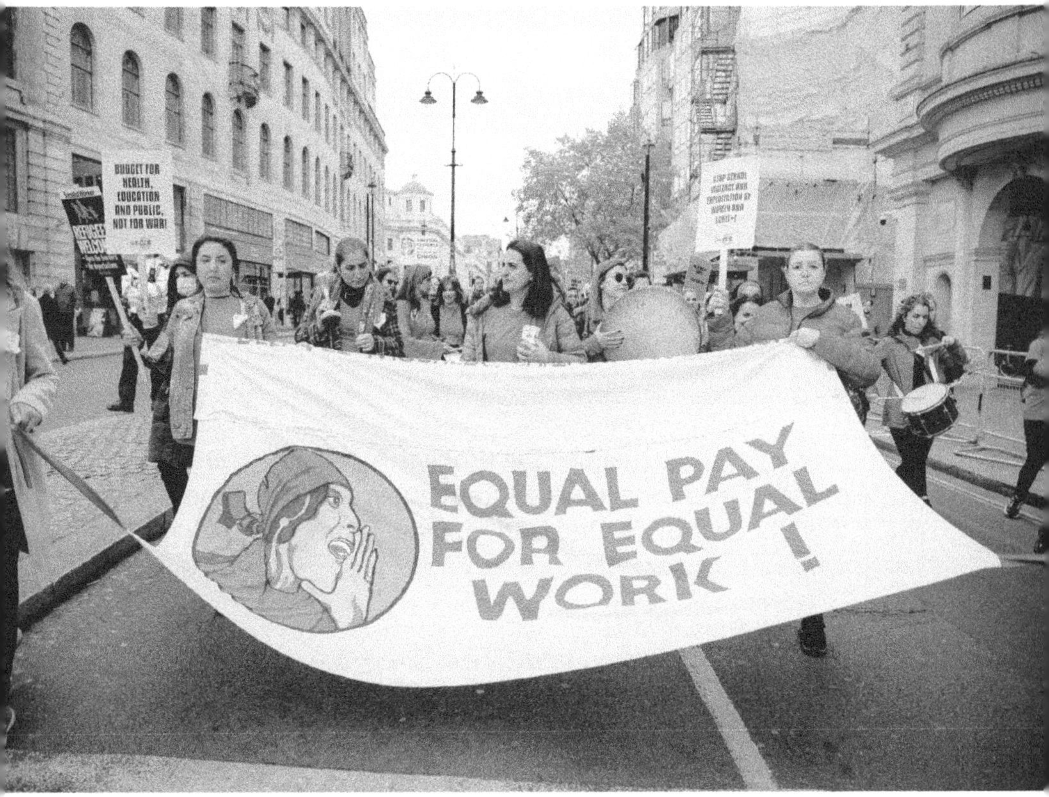

Figure 11.1 Activists continue to advocate for equal pay. SHUTTERSTOCK

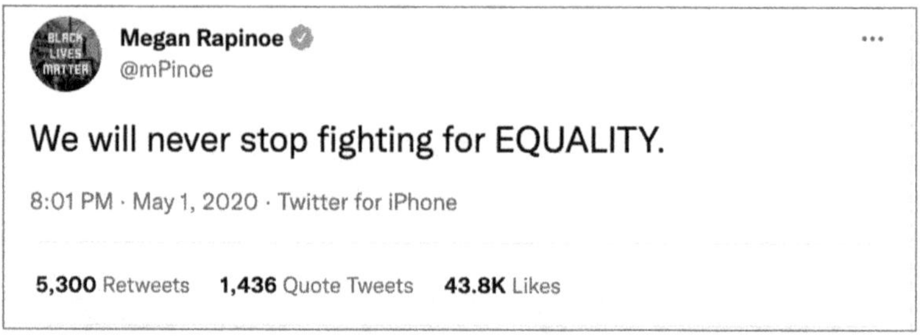

Figure 11.2 US Women's National Soccer Team captain Megan Rapinoe reacts to 2020 California ruling. POSTED ON X

THE HASHTAG #EqualPlayEqualPay was trending after the US women's soccer team won the Women's World Cup in 2019. According to activists, US women's soccer players made just $0.38 for every dollar US men's soccer players earned (Ziv 2019). In March 2019, the US women's soccer team filed a lawsuit against the US Soccer Federation (USSF) claiming systematic gender discrimination in their compensation (Das 2019b). The lawsuit claimed that the women's soccer team earned more profit for the federation than the men's team, but only earned a fraction of the income (Goodman 2019). In November 2019, a federal judge granted the women's national soccer team class status. This allowed the soccer players to be treated as a group (or "class") instead of individuals (Das 2019a).

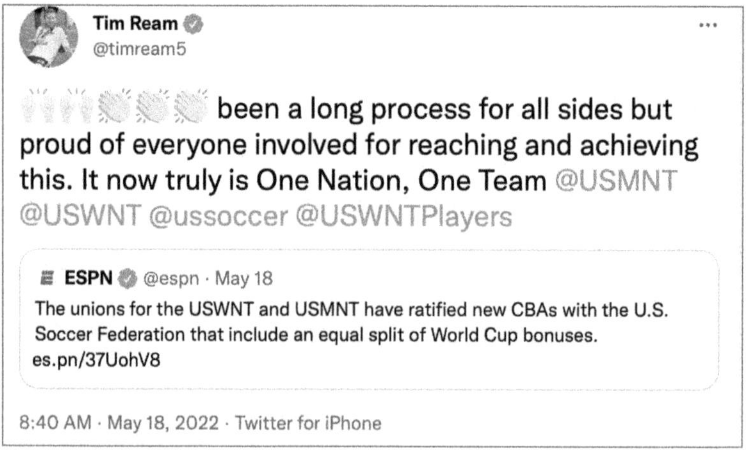

Figure 11.3 Outspoken opponent of the USWNT's lawsuit reacts favorably to the 2022 USSF agreement. POSTED ON X

In March 2020, the USSF submitted a memorandum claiming that men's and women's soccer players do not complete equal work—that is, that men's players must work harder and have a wider skill set (McCann 2020). A California judge agreed, dismissing multiple claims by the women's soccer team, including discrimination under the Equal Pay Act and unequal working conditions (grass versus turf fields) (Cater 2020).

Despite the persistent legal opposition, the US women's soccer team (USWNT) secured a historic win. In May 2022, the US Soccer Federation reached a collective bargaining agreement that guaranteed equal payment for the men's and women's soccer teams (Hernandez 2022a). The bargaining agreement also included a $24 million settlement and back pay to the women's team (J. Barnes 2022). This public fight about equal pay forced the gender pay gap into the public arena. *Is the gender pay gap even real? Let's discuss.*

LEARNING GOALS

By the end of this chapter, you should be able to

1. Define the gender pay gap
2. Explain the individual and societal reasons for gender inequality in the workplace
3. Assess potential social change efforts to end the gender pay gap

THE GENDER WAGE GAP

Since World War II, women's inclusion in the workforce has steadily increased, from 32.7 percent in 1948 to 70 percent in 2017 (Dalrymple and Landivar 2020; National Women's Law Center [NWLC] 2021b). Working mothers have become the norm with 70 percent of women with children under eighteen employed, and 75 percent of those women working full-time (Dalrymple and Landivar 2020). According to the Pew Research Center, 2019 was the first year that women surpassed men in the college-educated workforce at 50.2 percent (Fry 2019). Despite this accomplishment, women still experience the **gender wage gap** or the difference in hourly pay between men and women after controlling for individual differences. In 2023, women made approximately 82 cents for every dollar men made (Haan 2023).

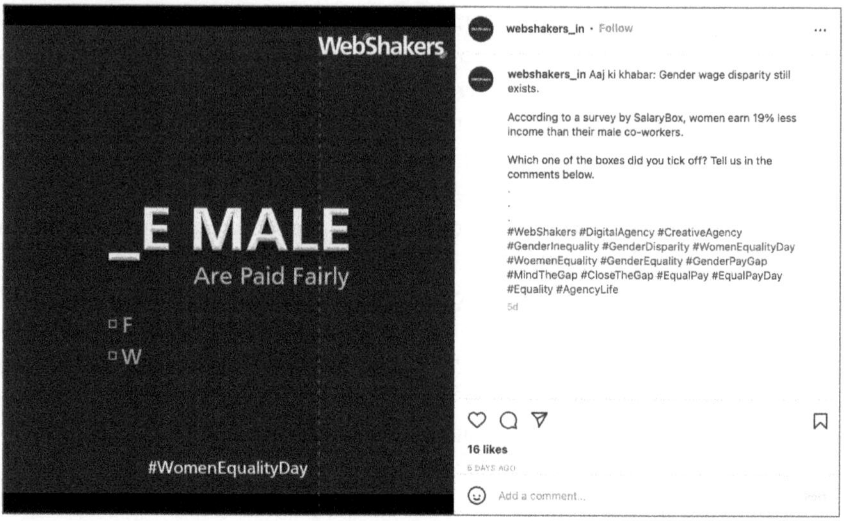

Figure 11.4 Social media is used as a resource to raise awareness about pay disparities.
POSTED ON INSTAGRAM

The gender pay gap is the disparity in wages based on gender, but other forms of discrimination complicate this. To understand more fully, we must analyze this problem using an intersectional perspective. **Intersectionality** is a way of viewing forms of oppression as interconnected and interlocking. Pay is not only affected by sexism (or societal gender prejudice) but also by racism (or racial and/or ethnic prejudice). **Racism** is the belief that a specific racial category of people is superior (usually white people) coupled with the societal power to make laws, policies, and public opinion support that ideology.

Women of color women experience a **double wage gap** or inequality in earning based on race/ethnicity and gender (Economic Policy Institute 2019). According to the Bureau of Labor Statistics (2022), Black women's median earnings are 67.4 percent compared to white men's (IWPR 2023b). Latina workers have to work ten months into 2022 to earn the same pay as white men, with Latina workers earning 53 cents to every white man's dollar (Gould 2019). While the inequality narrows a bit when controlling for education, immigration status, location, and years of experience, the pay gap remains with Latinas earning 52 cents per white man's earned dollar (Pierre-Bravo 2023). This translates into approximately $25,000 less in annual earnings for women of color (NWLC 2019a). Native women earn just 54.7 cents per dollar paid to white men. At this rate, they will not reach pay equity with white men until the year 2144 (IWPR 2023a).

This wage gap increases throughout the life course with full-time working women over the age of sixty-five earning only 76 cents to the male dollar (NWLC 2019a). Research indicates that transgender women's earnings drop after they complete gender reassignment surgery; their wages fall by nearly one-third (Schilt and Wiswall 2008). Nonbinary, genderqueer, or gender-fluid full-time workers are paid 70 cents for every dollar cisgender workers are paid (NWLC 2023). This analysis requires more data, however, because questions about sexuality and gender are not included in most labor surveys.

In addition to salary disparity, researchers found the average bonus for women was less than 66 percent of that for their male counterparts, even when controlling for experience, age, and base salary (Goldar, Ryan, and Yildirmaz 2019).

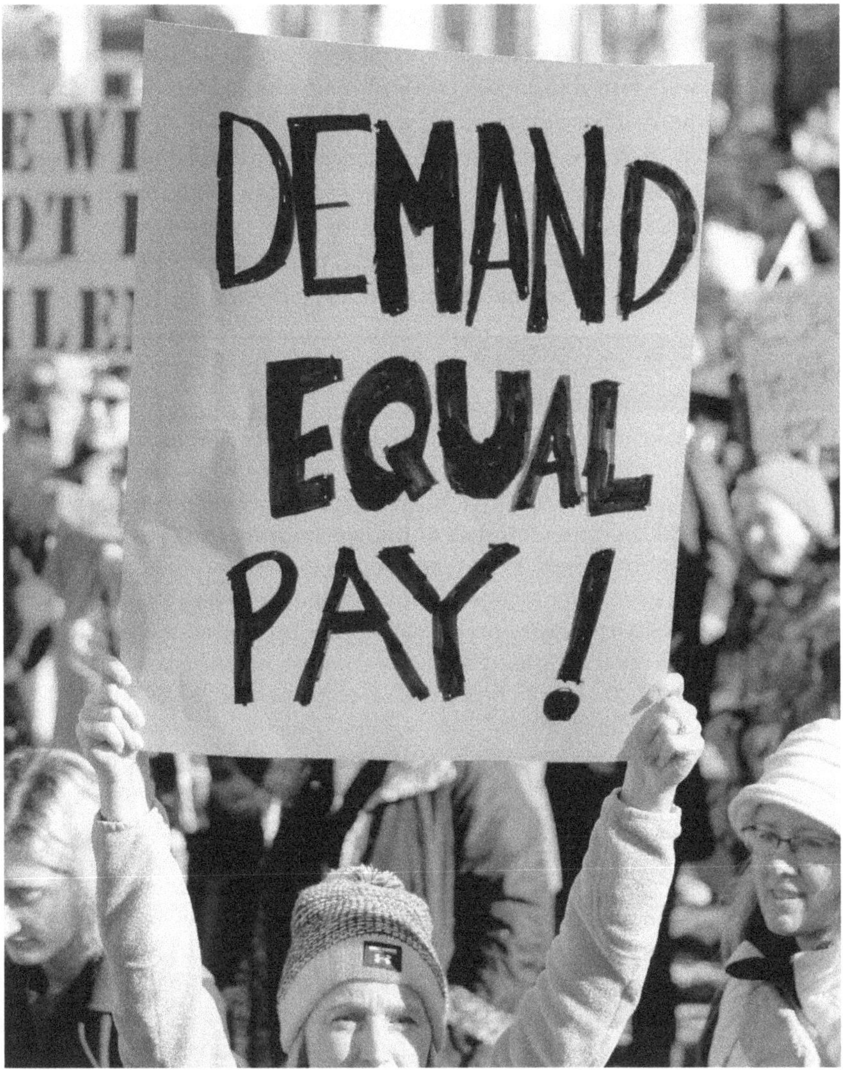

Figure 11.5 Despite improvements, unequal pay based on gender, race, and other social identities persist. Wikimedia Commons

Women with children experience the **motherhood penalty**, or the loss of wages women experience as they have children. The average mother in the United States working full-time makes 75 cents for every dollar a working father makes (NWLC 2021a). This is often due to employers putting women on the so-called mommy track. The **mommy track** assumes that women workers will be less committed to their jobs due to family obligations and are therefore willing to sacrifice workplace equality as a trade-off (Wade and Ferree 2019). Years of research indicate that the lack of free, reliable early childhood education and childcare is one pervasive element in creating gender inequality in the workplace (Miller 2017). The impact of COVID-19 cannot be understated as elementary schools and childcare centers closed due to the pandemic. Working mothers were forced to choose between their jobs and families, which one author hypothesized "is going to set . . . women back 10 years" (Taub 2020).

Conversely, men who are fathers experience the **fatherhood premium** or the wage increase that happens as men marry and have children. The assumption is that men who are married with children have "settled down," and are more committed to their work so that they can provide for their families. Even when controlling for educational attainment, degrees earned, occupation, race,

In the News . . .

Never has the motherhood penalty been more apparent than during the COVID-19 pandemic. For white-collar families with children home from school, parents were left wondering how they would manage work, childcare, and the unending list of unpaid household tasks. For most families, the mother's job is the least paid, and therefore it is most likely that the mother will quit her job to accommodate the families' needs (Lewis 2020). Blue-collar jobs were most likely to be lost during the pandemic, so women in those jobs, especially single mothers, were hardest hit (Baker 2020). By July 2020, women had shouldered 56 percent of COVID-19 job losses (Madgavkar et al. 2020).

For women who do keep their jobs, their time and concentration focused on work was often limited due to the many roles assumed while working and schooling from home. Studies found that mothers were doing the majority of homeschooling (Fleischer 2020). Indeed, women spent over twelve hours a day on childcare and housework during COVID-19 (Andrew et al. 2020). It follows that women were spending less time doing work-related tasks and experienced an estimated one-third of the uninterrupted work time that fathers enjoyed, making them 23 percent more likely to be fired (Andrew et al. 2020; Topping 2020). Working moms' mental health suffered; trying to juggle these multiple roles during lockdown became "too much."

and region, 38 percent of the disparity in women's pay remains unexplained (Blau and Kahn 2016). Researchers attribute that remaining inequity to gender discrimination (NWLC 2019a).

The effects of this disparity are compounded when retirement benefits, such as 401(k) contributions, are calculated based on salary (Ziv 2019). The long-term financial security of women is significantly impacted in this way. Since employer contributions are often calculated as a percentage of salary, women save less for retirement over time. This gap will widen, of course, as invested funds receive compounded interest over the years. Social Security benefits are calculated based on a person's earnings and years on the job. Since women's salary is affected by the gender pay gap, their Social Security payouts are also reduced (US Congress Joint Economic Committee 2011). The average woman would need to work an additional nine years to make up the lost income due to the wage gap (NWLC 2019a).

Due to these ancillary forms of compensation, researchers have found that the gender wage gap doesn't fully encompass the extent of inequality. When combining other employee-provided perks, like health insurance, bonuses, and retirement contributions, research indicates that women earn 57 cents for every man's dollar (Stanford Poverty Law Center 2019). This data supports the **gender earnings gap**, or the calculation of gendered income disparities which include wages *and* other forms of employee compensation to measure income.

It's easy to think of this as just numbers—statistics that tell us about an often-lamented social problem. Have you ever thought about the real-life consequences of the gender pay gap? Paying women equally would provide economic stability for families across the United States. If the gender pay gap was eradicated, the poverty rate among women would be cut in half. This change would positively affect children, too, moving 2.5 million children out of poverty (Whaley 2018).

Student loan debts would be paid off quicker with pay equity. A 2018 study found that only 33 percent of female 2007 and 2008 graduates had paid off their student loan debt by 2012. However, 44 percent of men had paid off their student loans (Whaley 2018). In day-to-day terms, closing the wage gap would mean approximately $10,000 more per year for the average working woman. That could mean a three-month supply of groceries ($2000), three months of childcare payments ($2500), three months of rent ($2500), three months of health insurance premiums ($1500), four months of student loan payments ($1000), and nine tanks of gas ($500) (National Women's Law Center 2021b; based on 2019–2020 data).

In the News . . .

In October 2020, Princeton University agreed to a settlement with the US Department of Labor. A 2012–2014 review of professors' pay found systematic and pervasive bias in pay against female faculty. The Department of Labor found that female faculty were earning less than male faculty, even though they had the same education, credentials, and experience (Heyboer 2020). After initially contesting these findings, Princeton University agreed to a $1.2 million settlement which includes back pay and future salary adjustments (Associated Press 2020b). In addition, Princeton agreed to pay-equity training for staff and conducted statistical analyses to ensure no future discrimination. As a condition of the settlement, Princeton University publicly admitted no wrongdoing (Heyboer 2020).

Gendered Work

Society uses a gendered lens to determine which circumstances and tasks are labeled "work," and therefore which labor should be paid versus unpaid. Care work, such as raising children, aiding the sick, or assisting the elderly has largely been deemed "women's work"—and therefore unpaid. Even when work is deemed worthy of compensation, our society continues to gender work titles and job functions. **Gendered job segregation** refers to tracking people into specific occupations that are deemed "masculine" or "feminine." For example, the Bureau of Labor Statistics found that 98 percent of speech-language pathologists are women, while only 11 percent of civil engineers are women (DeWolf 2017). Women in STEM (science, technology, engineering, math) fields are still underrepresented.

The working world still largely subscribes to the **glass slipper ideology** or the belief that leadership is associated with man and manhood. Women aren't seen as able to lead—just attend to more "feminine" concerns (just like Cinderella) (Rennison and Bonomi 2020). Women experience the **glass ceiling**, or barriers restricting women from rising to the highest leadership positions. Hillary Clinton, in her presidential concession speech in 2016, acknowledged the glass ceiling associated with high-ranking positions of power. She said, "I know we have still not shattered that highest and hardest glass ceiling, but someday someone will—and hopefully sooner than we might think right now" (Clinton 2016).

Letters of recommendation for women are shorter and stress work ethic, while letters written for men often express their superior intellect and skill

(Dutt et al. 2016). Women in computer-related jobs have decreased since 1990 (DeWolf 2017). Indeed, research indicates that even as women move into these work spheres, those jobs become gradually devalued and underpaid over time (NWLC 2019a). This is called **job feminization**—the phenomenon in which job prestige and associated salaries are reduced simply because women become more common employees in that field.

Simply having a feminized name can be a liability in the workforce. One study found that when a man's name replaced a woman's name on a résumé, managers were 60 percent more likely to hire the applicant (Carter 2023). For example, women in STEM careers are less likely to be hired, have their research funded, or receive the materials and mentorship necessary for success (Colwell 2020). A 2019 study of National Institutes of Health grant funding found that male first-time principal (lead) investigators are granted substantially larger monetary awards than female PIs—an average of $41,000 more (Oliveira et al. 2019). The COVID-19 pandemic increased the need for scientists, and female researchers at the frontlines of this research. For example, Kimberly Prather (UC San Diego) was one of the lead scientists who determined COVID-19 was airborne (Hoffman 2020). A well-known researcher from UC Berkeley, Jennifer Doudna, focused her research on enhancing the efficiency and effectiveness of COVID-19 testing (Colwell 2020). However, the question remains: how much further would we be in fighting COVID-19 if we had "all hands on deck?"

We must remember that institutional discrimination is a much larger system of oppression than just the sum of a few women's choices. Indeed, these forms of gender bias create a double bind for women leaders. Women leaders who are direct and decisive—qualities our society characterizes as masculine—are seen as "not nice"; however, women who seek to build consensus and community—qualities deemed as feminine—are seen as "too nice" (McCollum 2023). These two opposite traits are usually perceived by employees as either/or but rarely as a happy medium. Second, women must work doubly hard to obtain the same amount of respect and credibility as men, and yet they earn fewer rewards than their male leader peers. Finally, women leaders are seen as liked or competent, but not both (McCollum 2023). This scenario leaves women in positions of power the painstaking task of meeting a standard that they are unlikely to attain.

Of course, there has been progress over time. The Bureau of Labor Statistics found that women working in managerial and professional occupations have increased; however, many of those positions are a so-called glass cliff.

Glass cliffs are the propensity to hire women to the highest positions only when the business is likely to fail. This leaves the woman executive to take the blame for the organizational downfall (Ryan and Haslam 2005). For example, in 2023 Twitter (now X) faced heavy debt, low advertisement revenues, and negative cash flow after Elon Musk purchased the company (Macias and Kolodny 2023). During these financially unstable times, Linda Yaccarino was promoted to CEO. This promotion was only granted after the company showed significant losses in revenue and routinely negative press coverage (Hetler 2023).

Women of color experience additional barriers, as promotion decisions are often based on personal relationships and mentor connections. Despite their ambitions, research shows that Black women are less likely to find mentors to help them rise in their careers (Melaku 2019). Women of color often experience the broken rung. The **broken rung** refers to the phenomenon where women are less likely than men to be promoted to their first role as managers. For every one hundred men promoted to manager, eighty-seven women were promoted. For women of color, only seventy-three were promoted to manager (McKinsey & Company 2023). This is sometimes due to unconscious bias as well as intentional exclusion (Wingfield 2020).

GENDER PAY GAP AND PUBLIC POLICY

In the workplace, secrecy about pay is one reason the gender pay gap remains. After all, how can you determine pay disparity if you're unaware of wage differences? The **National Labor Relations Act (1935)** requires employees to be allowed to discuss pay and other compensation, but evidence suggests that employers still routinely discourage workers from wage conversations (NWLC 2019a). Making pay and other types of compensation accessible to all workers is one way to reduce the gender pay gap. In August 2022, California joined New York, Colorado, and Washington in passing a law that requires employers to list salary ranges for all jobs, as well as share data about median gender and racial wage gaps. Research indicates that as pay transparency increases wage gaps decrease (Green and Stecker 2022).

Since mothers routinely experience discrimination, policies that support working families, like affordable childcare initiatives and paid maternity and family leave, will increase positive outcomes. For example, Gov. Gretchen Whitmer of Michigan moved the Michigan Women's Commission from the Department of Civil Rights to the Department of Labor and Economics.

This move signals that equal pay and economic security are critical to gender equity (Whitmer 2020).

Research indicates that unionization has a direct effect on the gender pay gap, as unions are likely to fight for accessible compensation and fair wages for all. Protecting workers to collectively bargain and unionize is important to reducing the wage gap (NWLC 2019a). The **1963 Equal Pay Act** states that employers cannot determine salary based on gender. Despite this important legislation, the influence of sexism on the economy continues to define financial success and independence. Legislatively, the Equal Pay Act has proven to be ineffective in closing the pay gap completely.

To address this, the **Lilly Ledbetter Fair Pay Act** (2009) was signed into law to allow employees to sue employers for lost wages due to discrimination (Nilsen 2019). Lilly Ledbetter was one of the few women supervisors at a Goodyear plant in Alabama in the 1990s. Despite earning a "top performance" award, she was making significantly less money than her men coworkers. Ledbetter did not know about the pay disparity because employees were prohibited from talking about compensation. In 1998, Ledbetter was checking her office mail when an anonymous note dropped out that listed three men coworkers' salaries, each much higher than her own (Houchins 2015).

Ledbetter filed a claim under the Equal Employment Opportunity Commission, which led to her first trial. The jury awarded her millions of dollars in back pay and damages. However, Goodyear appealed the decision, stating that the discriminatory pay complaint had reached the 180-day time limit. The original claim was overturned. A subsequent appeal to the Supreme Court led to the same results. Congress acted, writing an amendment to the Civil Rights Act of 1964 allowing employees to dispute discriminatory pay by resetting the 180-day limit each time an unfair paycheck is received (Houchins 2015).

MOVING FORWARD

According to a 2020 study, 69 percent of Americans believe that women have not achieved gender equality in the workplace (Saad 2020). Social media campaigns continue to be useful in creating public awareness and social change about the gender pay gap. In the fall of 2020, a cartoon went viral on social media depicting three men and three women wearing business suits at the starting line of a track. The cartoon shows the men ready to run the race, while the women look somberly at the additional barriers of housework blocking their way.

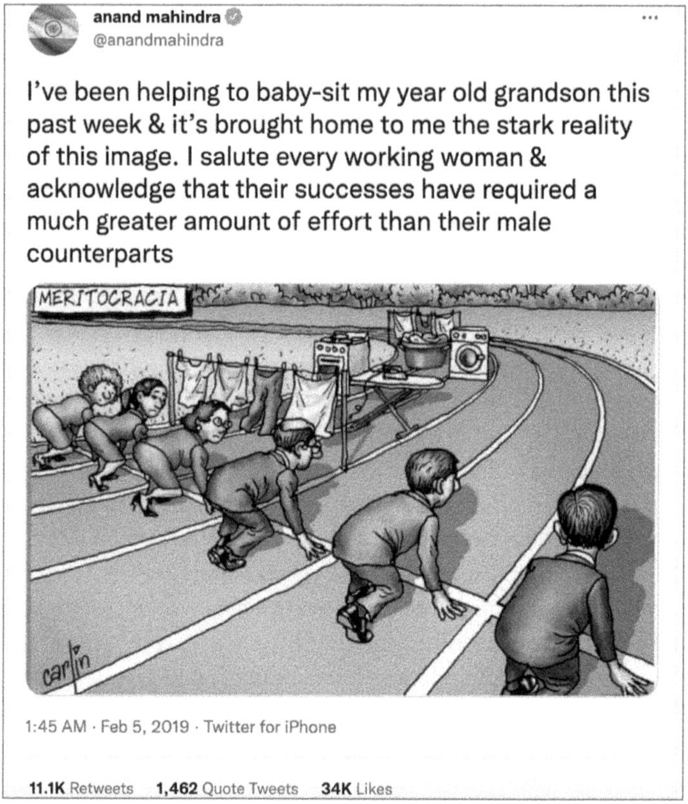

Figure 11.6 This cartoon depicts the many barriers that contribute to gendered work inequality. Posted on X

Although increases in women's rights have reduced the wage gap, closing this pay disparity is necessary for the economic stability of women (National Women's Law Center 2019). Building public awareness about the gender wage gap is critical to creating social change. One public campaign is Equal Pay Day. **Equal Pay Day** takes place on the date (usually in the first four months of a new year) that women must work into the new year to earn what men made in the previous calendar year. Equal Pay Day was first recognized in 1996 by the National Committee on Pay Equity. In 1996, Equal Pay Day was April 11 (Burrows 2023). In 2024, Equal Pay Day was March 12.

Women, particularly women of color, are overrepresented in low-paying jobs (i.e., fast food, home health aides) and likewise underrepresented in high-paying jobs (i.e., STEM careers) (NWLC 2019a). Therefore, any policy that increases the minimum wage will have a disproportionately positive effect on women's earning potential. In addition, public policy and educational initiatives that support women moving into STEM careers have proven successful in engaging women in high-earning work. Barbie (under the Mattel Corporation) has started the Dream Gap campaign, #closethedreamgap. In addition, the campaign #shecanSTEM provides resources for recruiting girls into science and technology fields.

Women of color experience the double discrimination of sexism and racism in the workplace, so it is imperative to address this problem head-on. Research shows that good intentions or easy platitudes about equality do not lead to measurable change. Policies must be implemented around diversity in hiring and followed without fail (Wingfield 2020). Corporations that profess belief in diversity must also work to end systemic racism and sexism. Enter the Gender Pay Gap Bot. This UK-based app is an automated X (formerly Twitter) account that responds to companies' International Women's Day posts with publicly available employee compensation data. These posts expose the pervasive gender and racial pay inequalities at each company and highlight that companies' supportive tweets are rarely backed by real action (Fensome 2022).

Finally, the **Paycheck Fairness Act** was introduced in Congress to strengthen the Equal Pay Act of 1963 (US 116th Congress 2019–2020). The goal of this legislation is to protect employees from employer reprisal for discussing pay and limit the use of previous payment in job hiring (among other protections) (NWLC 2019a). At the time of publication (2024), this legislation passed in the House of Representatives but was still awaiting a vote in the Senate.

Key Takeaways

- The gender wage gap is the difference in hourly pay between men and women after controlling for individual differences.
- Women of color are affected by a double pay gap, which lowers their pay based on sexism and racism.
- Gendered job segregation funnels people into jobs based on gender, while the glass ceiling prevents women from rising to the highest levels of occupations.
- The Equal Pay Act, the Lilly Ledbetter Fair Pay Act, and the National Labor Relations Act are examples of just some the federal legislation aimed to end workplace gender inequality.
- Changes in minimum wage, affordable childcare, and increasing unionization are all ways to create lasting changes to the gender pay gap.

12

GENDER AND POLITICS
#VOTE

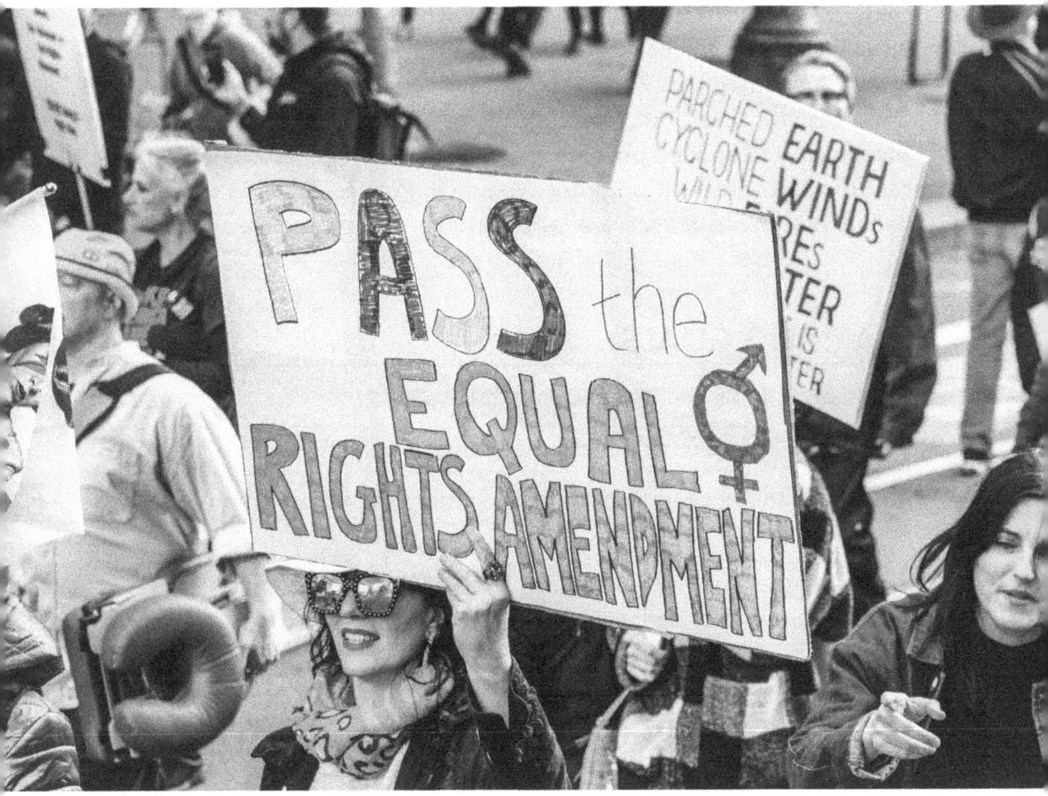

Figure 12.1 Activists participate in a rally supporting the Equal Rights Amendment (ERA).
SHUTTERSTOCK

A 2020 GALLUP SURVEY found that the majority of Americans doubt the presence of gender equality in politics (Saad 2020). Yet a more recent Gallup poll states that 93 percent of US adults believe that a woman president is possible in the next ten years (Reinhart 2021). Data from a global survey found that the majority of respondents from all countries surveyed viewed men as more capable leaders than women (Peck 2019a). Historically, most positions of political power are held by men.

The 2022 election showed a record-breaking number of women elected to Congress—a total of 149 seats held by women (Center for American Women in Politics 2023). Despite recent historic gains, only 25 percent of Senate seats and 28.5 percent of House of Representatives seats are held by women. Of those 149 seats, 1.9 percent are held by Asian/Pacific Islander women, Black women held 5 percent, Latina/Hispanic women held 3.6 percent, 0.2 percent are held by Middle Eastern/North African women, and 0.4% are held by Native American/Alaska Native women (Center for American Women in Politics 2023). You guessed it; 94 percent of women in US Congress are white. The year 2022 also saw a record-breaking number of women elected as state governors, and yet this number is still only 23.5 percent of all governors (Center for Women in Politics 2023). *What role does gender play in the political arena? Do women still experience sexism in politics, or is gender inequality a thing of a past? Let's take a look.*

LEARNING GOALS

By the end of this chapter, you should be able to

1. Identify examples of gender inequality in politics
2. Explain the positive and negative influences of the women's suffrage movement
3. Assess the current public policy and nonprofit interventions to increase gender parity in politics

GENDER PERFORMANCE IN POLITICS

Performance of gender is at the center of American politics, particularly in the race for the presidency. Research suggests that the traits Americans associate with the presidency, such as toughness, aggressiveness, and ambition, are also linked with masculinity (Schneider and Bos 2014). Because our societal norms associate the presidency with masculinity, men have an easier time running for office as they enjoy the basic assumption that they are qualified; however, women must be overprepared to be considered electable (Thomson-DeVeaux 2019).

Women who run for office must confront sexist stereotypes and double standards that men candidates do not face (Thomson-DeVeaux 2019). The bias is declining, however. In 2018, the General Social Survey (GSS) found that only 13 percent of Americans believe that men are "better suited emotionally" than women for politics (Carnevale, Smith, and Campbell 2019). People of all ages and all social classes are becoming more tolerant of women in politics, but those Americans who identify as "strong Republicans" are more likely to believe that men are better suited emotionally for politics (approximately 40%) than those who identify as "strong Democrats" (approximately 18%). People with higher educational attainment are more likely to support women in politics (Carnevale, Smith, and Campbell 2019).

Despite these trends, we must remember that in 2016, Democratic presidential nominee Hillary Clinton won the popular vote by 2.9 million votes but lost the election to Republican nominee Donald Trump in the Electoral College vote (Carnevale, Smith, and Campbell 2019). Even though gender bias is historically at its lowest, even small amounts of inequality can make a big difference, as the 2016 election illustrates.

While women politicians are less likely to exude traditionally feminine qualities—such as empathy and compassion—they also bear criticism if they project traditionally masculine traits (Schneider and Bos 2014). However, some traditionally feminine qualities can work in women candidates' favor. For example, research shows that more women candidates than their men counterparts are seen as honest, better role models for children, and able to compromise. If

In the News . . .

Governor Gretchen Whitmer, also known as "that woman from Michigan" and "Big Gretch," was the focus of a kidnapping plot meant to "punish" her for her policies during the COVID-19 pandemic. While this attack was politically motivated, researchers argue that misogyny toward women in power was also a factor (Krook 2020). The assailants used multiple slurs, calling Whitmer a "tyrant bitch" and hung a naked brown-haired effigy by the neck.

In August 2022, three of the would-be kidnappers were convicted of all charges, including conspiracy and explosives/weapons of mass destruction charges. In December 2022, a judge sentenced one of the kidnappers to sixteen years in prison for his role in the attempted kidnapping (Li 2022).

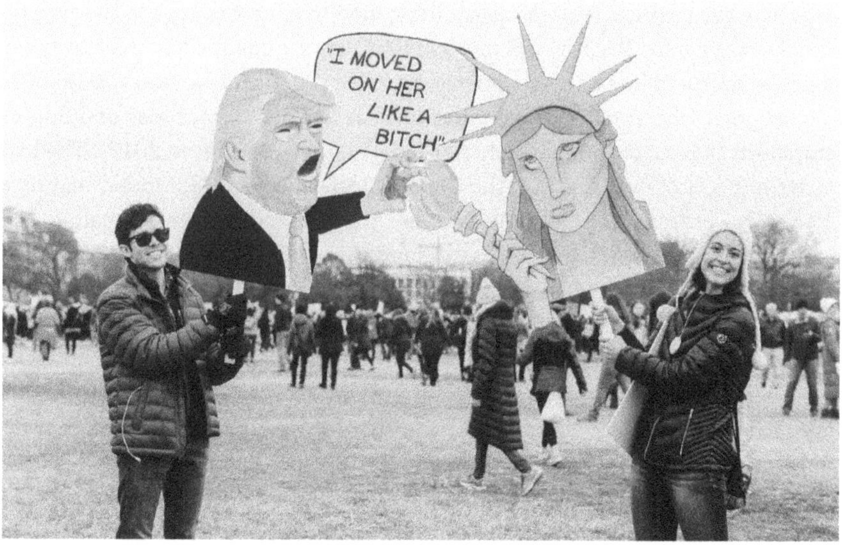

Figure 12.2 Hypermasculine language and imagery was a cornerstone of Trump's 2016 presidential campaign. POSTED ON X

this image is flawed due to scandal or misstep, however, voters are much less forgiving of women politicians (Thomson-DeVeaux 2019).

While these stereotypes are rarely explicitly stated, we can see glimpses in political commentary. News outlets reported former President Donald Trump appealing to white men voters using traditional masculine tropes that are interpreted as "strength" (Katz 2019). Trump's language toward women and minorities illustrates this ideology. Indeed, during his 2019 impeachment trial, Trump routinely used language that emasculated Democratic men to rally support (Katz 2019).

The 2020 presidential election displayed a battle between two white men over the age of seventy who performed two different kinds of masculinity. Former president Donald Trump is known for his hypermasculine posturing, described as ornamental masculinity defined by machismo demeanor and swagger (Faludi 2020). White men were his biggest supporters. Some researchers argue that Trump's appeal to the hypermasculine, bully archetype secured this vote (Katz 2020). Conversely, President Joe Biden portrayed a different version of masculinity, speaking openly about loss and relationships (Hesse 2020).

Both candidates, however, know the masculine tropes necessary for election. In 2018, Biden stated that he would "beat the hell out of" Trump if they were in high school (Stracqualursi 2018). After Trump continued to criticize his age and mental state, Biden challenged him to a push-up contest as a show

In the News . . .

In 2018, Dr. Christine Blasey Ford testified in front of the US Senate Judiciary Committee about being sexually assaulted while in high school by then-Supreme Court nominee Brett Kavanaugh. She spent hours retelling the events of her traumatic experience. Despite her bravery, Brett Kavanaugh was sworn in as a Supreme Court justice on October 6, 2018, and now holds a lifetime appointment to the highest court in the United States. Dr. Ford continues to be the focus of personal and professional attacks (Katz and Banks 2019).

Ford had to move four times after her testimony due to death threats (Jackson 2022). In 2022, activists protested at the home of Justice Kavanaugh following the Supreme Court's overturning of *Roe v. Wade*. Some argued that this protest was unjust, but others used X (formerly Twitter) to remind constituents of the burden carried by Ford. Her name was discussed so frequently that it became a trending hashtag on Twitter (Jackson 2022).

of strength (Wagner 2019). Despite Biden's different brand of masculinity, he knew what persona was required to win. For example, one Biden campaign video described his so-called masculine traits of "strength" and "courage" but also included "compassion" and "resilience" (Hesse 2020).

GENDERED ELECTIONS

Despite the 2022 midterm election gains, gender parity in politics is still lacking. Created by the nonprofit Represent Women, the **gender parity index (GPI)** assigns grades to each state individually and the United States as a whole. The index assigns a score between 0 and 100: 0 means no women are elected officials, and 100 means all elected officials are women (Ahrens 2019). States with perfect gender parity (same number of men and women elected officials) would have a GPI of 50. Based on the 2023 GPI, Maine (53.6) and Oregon (53.2) have the highest GPI while North Dakota (11.5) and Louisiana (9.2) have the lowest GPI scores in the United States (Lamendola and Scaglia 2023).

Recent data suggest that women and men win elections at the same rate. Therefore, if more women run for office, we should see an uptick in women in politics (Anastasopoulos 2016). However, other research indicates that women must be more qualified to be elected, which assumes a gender bias (Lawless and Pearson 2008). It is also possible that sexism in politics has remained the same, but women politicians have become savvier at navigating it (Dittmar 2015).

Representative Alexandria Ocasio-Cortez (AOC) (D-NY) has proven to be particularly adept at responding to gender-based attacks about her wardrobe, hair, and general appearance. In 2018, she became the youngest congresswoman elected at the age of twenty-eight. AOC is one of four congresswomen of color in a group called "The Squad" because of their willingness to battle the status quo of Washington, DC (Sullivan 2019). In 2018, Ilhan Omar (D-MN), Rashida Tlaib (D-MI), Alexandria Ocasio-Cortez (D-NY), and Ayanna Pressley (D-MA) joined together for an interview. Afterward, a group photo was uploaded to Instagram with the caption #squad (Izadi and Epstein 2019). While this label has become politically divisive for some, others see it as a rallying cry to those who are willing to do the hard work of making social change.

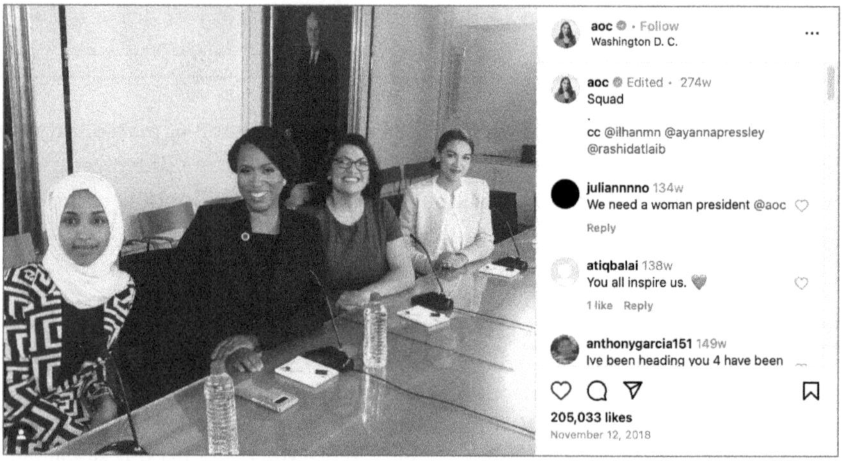

Figure 12.4 #squad. Posted on Instagram

Inclusion and visibility of other minority groups continue to be lacking, but there are some notable exceptions. In 2023, there were 1,185 LGBTQIA+ elected officials accounting for 0.23 percent of all elected officials (Parker 2024). While this is a 13.6 percent increase since June 2022 in LGBTQIA+ representation, America must elect 36,232 LGBTQIA+ officials to achieve equitable representation in state and federal government (Parker 2024). For example, elected to the Virginia House of Delegates in 2017, Danica Roem was the first openly transgender lawmaker in the United States (Lakritz 2021). President Joe Biden appointed the first openly transgender person to be confirmed by the

Senate—Dr. Rachel Levine was appointed as the assistant secretary for health (Stolberg 2021). Pete Buttigieg was the first openly gay candidate to run for president and then became the first openly gay cabinet secretary confirmed by the Senate. In 2021, he was confirmed as the head of the US Department of Transportation under President Joe Biden (Shepardson 2021).

How do we ensure that women's and LGBTQIA+ people's political positions continue to move toward true parity? The **concrete floor** is a term scholars use to analyze a "new normal" that is created toward gender equality. As more women are elected to office, that new level of representation becomes the new expectation. For example, Spain was the first country to have two-thirds of its federal cabinet positions held by women, the most inclusive government in the world (Franceschet and Beckwith 2018). This reflects a global trend: once women are included in powerful positions in government, those numbers tend to rise.

GENDERED POLITICAL PARTICIPATION

Research shows that women are three times more likely than men to state that the number one reason they do not get involved in politics is because they do not know enough about political issues. This does not mean that women *actually* do not know as much as men about politics—it just means that there is a confidence gap (American University 2020). Despite this reluctance, women have registered and voted at higher rates than men in every presidential election since 1980 (Center for American Women and Politics [CAWP] 2023). This voter turnout data remains constant regardless of race. Black, Hispanic, Asian American/Pacific Islander, and white women voted more than men. The disparity between men and women voters is most seen in Black voters with 66.3 percent of Black women versus 58.3 percent of Black men voting (CAWP 2023). According to a 2020 survey, women on both sides of the political aisle agree that they get involved in politics to make the world a better place (American University 2020). Democratic voters report wanting to elect a woman president, but it is not the primary goal (Kurtzleben 2019). A 2019 poll found that the main concern of Democrats in the 2020 election was defeating President Trump (82%) instead of electing an ethnic minority (38%) or a woman candidate (40%) (Ipsos 2019).

Regardless of gender or political affiliation, voters overwhelmingly agree that it is important that they "like" the candidate for which they vote (84% of men; 90% of women). Political pundits will often ask if a woman candidate is "likable" (Johnson 2019). Voters described "likeability" as a combination of confidence, presentation, and track record (Barbara Lee Family Foundation 2016). While some of these aspects can be controlled, other factors are external.

For example, research shows that voters pay particular attention to women's race and physical appearance. Indeed, women politicians were deemed more likable the younger and more physically attractive they were. In addition, tone of voice was of particular importance as women candidates were more likely to be called "shrill" and "boring" (Barbara Lee Family Foundation 2016).

GENDERED POLITICS AND PUBLIC POLICY

The **women's suffrage movement** reflects the work of women (and men) who fought tirelessly to pass the **Nineteenth Amendment** ensuring women's right to vote in the United States. When we talk about women having the right to vote, we often forget about the intense sacrifice first-wave feminists made to secure that privilege. In 1917, the National Women's Party became the first group to picket in front of the White House. These **Silent Sentinels** held banners and signs that were intentionally provocative to gain attention and support for the cause (Marino 2023). Initially, public response was mixed, and often mocking of the women; however, as the United States entered World War I, people were angered by the women's insistence to continue their protest. Many of the sentinels were routinely arrested.

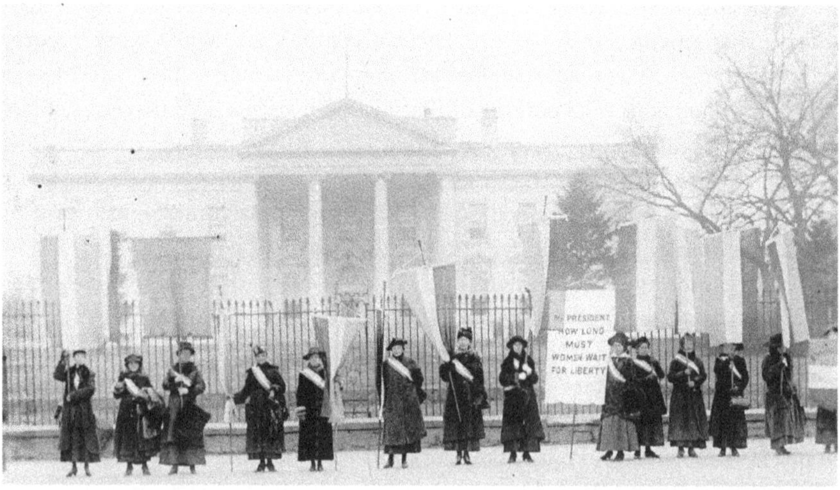

Figure 12.3 Suffragettes gather outside of the White House in support of women's right to vote (1917). Library of Congress

Often forgotten, the **night of terror** took place on November 14, 1917. A Washington, DC, police superintendent ordered forty guards to "teach the women a lesson" (Marino 2023). Thirty-three suffragettes were beaten with clubs, arrested, imprisoned, and endured physical and psychological terror. Affidavits later state that the women were punched, kicked, and pinched. Some were knocked unconscious, left hanging from ceiling bars through the night, and hit with an iron bed. All were denied medical treatment (Marino 2023). This event caused significant negative press and persuaded President Woodrow Wilson to act. He declared women's suffrage a "war measure" that needed immediate attention. The Nineteenth Amendment was officially passed on August 26, 1920.

The women's suffrage movement was not without issues. The movement originated with the joint purpose of passing the Fifteenth Amendment—the right for Black men to vote (Little 2021). Influential suffragists Elizabeth Cady Stanton and Susan B. Anthony worked tirelessly to obtain the right to vote for women—but not all women. Racism split the activists; Stanton and Anthony spoke against the right for Black men, particularly poor Southern Black men, to vote (Little 2021). They were enraged that Black men would have the right to vote (under the Fifteenth Amendment) before white women (Block 2020). In addition, racism stopped many lawmakers from supporting women's suffrage. Lawmakers who opposed voting rights for Black men railed against women's voting rights, as this would allow for more Black voters (Block 2020).

White feminist activists did not prioritize the expansion of voting rights for all women. Despite the passing of the Fifteenth and Nineteenth Amendments, Black Americans (particularly in the Southern states) were still actively disenfranchised by poll taxes, literacy tests, and violence (T. Brown 2018). Shortly after the passing of the Nineteenth Amendment, Black suffragist Mary Church Terrell stated that Black women in the South were "shamefully treated" and "not allowed to vote." Asian Americans, Native Americans, and other ethnic minorities were not permitted to vote until the passing of the 1965 Voting Rights Act (Block 2020).

One tireless advocate of elevating Black women in politics was Shirley Chisholm, enduring the obstacles placed by both sexism and racism in the 1960s. She was the first Black woman to be elected to Congress from the South, and the first Black person to run for president of a major party (Turner 2021).

The year 2020 marked the one hundredth anniversary of the Nineteenth Amendment, and a commemorative coin was issued to celebrate (Hannon 2019). A 2020 Gallup survey found that two-thirds of Americans consider the ratification of the Nineteenth Amendment to be the most important step in advancing women's rights (Saad 2020). However, activists note that voter

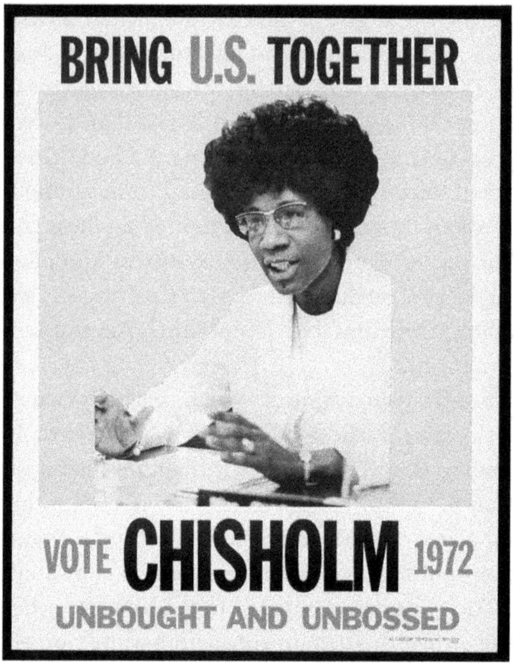

Figure 12.5 Presidential candidate and US Representative Shirley Chisholm's campaign poster makes clear that she's "unbought and unbossed." LIBRARY OF CONGRESS

disenfranchisement, particularly for Southern people of color, continues to suppress many women's participation in the political sphere (Block 2020).

Equal Rights Amendment

In 2016 the ERA Coalition conducted a survey which found that 80 percent of Americans polled believe that the US Constitution guarantees men and women equal rights (ERA Coalition 2016); however, this is untrue. The United States is one of only twenty-eight countries that do not explicitly guarantee gender equality or equal rights based on gender identity or sex. Globally, every constitution adopted after 2000 includes a sex/gender equality provision (Heymann, Raub, and Sprague 2020).

The **Equal Rights Amendment** (ERA) was first introduced into the US Congress in 1923 by Alice Paul, a prominent leader in the feminist movement (Lyons, Astor, and Salam 2020). The first general protections for women were in the Equal Protection Clause of the Fourteenth Amendment, which was ratified in the 1970s (Heymann, Sprague, and Raub 2020). Despite general protections in the Constitution, loopholes are often found. The ERA is three sentences

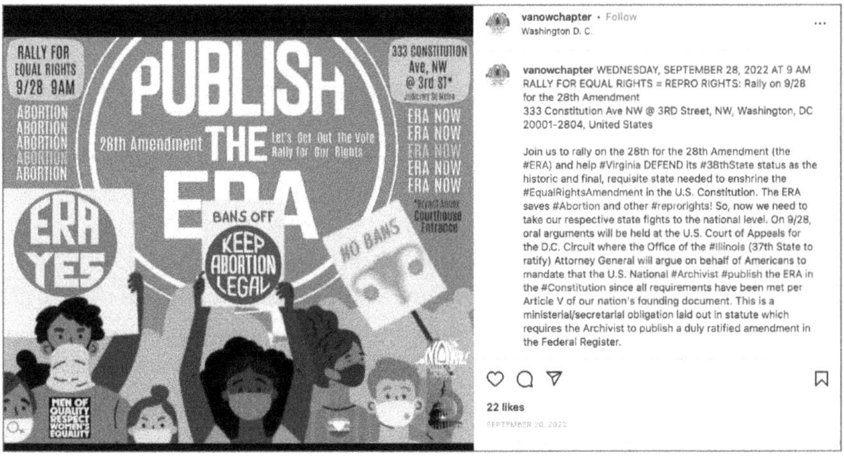

Figure 12.6

long, the last two guiding how to implement the amendment. The first sentence reads, *"Equality of rights under the law shall not be denied or abridged by the United States or any State on the account of sex."*

This amendment has been polarizing every time it is reintroduced to Congress. Presently, proponents of the amendment state that the bill would put an end to gender discrimination, including the gender pay gap and pregnancy discrimination. However, opponents believe that the amendment would undermine religious freedoms and family structure (Lyons, Astor, and Salam 2020). Those who are antiabortion oppose this bill, as legislation is currently unclear whether the lack of access to family planning is a violation of rights (Matson 2020).

In January 2020, Virginia voted on the Equal Rights Amendment and was the thirty-eighth state to ratify the legislation (Matson 2020). This was important because thirty-eight states are necessary to ratify the amendment in Congress (Schneider, Vozzella, and Sullivan 2020). However, the US Department of Justice issued a statement (January 2020) that the deadline had expired and the process of ratification would need to start again (Associated Press 2020a). Activists argue that this timeline was arbitrary and that the ERA is the twenty-eighth amendment (Baker 2022).

MOVING FORWARD

In the 2020 election, 24 million Gen Z citizens (ages 18–23) were eligible to vote for the first time (Cilluffo and Fry 2019). Combined with millennials (ages 24–39), this youngest demographic group made up 34 percent of 2020 voters (Kight 2019). It is safe to say that the youngest Americans have the potential to completely shift our political climate. In the 2022 midterm elections, eighteen- to twenty-nine-year-old voters (mostly Gen Z) had a significant rise in voter turnout—particularly young women. Young voters are largely credited with preventing the predicted "red wave" of Republican candidates in the 2022 midterms (Frey 2022).

However, navigating the US voting process can be challenging. VOTE411.org is a nonpartisan website that contains all the information voters need to get registered, find their polling location, and review local ballots. The organization also has an Election Day hotline available in several languages to report election problems. Analytics of website use found that the polling place locator is the most used feature in the days leading up to Election Day (VOTE411 2020). This organization is helping every voter to be empowered and informed.

Several organizations are working to empower women to be political candidates. Ready to Run is a nonpartisan organization that supports electing more women to public office regardless of party affiliation. They provide training about fundraising, campaigning, and media interactions. She the People is a national network of women of color seeking to mobilize voters to elect women of color. The organization sponsors debate watch parties, town hall meetings, and other social gatherings to build networks and relationships among women of color (She the People 2024).

She Should Run provides self-paced, online learning modules and virtual cohorts to create communities of women considering political office. The organization also engages citizens in supporting women candidates in office and teaching young girls to lead (She Should Run 2020). She Should Run launched the Team250K project, which is working toward the goal of having 250,000 women running for office by the year 2030. These social change organizations (and others) are working towards tangible differences in the gender parity of our elected officials.

Finally, the 2020 presidential race included a record number of people of color and women running in the primaries (Williams 2020). Democratic front-runners included popular candidates like Elizabeth Warren (Massachusetts) and Kamala Harris (California). While all women candidates ended their campaigns, their presence in the primary normalized women in the race and is likely to encourage more women candidates in the future (Williams 2020). The Democratic nominee, former vice president Joe Biden, chose Senator Kamala Harris as his running mate. However, an in-depth report of media coverage of Harris found racist and sexist remarks dominated news coverage of this event. According to a Time's Up Now study, 61 percent of news coverage of Harris mentioned race or gender, compared to only 5 percent of the coverage on her white man opponent. In addition, 36 percent of news coverage focused on Harris's ancestry instead of her accomplishments and credentials and skewed negatively, using words like "phony," "nasty," and "mean" (Time's Up Now 2020). The "angry Black woman" trope was a common theme in 13 percent of news reports about her (McShane 2020).

Nevertheless, on November 8, 2020, Kamala Harris gave her first speech as vice president–elect wearing a suffragette white suit. She stated, "While I may be the first woman in office, I will not be the last. . . . Every little girl that's watching tonight sees that this is a country of possibilities" (Aschbrenner, Fritze, and Hayes 2020).

Key Takeaways

- Gender plays a critical role in politics. Because positions of political power are deemed "masculine," men are seen as more qualified candidates.
- Gender parity, or equality of men and women elected officials, is significantly lacking in the United States.
- The woman's suffrage movement endured intense scrutiny and violence to advocate the passing of the Nineteenth Amendment.
- While the US Constitution does not guarantee equality, the Equal Rights Amendment, if passed, would prohibit discrimination on the basis of sex or gender identity.
- With the increasing numbers of Gen Z voters, the 2024 election will be largely influenced by the youngest voters—if they vote!

13

GENDER AND SOCIAL CHANGE
#FEMININST

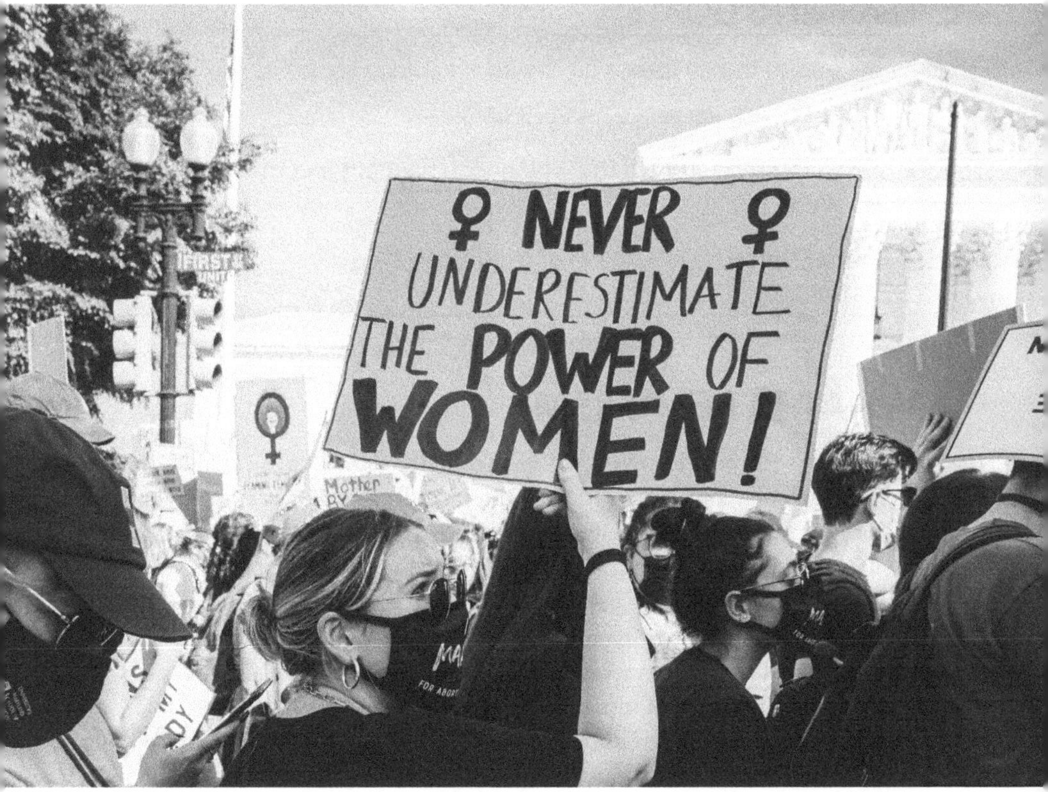

Figure 13.1 Feminism is a social movement that embraces the power of collective action.
UNSPLASH

FEMINISM HAS MORE support now than ever (Marcotte 2019). The popularity of feminism can be seen in the Women's March that took place in 2017. Thousands of women joined together to express rage and grief. In response to a leaked 2005 *Access Hollywood* interview where Donald Trump bragged about perpetrating sexual misconduct against women, women wore pink cat-ear knitted hats in protest. The Women's March saw three times the number of protesters than those at the Presidential Inauguration the day before (Wallace and Parlapiano 2017) and is lauded as likely the largest single-day demonstration in American history to date (Chenoweth and Pressman 2017).

Merriam-Webster named "feminism" their word of the year in 2017, largely due to the increased political activism of women following the 2016 presidential election (Merriam-Webster, 2017). Many cite feminism as the ideological framework for this social change movement. *So what is feminism? Who can be a feminist? Let's take some time to clear up some misconceptions.*

LEARNING GOALS

By the end of this chapter, you should be able to

1. Identify the main frameworks of feminism
2. Explain the herstory of the women's movement and the subsequent backlash
3. Assess the strengths and challenges of each wave of the feminist movement

WHAT IS FEMINISM?

Throughout the past chapters, we've highlighted some of the challenges and victories women have endured over the past decade. For example, women's political representation is at its highest. In 2016, Hillary Clinton was the first woman to be a major political party presidential nominee, and the first woman to earn the popular vote for president. Women became the majority of students in law school for the first time in 2010 and were 54 percent of enrolled law students in 2019 (Heelan-Stanzoine 2019). Similarly, women made up the majority of medical school students in 2019 (Pawlowski 2019). The Affordable Care Act reduced the number of uninsured women by almost half and required that people could not be denied care because of sex or race discrimination (Coombs 2019). In 2012, President Obama required that all employers cover contraception without copays (Baker and Fleisher 2019). In 2015, marriage equality became legal in all fifty states (*Obergefell v. Hodges*). Currently, twenty-three states and Washington, DC, have laws that require employers to accommodate pregnant workers. In 2019, Congress voted to require paid family leave for all federal employees (Ness 2019). By all accounts, we've come a long way, baby.

Many of these successes can be attributed to feminist activism; however, using the label "feminist" often is met with mixed responses. A 2018 poll found that 38 percent of American women and 22 percent of American men identify themselves as "feminists" (Ballard 2018). Younger women are more likely to identify as feminists, so this brand of activism is not going away. While this is an increase from 2016, it still means that most Americans do not identify with that label (Ballard 2018). Why the controversy of this word? At its basic core, **feminism** is "a movement to end sexism, sexist exploitation, and oppression" (hooks 2000, viii). Therefore, a **feminist** is a person who believes in the concepts of feminism and actively works toward the end of sexism.

Social stigma still exists about feminists with the assumption that they hate marriage, men, and children. One X (formerly Twitter) user posted that he had never met a "happy feminist" (Perry 2020). What unleashed was a storm of replies, reminding the original poster that the common factor in all of these interactions was him (not feminism).

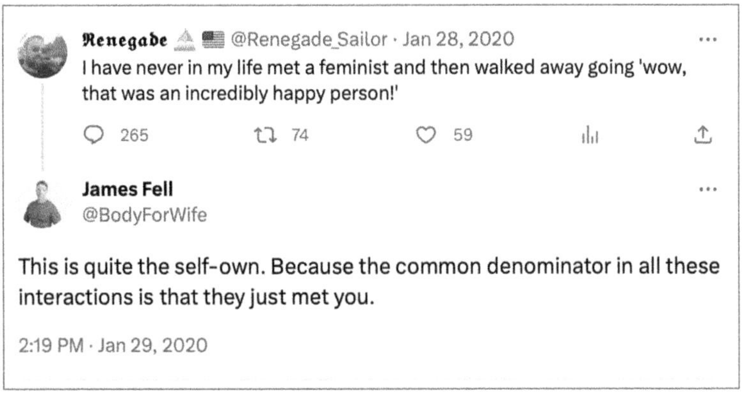

Figure 13.2 Never met a happy feminist? Maybe you're the problem.
JAMES FELL. POSTED ON X

Can men and nonbinary people be feminists? Before answering this question, let's review the definition of feminism: "Feminism is a movement to end sexism, sexist exploitation, and oppression" (hooks 2000, viii). This definition clearly states that sexism—not men, government, or religion—is the problem. **Sexism** is the societal devaluation of girls, women, and those feminine presenting. We must remember that all people, regardless of gender, have been socialized into our sexist society. Because the United States operates as a patriarchy with institutionalized sexism, we all (regardless of sex or gender) must consciously unlearn this way of seeing the world (hooks 2000). Indeed, for the feminist movement to succeed, men allies must be willing to change the narrative using the power given to them through patriarchy. The number of men feminists continues to rise.

Many men subscribe to **gender egalitarianism**, or the general belief in women's equality (Andersen 2015). Research states that men who have increased education are more likely to espouse gender egalitarian views. In addition, men who are in dual-earner families are more likely to be egalitarian (Pampel 2011).

Frameworks of Feminism

Although all feminists believe in ending sexism, the methods and means of how to get there have created many rifts within the community. As such, several frameworks (or theories) of feminism emerged with different ideas about sexism. There are many types of "personal feminisms" claimed by individuals; however, they usually fall under one of five feminist frameworks (see table 13.1). The key questions each framework asks are (1) why does sexism or patriarchy exist in society? and (2) what should be done to end it? This table distills the main points of each feminist framework into brief knowledge nuggets and is not meant to be a comprehensive overview.

HERSTORY OF THE WOMEN'S MOVEMENT

Social movements are groups of people who work to promote or resist a change in society. Historically, groups emerge when they have experienced a perceived injustice (Andersen 2015). Some social movements include a series of networked **social change organizations**, or formally defined entities with paid advocates, who work on a cause. Other social movements rely solely on the work of grassroots activism. **Grassroots activism** refers to everyday people—those without formal power—who experience an injustice standing together to make a change.

The women's movement relies on organizational power and grassroots activism to make social change and is one of the most successful social movements to date (Andersen 2015). The women's movement advocated for women's

TABLE 13.1 Feminist Frameworks: The Basics

	Why does sexism exist?	How do we end sexism?	Critiques of the framework
Liberal Feminism	Unequal laws and public policies that disadvantage women	Make all laws and public policies gender neutral (and color-blind)	Society is not gender-neutral or color-blind; does not address the realities of people's lived experiences
Socialist (Marxist) Feminism	The system of capitalism, with particular analysis of the intersection of productive and reproductive labor	Overthrow capitalism; end hierarchy altogether	Capitalism is not the only cause of gender inequality
Radical Feminism	Patriarchy, or men having power over women with particular analysis of sexual violence	End patriarchy; re-create society as a women-centered culture	Oversimplified view of sexism; not all men are victimizers; not all women are victims
Intersectional Feminism	Race, class, gender, and sexuality interlock to construct dominant, oppressive institutions	Use intersectional theory as a foundation; dismantle socially constructed definitions on both micro (individual) and macro (societal) levels	Analysis is too individualized; hard to mobilize
Postmodern Feminism	Gender is a social construction that is embedded into social discourses to exert social control	Change social interpretations of gender ideologies, or deconstruct the idea of gender altogether	Although the concepts connected to gender are socially constructed, the consequences are real

So there it is. Does one of these theories stand out to you? Which are you most likely to follow?

right to education. Women's education, supporters argued, would increase the knowledge base of the entire country, which was a benefit to all. Because of their advocacy, women (upper-class and white) were allowed entrance into the first college in 1836 (Andersen 2015).

The origins of the women's movement do not just begin with white women, however. The **abolitionist movement** of the 1830s, or the social change movement to end slavery, worked alongside the women's movement. For example, Charlotte Forten was a Black activist who founded the Anti-Slavery Society of Philadelphia and worked with well-known white activists Sarah and Angelina Grimké toward ending slavery and advancing the equal rights of women (Andersen 2015).

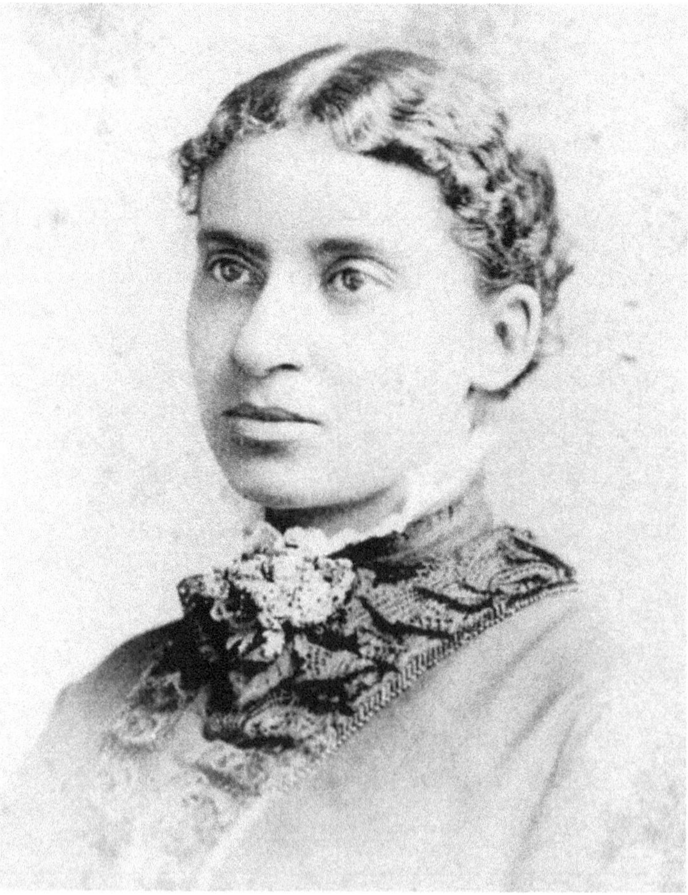

Figure 13.3 Abolitionist and educator Charlotte Forten (1837–1914).
WIKIMEDIA COMMONS

In 1848, over 300 men and women attended the **Women's Rights Convention** in Seneca Falls, New York. Attendees developed the **Declaration of Sentiments** with twelve resolutions that fought for equality between the sexes. This declaration was the beginning of the woman's suffrage movement. Thus, began **first-wave feminism**, focusing on women's right to vote and the passing of the Nineteenth Amendment. In addition, attendees of the conference were the first to draft the Equal Rights Amendment and campaign for its passage (Wade and Ferree 2019).

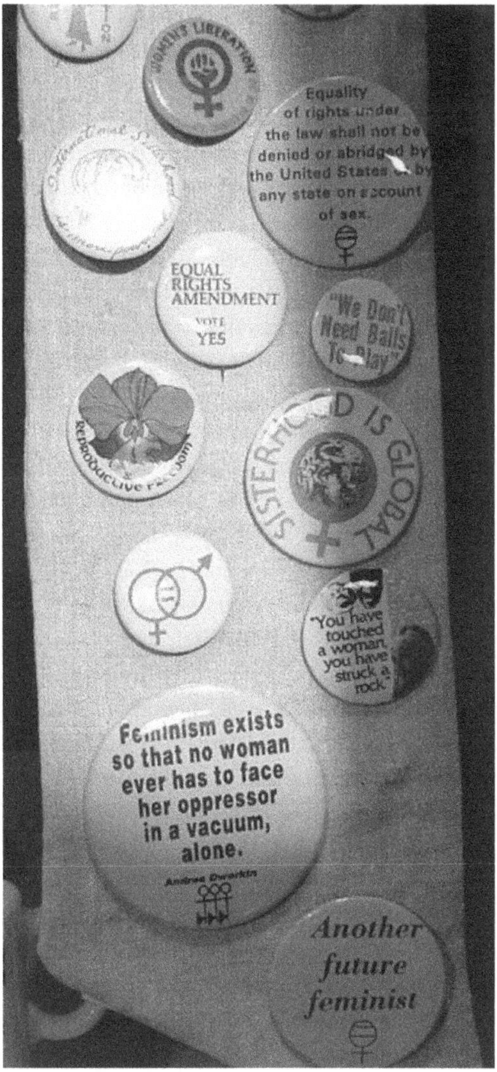

Figure 13.4 Intersectional feminism is a critique of early feminists' focus on white women.
Edward Kimmel, Women's March (1743), CC BY-SA 2.0

The 1960s increase in women's labor-force participation illuminated the contradiction of societal expectations of women's roles as homemakers and the actual participation of women in all aspects of society. As the civil rights movement of the 1950s began to challenge the existence of racial oppression, women saw their own struggles reflected (Andersen 2015). By the late 1960s, feminism was a defined social movement, with women participating in consciousness-raising groups, local feminist organizations, and political advocacy. This was the start of **second-wave feminism**, which focused on changing public policy and legislation to be gender-neutral. Second-wave feminists fought for equality in education, wages, and reproductive rights (Wade and Ferree 2019).

Second-wave feminists won significant battles for the inclusion of women in society. As time progressed, the next generation of feminist women found that their concerns as women differed from their mothers'. **Third-wave feminism** began in the mid-1990s and focused on using an intersectional lens to end patriarchy. Third-wave feminists addressed heteronormativity and racism within the women's movement (Wade and Ferree 2019). **Heteronormativity** is the belief (both individually and societally) that heterosexuality is the only sexual and romantic relationship structure that is good, right, and moral.

Third-wave feminists also increasingly addressed the backlash against the women's movement that was made easier by the advent of the internet. In 2001, feminist bloggers began shaping spaces within the internet that advocated for the rights of women. During this time, many writers were claiming a "postfeminist" America—or the stance that women's equality had already been achieved and the feminist movement was now moot (Roberts 2019). Many of these first blogging sites were run by white women; *Feministe*, *Feministing*, and *Jezebel* were among the first.

Intersectional discussions about women's issues were lacking at this time, so feminist women of color began carving their own corners of the blogosphere. *Reappropriate* was the first Asian American feminist blog in the early 2000s. While the feminist websites that focused on women of color gained moderate followers, the sites run by white feminists gained widespread notoriety. Jessica Valenti started the blog *Feministing* and gained fame for her site; she later published critically acclaimed books like *Full Frontal Feminism* and *The Purity Myth*.

In the late 2000s, feminist blogging reached a new peak and was getting attention from mainstream media outlets. Unfortunately, the same attention was coming from antifeminist trolls. While the early motto was "nothing on the internet can hurt you," bloggers soon learned that internet threats were real (Roberts 2019). Women of color were more often targets of these attacks. They endured many types of harassment, including **doxing**, or the online publication of someone's personal information and identity.

Backlash

As feminism grows in popularity, it also signals a **backlash**—or the focused actions intended to swing the ideological pendulum back to antifeminist beliefs (Faludi 1991). For example, research shows that very little has changed from the 1950s regarding household tasks and traditional gender roles. According to a recent poll of heterosexual married or cohabiting couples, 58 percent of women were responsible for laundry, and 51 percent of women were responsible for household cleaning and cooking. Following traditional gender roles, men are most likely to keep the car in working order (69%) and maintain the lawn (59%) (Brenan 2020). Although younger demographics tend to espouse egalitarian beliefs, a recent study found that high school seniors believe the ideal family arrangement included a full-time working husband and stay-at-home mother (Dernberger and Pepin 2020).

One of the most obvious examples of antifeminist backlash came in the form of Gamergate. Starting in the summer of 2014, Gamergate was an internet-based "social movement." Gamergate can best be described as a culture war between "new wave" gamers pushing for inclusivity and representation in gaming, and "traditional" gamers who want video games to stay the same (i.e., explicit violence and hypersexualization of women) (Dewey 2014). Several women in gaming were forced to leave their homes due to threats, including indie-game developer Brianna Wu, who left her home due to violent death and rape threats after criticizing followers of Gamergate on Twitter (now X) (Scimeca 2020).

Additionally, Men's Rights groups and so-called incels are becoming more violent (Marcotte 2019). **Incel** is short for "involuntarily celibate" and describes

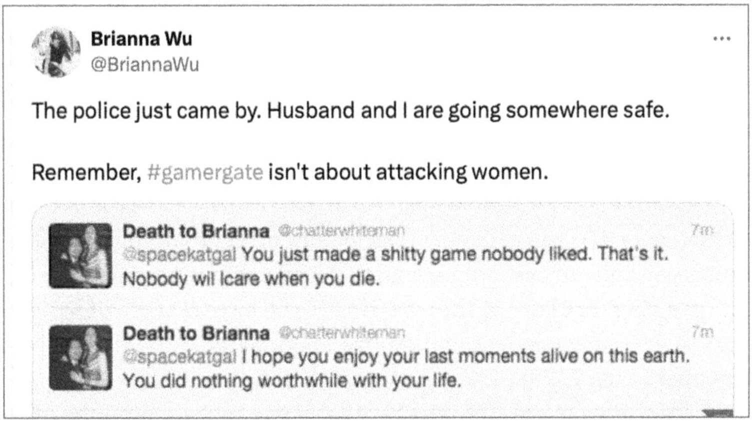

Figure 13.5 Game developer Brianna Wu received over a hundred death threats during #GamerGate. POSTED ON X

In the News . . .

In 2014, Elliot Rodger (22), stated that the "incel revolution has begun." He killed six people and injured fourteen (BBC News 2018). In 2018, Alex Minassian (25), a member of incel forums since 2014, drove a rented van into a crowded Toronto intersection killing ten and wounding sixteen (Brockbank 2019). In 2019, Scott Paul Beierle (40), an avowed hater of women, walked into a Florida yoga studio and shot six women, two fatally, before killing himself (Hendrix 2019). As incel online forums grow in popularity, they create a cycle where men validate each other's shortcomings, sending them deeper into their self-loathing and misogyny. For some, these forums have further fueled their anger and self-radicalization.

mostly young men who believe that society's standards and women in general are the reason they are still virgins. These groups have joined online communities on Reddit or incels.co under the hashtag #ForeverAlone to offer each other support and trade stories of rejection and embarrassment (Emba 2019). Incels create elaborate theories about the few, attractive men who lure vapid, gullible women, which is why women are no longer attracted to the "average guy"—or the incel, or so their theory suggests (Emba 2019).

MOVING FORWARD

Fourth-wave feminism is happening now! Fourth-wave feminists are the most diverse of the women's movements (Wade and Ferree 2019). A 2020 survey conducted by the Pew Research Center found that 40 percent of women said the feminist movement has helped them (Horowitz and Igielnik 2020). One of the most prominent examples of fourth-wave feminism is found in the Women's March. However, since the first march in 2017, organizers note that activism is waning; compassion fatigue has become a real concern (Lang 2020).

Criticism of organizational leadership, particularly the lack of racial and ethnic diversity, has caused many former supporters to decline membership. Feminists continue to ask if organizational leadership is necessary, or if grassroots organizing should be at the core. Due to the increased use of social media platforms, everyday people can organize major activist events just by using their phones (Lang 2020).

Men feminist allies are joining the cause more than ever. Fourth-wave feminists include Richie Edmond-Vargas, the creator of the nonprofit

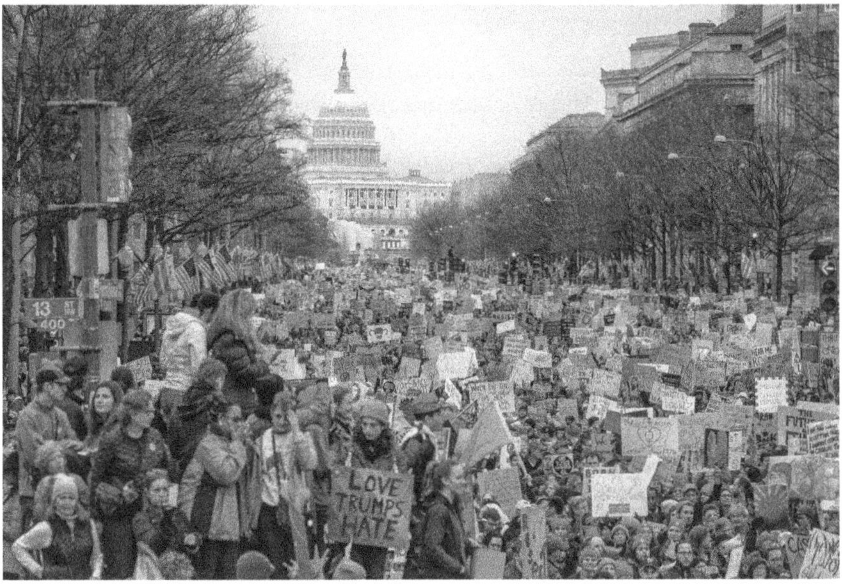

Figure 13.6 Crowds of protesters converge on Washington, DC, in 2017.

organization Success Stories. Success Stories runs a twelve-week course that trains male prisoners between the ages of eighteen and thirty-five to confront patriarchy within the prison system (Nonko 2019). During the course, men are asked to do the hard work of unlearning patriarchy using the work of intersectional feminist bell hooks (Nonko 2019). He created a podcast titled *Engendered* to educate about misogyny.

Finally, financial support is necessary, and fourth-wave feminism has friends in high places. Melinda French Gates is inspired by the current women's movement (Gates 2019). In 2019, Gates observed the media coverage of the courage shown by the #metoo movement, the historic number of women in Congress in 2018, and the small, everyday victories of women who work, parent, and contribute to society. To maintain this momentum, Gates has committed to donating $1 billion (yes, *billion*) to promote gender equality in the United States. Her company Pivotal Ventures will focus its efforts on removing barriers to women's professional advancements, fast-tracking women into underrepresented fields (i.e., politics, STEM, and media), and mobilizing other stakeholders to pressure organizations for reform (Gates 2019).

So when will we achieve gender equality? It's hard to predict an exact timeline. However, a 2020 Gallup survey found that only a small percentage of

In the News . . .

When the film *Barbie* was released, one scene was hailed as one of the most talked-about scenes in a movie in 2023 (Aguilar 2024). In the movie, America Ferrera (playing Gloria) delivers a monologue about the realities of women in a patriarchal society. She states, "It is literally impossible to be a woman. . . .You have to be thin, but not too thin. . . . You have to have money, but you can't ask for money because that's crass. You have to be a boss, but you can't be mean. . . . You're supposed to stay pretty for men, but not so pretty that you tempt them too much or that you threaten other women. . . . Always be grateful, but never forget that the system is rigged." Ferrera performed that monologue over thirty times over two days of shooting (Ford 2023). While some critics believe the monologue oversimplifies the experiences of women, Ferrera argues that some people need to hear Feminism 101 (Ford 2023). America Ferrera's performance earned her an Oscar nomination for Best Supporting Actress (Ulaby 2024).

Americans believe that equality will be reached within the next decade (12% for the workplace; 13% for politics). The vast majority think equality will take about eleven to thirty years—if ever (Saad 2020). Based on the caliber of students I teach who are committed to this cause, I tend to be more optimistic.

Key Takeaways

- Despite misconceptions, feminism is simply a movement to end sexism, sexist exploitation, and oppression.
- Men feminist allies are essential to the movement's success.
- Feminist frameworks emerged over differences of opinion about why sexism emerges and how it can be stopped.
- First-, second-, third-, and fourth-wave feminist movements all contribute to the current successes of women in society

References

Abramson, Ashley. 2023. "Are You Guilty of 'Weaponized Incompetence'? Here's How to Fight It." *Fatherly*, August 9. https://www.fatherly.com/life/what-is-weaponized-incompetence.

Adams, Rachel. 2019. "Artificial Intelligence Has a Gender Bias Problem—Just Ask Siri." *The Conversation*, September 22. https://theconversation.com/artificial-intelligence-has-a-gender-bias-problem-just-ask-siri-123937?fbclid=IwAR2YYJkmAvHYU4nqC5dlJay8ZwZfeYwseNzl0E0gwLtcHAS7XQXb6TimWlc.

Advocates for Youth. 2021. "Pink, Blue and Purple: A Lesson Plan from Rights, Respect, Responsibility: A K-12 Curriculum." https://www.advocatesforyouth.org/wp-content/uploads/2021/08/3Rs_Grade1_PinkBluePurple_2021.pdf.

Aguilar, Carlos. 2024. "America Ferrera and the 'Barbie' Monologue We All Talked About." *New York Times*, January 1. https://www.nytimes.com/2024/01/01/movies/america-ferrera-barbie.html.

Aguillon, Stepfanie M., Gregor-Fausto Siegmund, Renee H. Petipas, Abby Grace Drake, Sehoya Cotner, and Cissy J. Ballen. 2020. "Gender Differences in Student Participation in an Active-Learning Classroom." *CBE Life Sciences Education*, 19(2). https://www.ncbi.nlm.nih.gov/pmc/articles/PMC8697656/.

Ahrens, Corrinne. 2019. "Where We Are Now: Breaking Down Represent Women's 2019 Gender Parity Index." *Ms. Magazine*, October 22. https://msmagazine.com/2019/10/22/where-we-are-now-breaking-down-representwomens-2019-gender-parity-ndex/?fbclid=IwAR2_zGNG0DjFb0ZZ13-Pv9DjVAqh2nIJQJaFXx-xB3D-mowcJW7nEUizbYA.

Aid Access. 2020. "Aid Access: For a Safe Abortion." February 10. https://aidaccess.org/en/.

Ainsworth, Amber. 2023. "What Makes You 'Middle Class' in Detroit? Here's How Much Money You Need to Earn." Fox2 Detroit. April 19. https://www.fox2detroit.com/news/what-makes-you-middle-class-in-detroit-heres-how-much-money-you-need-to-earn.

Airgood-Obrycki, Whitney. 2022. "The Record-Breaking Rental Market." *Housing Perspectives: Research, Trends, and Perspective from the Harvard Joint Center for Housing Studies*, February 1. https://www.jchs.harvard.edu/blog/record-breaking-rental-market.

Alber, Rebecca. 2017. "Gender Equity in the Classroom." *Edutopia*, January 17. https://www.edutopia.org/blog/gender-equity-classroom-rebecca-alber.

Ali, Russlynn. 2011. "Dear Colleague Letter." US Department of Education, Office of the Assistant Secretary. April 4. https://www2.ed.gov/about/offices/list/ocr/letters/colleague-201104.html.

Alter, Charlotte. 2023. "She Wasn't Able to Get an Abortion. Now She's a Mom. Soon She'll Start 7th Grade." *Time Magazine*, August 14. https://time.com/6303701/a-rape-in-mississippi/?utm_medium=email&utm_source=sfmc&utm_campaign=newsletter+inside-time-saturday+default+ac&utm_content=+++20230819+++body&et_rid=240530819&lctg=240530819.

American Association of University Women (AAUW). 2023a. "Early Gender Bias." https://www.aauw.org/issues/education/gender-bias/.

———. 2023b. "Support the Gender Equity in Education Act." June 23. https://www.aauw.org/act/two-minute-activist/geea/.

American Bar Association. 2023. "School-to-Prison Pipeline Statistics." July 11. https://www.americanbar.org/groups/diversity/racial_ethnic_justice/projects/school_to_prison/statistics/.

American Psychiatric Association. 2023. "Gender Dysphoria Diagnosis." https://www.psychiatry.org/psychiatrists/diversity/education/transgender-and-gender-nonconforming-patients/gender-dysphoria-diagnosis#:~:text=With%20the%20publication%20of%20DSM–5%20in%202013%2C%20"gender,%2C%20medical%2C%20and%20surgical%20treatments).

American Psychological Association. 2018. "APA Guidelines for Psychological Practice with Boys and Men." APA Boys and Men Working Group. August. https://www.apa.org/about/policy/boys-men-practice-guidelines.pdf .

———. 2023. "Disability & Socioeconomic Status." https://www.apa.org/pi/ses/resources/publications/disability.

American University. 2020. "Stepping Up and Standing Out: Women's Political Participation in 2020." *Gender on the Ballot*, January 21. https://www.genderontheballot.org/women-voters-research/.

Amra & Elma. 2023. "100 Top Mom Influencers in 2023." *Amra & Elma*. https://www.amraandelma.com/100-top-mom-influencers/.

Anastasopoulos, Lefteris. 2016. "Estimating the Gender Penalty in House of Representative Elections Using Regression Discontinuity Design." *Electoral Studies*, 43: 150–57.

Andersen, Margaret. 2015. *Thinking about Women: Sociological Perspectives on Sex and Gender*, 10th ed. Boston: Pearson.

Andrew, Alison, Sarah Cattan, Monica Costa Dias, Christine Farquharson, Lucy Kraftman, Sonya, Krutikova, Angus Phimister and Almudena Sevilla. 2020. "Inequalities in Children's Experiences of Home Learning during the COVID-19 Lockdown in England." *Fiscal Studies: The Journal of Applied Public Economics*, July. https://onlinelibrary.wiley.com/doi/full/10.1111/1475-5890.12240.

Andrew, Scottie. 2020. "More than 200 Medical Professionals Condemn Bills Trying to Restrict Transgender Kids from Getting Gender Reassignment Treatments." CNN Health, February 7. https://www.cnn.com/2020/02/07/health/doctors-condemn-anti-trans-health-care-trnd/index.html?fbclid=IwAR27JqOgnUhDtD5tMpBphXcAHDUGJzYi8ilzjNJn2z2Y3mo3qn8WYZguDc4.

Aragáo, Carolina, Kim Parker, Shannon Greenwood, Chris Baronavski, and John Carlo Mandapat. 2023. "The Modern American Family." Pew Research Center. September 14. https://www.pewresearch.org/social-trends/2023/09/14/the-modern-american-family/.

Archie, Ayana. 2023. "There Have Been Attempts to Censor More than 1,900 Library Book Titles So Far in 2023." National Public Radio. September 20. https://www.npr.org/2023/09/20/1200647985/book-bans-libraries-schools.

Armstrong, Elizabeth A., Laura Hamilton, and Brian Sweeney. 2006. "Sexual Assault on Campus a Multilevel, Integrative Approach to Party Rape." *Social Problems*, 483–99.

Aschbrenner, Annah, John Fritze, and Christal Hayes. 2020. "Kamala Harris Wears Suffragette White in First Speech as History Making Vice-President-Elect." *USA Today*, November 08. https://www.usatoday.com/story/news/politics/elections/2020/11/07/kamala-harris-wears-white-nod-suffragettes-women-before-her/6210019002/?fbclid=IwAR0qe_F5awNQaj-utb2iO2sDhNDitlLTfNpwpnIpAvJni6KieD4q-4sEMCo.

Asma-Sadeque, Samira. 2022. "US Jury Finds in Favor of Pharmacist Who Denied Woman Morning-After Pill." *The Guardian*, August 6. https://www.theguardian.com/us-news/2022/aug/06/morning-after-pill-contraception-judge-minnesota.

Assault on Campus?" *Chronicle of Higher Education*, October 6. https://www.chronicle.com/article/the-fraternity-dilemma?utm_source=Iterable&utm_medium=email&utm_campaign=campaign_2985946_nl_Academe-Today_date_20211007&cid=at&source=ams&sourceid=&fbclid=IwAR1AEnGIE6_oknGrD-w8eFpz-JUqCmKLrDxe3ASL73JFSsxTN2X0kStlCEY.

Associated Press. 2020a. "DOJ Says It's Too Late to Pass the Equal Rights Amendment." NBC News, January 09. https://www.nbcwashington.com/news/local/doj-says-its-too-late-to-pass-the-equal-rights-amendment/2198111/.

Associated Press. 2020b. "Princeton University Faces Federal Inquiry after Acknowledging Racism." NJ.com. September 20. https://www.nj.com/education/2020/09/princeton-university-faces-federal-inquiry-after-acknowledging-racism.html.

Astor, Maggie. 2023. "G.O.P. State Lawmakers Push a Growing Wave of Anti-Transgender Bills." *New York Times*, June 20. https://www.nytimes.com/2023/01/25/us/politics/transgender-laws-republicans.html.

Badgett, M. V. Lee, Soon Kyu Choi, and Bianca D. M. Wilson. 2019. "LGBT Poverty in the United States: A Study of Differences Between Sexual Orientation and Gender Identity Groups." Williams Institute, UCLA School of Law. October. https://williamsinstitute.law.ucla.edu/wp-content/uploads/National-LGBT-Poverty-Oct-2019.pdf.

Baker, Carrie N. 2020. "New Research Proves Restricting Abortion Harms Women." *Ms. Magazine*, June 30. https://msmagazine.com/2020/06/30/the-turnaway-study-new-research-proves-restricting-abortion-harms-women/?fbclid=IwAR1B4Ghw4breO0EyQNa2IfydmZ7AtNvJutHk0U5nkWitnwz7bYzEFdWTxco.

———. 2021. "California Law Eliminates Spousal Rape Exemption—But 'Patriarchy Still Dies Hard.'" *Ms. Magazine*, October 13. https://msmagazine.com/2021/10/13/can-your-husband-rape-you-california-law-spousal-rape-exemption/?fbclid=IwAR0TwgnkR5A3utKa2WiBO80svB8i-bJjLfAqEOAi9AKdAcZh1n6amMirPWs .

———. 2022. "'Equal Rights Amendment Has Been Ratified.' It Is law.' US House Resolution Declares ERA 28th Amendment." *Ms. Magazine*, January 27. https://msmagazine.com/2022/01/27/equal-rights-amendment-resolution-us-house-28th-amendment-constitution/.

Baker, Carrie, and Katie Fleisher. 2019. "A More Perfect Union: Eight Feminist Victories from the Last Decade." *Ms. Magazine*, December 26. https://msmagazine.com/2019/12/26/a-more-perfect-union-eight-feminist-victories-from-the-last-decade/.

Balingit, Moriah, and Anderson, Nick. 2022. "Sweeping Title IX Changes Would Shield Trans Students, Abuse Survivors." *Washington Post*, June 23. https://www.washingtonpost.com/education/2022/06/23/title-ix-biden-trans-sexual-assault-college/.

Ballard, Jamie. 2018. "American Women Are More Likely to Identify as Feminists Now than in 2016." YouGov. August 9. https://today.yougov.com/topics/lifestyle/articles-reports/2018/08/09/feminism-american-women-2018.

Bao, Angela BeiBei. 2020. "Preventing Intergenerational Transmission of Domestic Violence." *Social Work Today*, April 16. https://www.socialworktoday.com/archive/exc_011813.shtml.

Barbara Lee Family Foundation. 2016. "Politics Is Personal: Key to Likeability and Electability for Women." April. https://www.barbaraleefoundation.org/wp-content/uploads/BLFF-Likeability-Memo-FINAL.pdf.

Barnes, James. 2023. "I'm a Trans Man. I Didn't Realize How Broken Men Are." *Newsweek*, August 6. https://www.newsweek.com/trans-man-broken-men-1817169?fbclid=IwAR1bzVQPxfeDe0W5CZSSKEymhE3SmYkfomjV9t2Szg8HyQ4we0g5XMFAtZY.

Barnes, Janae. 2022."*US Women's National Soccer Team Scores $24 Million Settlement and Equal Pay for Women's and Men's Players." Forbes, August 12.* https://www.forbes.com/sites/jenaebarnes/2022/08/12/us-womens-national-soccer-team-scores-24-million-settlement-and-equal-pay-for-womens-and-mens-players/.

Barnes, Katie. 2022. "Amid Protests, Penn Swimmer Lia Thomas Becomes First Known Transgender Athlete to Win Division I National Championship." ESPN. March 17. https://www.espn.com/college-sports/story/_/id/33529775/amid-protests-pennsylvania-swimmer-lia-thomas-becomes-first-known-transgender-athlete-win-division-national-championship.

Barone, Emily. 2019. "Many American Men Have a Skewed View on Gender Inequality, TIME Poll Finds." *Time Magazine*, September 26. https://time.com/5667397/gender-equality-/

Basile, Kathleen, Sharon Smith, Marcie-jo Kresnow, Srijana Khatiwada, and Ruth Leemis. 2016/2017. "The National Intimate Partner and Sexual Violence Survey: 2016/2017 Report on Sexual Violence." Centers for Disease Control and Prevention. https://www.cdc.gov/violenceprevention/pdf/nisvs/nisvsReportonSexualViolence.pdf.

Bauer-Wolf, Jeremy. 2019. "Fraternity House Sit-In." *Inside Higher Ed*, April 30. https://www.insidehighered.com/news/2019/04/30/swarthmore-students-sit-fraternity-house-after-sexual-assault-allegations.

BBC News. 2018. "Elliott Rodger: How Misogynist Killer Became 'Incel Hero.'" April 26. https://www.bbc.com/news/world-us-canada-43892189.

Bedera, Nicole. 2020. "Trump's New Rule Governing College Sex Assault Is Nearly Impossible for Survivors to Use. That's the Point." *Time Magazine*, May 14. https://time.com/5836774/trump-new-title-ix-rules/.

Belluck, Pam, and Adam Liptak. 2023. "Appeals Court Upholds Legality of Abortion Pill but with Significant Restrictions." *New York Times*, August 16. https://www.nytimes.com/2023/08/16/health/abortion-pill-ruling.html.

Bendix, Aria, and Joe Murphy. 2023. "The Modern Family Size Is Changing. Four Charts Show How." NBC News, January 12. https://www.nbcnews.com/health/parenting/how-modern-us-family-size-changing-charts-map-rcna65421.

Benson, Craig. 2022. "Poverty Rate of Children Higher than National Rate, Lower for Older Populations." United States Census Bureau. October. https://www.census.gov/library/stories/2022/10/poverty-rate-varies-by-age-groups.html.

Benson, Craig, Alemayehu Bishaw, and Brian Glassman. 2023. "Persistent Poverty in Counties and Census Tracts." United States Census Bureau. May 9. https://www.census.gov/library/publications/2023/acs/acs-51.html.

Berger, Michele W. 2023. "How Have Women in the Workforce Fared, Three Years into the Pandemic?" *Penn Today*, March 2023. https://penntoday.upenn.edu/news/how-have-women-workforce-fared-three-years-pandemic.

Bixby Center for Global Reproductive Health (BCGRH). 2020. "Turnaway Study." *Advancing New Standards in Reproductive Health*, July 18. https://www.ansirh.org/sites/default/files/publications/files/turnaway_study_brief_web.pdf.

Blackless, Melanie, Anthony Charuvastra, Amanda Derryck, Anne Fausto-Sterling, Karl Lauzanne, and Ellen Lee. 2000. "How Sexually Dimorphic Are We? Review and Synthesis." *American Journal of Human Biology*, 12(2): 151–66.

Blakemore, Erin. 2022. "How Historians Are Documenting the Lives of Transgender People." *National Geographic*, June 24. https://www.nationalgeographic.com/history/article/how-historians-are-documenting-lives-of-transgender-people.

———. 2023a. "How US Abortion Laws Went from Nonexistent to Acrimonious." National Geographic Explainer, April 11. https://www.nationalgeographic.com/history/article/the-complex-early-history-of-abortion-in-the-united-states.

———. 2023b. "What Was the Stonewall Uprising?" *National Geographic*, June 1. https://www.nationalgeographic.com/history/article/stonewall-uprising-ignited-modern-lgbtq-rights-movement.

Blau, Francine, and Lawrence Kahn. 2016. "The Gender Wage Gap: Extent, Trends, and Explanations." National Bureau of Economic Research, January. https://www.nber.org/papers/w21913.

Bleiweis, Robin, Diana Boesch, and Alexandra Cawthorne Gaines. 2020. "The Basic Facts about Women in Poverty." August 3. https://www.americanprogress.org/article/basic-facts-women-poverty/.

Block, Melissa. 2020. "Yes, Women Could Vote After the 19th Amendment—But Not All Women. Or Men." National Public Radio. August 26. https://www.npr.org/2020/08/26/904730251/yes-women-could-vote-after-the-19th-amendment-but-not-all-women-or-men.

Bocanegra, Michelle. 2020. "Domestic Violence Groups, Survivors Say New York's Pandemic Exacerbated Abuse." *Politico*, June 21. https://www.politico.com/states/new-york/city-hall/story/2020/06/21/domestic-violence-groups-survivors-say-new-yorks-pandemic-exacerbated-abuse-1293894.

Boerner, Heather. 2022. "What the Science on Gender-Affirming Care for Transgender Kids Really Shows." *Scientific American*, May 12. https://www.scientificamerican.com/article/what-the-science-on-gender-affirming-care-for-transgender-kids-really-shows/?fbclid=IwAR2EmkRHgXZcOENCxwhkdLm54HjciJGGFsT_AtLDohZMxv6jpAQBJuf2xxM.

Bonos, Lisa. 2020. "Ghosting Is Normal Now. That's Completely Bonkers." *Washington Post*, February 13. https://www.washingtonpost.com/lifestyle/2020/02/13/ghosting-is-normal-now-thats-completely-bonkers/?arc404=true.

Boodman, Eric. 2023. "Federal Judge Suspends FDA Approval of Abortion Pill." *Stat News*, April 7. https://www.statnews.com/2023/04/07/abortion-pill-texas-lawsuit-ban-fda/?fbclid=IwAR0raXHH3vfnl3NQWuG-ObJaWYd3ZAluXKgWFJpMKkB-8bLGyeeQRJCE5v8.

Booker, Christopher, Mori Rothman, and Connie Kargbo. 2019. "The Culture of Masculinity and Its Negative Impacts on Men." PBS. September 8. https://www.pbs.org/newshour/show/the-culture-of-masculinity-and-its-negative-impacts-on-men?fbclid=IwAR2dJYzZ2FmbTPlJh8RabqVJ5qtN9noqW8jbD8NVKS3nRrQWvsU3rXetWvc

Borkenhagen, Connie K. 1975. "Legal Bias against Rape Victims (The Rape of Mr. Smith)." *American Bar Association Journal.*

Boserup, Brad, Mark McKenny, and Adel Elkbuli. 2020. "Alarming Trends in US Domestic Violence during the COVID-19 Pandemic." *American Journal of Emergency Medicine*, 38(12): 2753–55.

Boyd-Barrett, Claudia. 2023. "When Your Baby Is Intersex." BabyCenter, March 14. https://www.babycenter.com/baby/newborn-baby/when-your-baby-is-intersex_20000898#.

Brenan, Megan. 2020. "Women Still Handle Main Household Tasks in the US." Gallup. January 29. https://news.gallup.com/poll/283979/women-handle-main-household-tasks.aspx.

Bridges, Ana J., Robert Wosnitzer, Erica Sharrer, Chyng Sun, and Rachael Liberman. 2010. "Aggression and Sexual Behavior in Best-Selling Pornography Videos: A Content Analysis Update." *Violence Against Women*, 1065–85.

Brockbank, Nicole. 2019. "Alek Minassian Reveals Details of Toronto Van Attack in Video of Police Interview." CBC. September 27. https://www.cbc.ca/news/canada/toronto/alek-minassian-police-interview-1.5298021.

Broussard, Meredith. 2019. "When Binary Code Won't Accommodate Nonbinary People." *Slate*, October 23. https://slate.com/technology/2019/10/gender-binary-nonbinary-code-databases-values .html?fbclid=IwAR0BygXHS_iVhcAGJYZVJX0X-kPgBfasy3Sks7xaDqDvqvTUjtgFkjkBtl8.

Brown, Anna. 2020. "Personal Experiences and Attitudes of Daters." Pew Research Center. August 2020. https://www.pewresearch.org/social-trends/2020/08/20/personal-experiences-and-attitudes -of-daters/?utm_content=buffer975ba&utm_medium=social&utm_source=twitter.com&utm_campaign =buffer.

———. 2022a. "About 5% of Young Adults in the US Say Their Gender Is Different from Their Sex Assigned at Birth." Pew Research Center. June 7. https://www.pewresearch.org/short-reads/2022/06/07 /about-5-of-young-adults-in-the-u-s-say-their-gender-is-different-from-their-sex-assigned-at-birth/.

———. 2022b. "More than Twice as Many Americans Support than Oppose the #MeToo Movement." Pew Research Center. September 29. https://www.pewresearch.org/social-trends/2022/09/29/more -than-twice-as-many-americans-support-than-oppose-the-metoo-movement/.

Brown, Sarah. 2021a. "Anti-Fraternity Protests Are Sweeping Campuses. This Is How We Got Here." *Chronicle of Higher Education*, October 1. https://www.chronicle.com/article/anti-frat-protests-are -sweeping-college-campuses-this-is-how-we-got-here.

———. 2021b. "The Fraternity Dilemma: Would Abolishing Frats Actually Reduce Campus Sexual Assault?" *Chronicle of Higher Education*, October 6. https://www.chronicle.com/article/the-fraternity -dilemma#:~:text=But%20some%20experts%20say%20that,might%20even%20make%20matters%20 worse.&text=here's%20no%20question%20that%20sexual%20assault%20in%20fraternities%20is%20 a%20problem.

Brown, Tammy L. 2018. "Celebrate Women's Suffrage, but Don't Whitewash the Movement's Racism." ACLU. August 24. https://www.aclu.org/news/womens-rights/celebrate-womens-suffrage-dont-white wash-movements-racism.

Buckley, Cara. 2019. "Why the Oscars, Emmys and Tonys Are Not Ready for They and Them." *New York Times*, October 16. https://www.nytimes.com/2019/10/16/movies/oscars-gendered-categories.html?fbc lid=IwAR0uch8fz7ieuq3Q8zX9tDdcnUmB5s9d53RsntspHI1W8VuqPv74CQRKvBk.

Bureau of Justice Statistics. 2013. "Female Victims of Sexual Violence, 1994–2010." Department of Justice, Office of Justice Programs.

———. 2017. "National Crime Victimization Survey, 2010–2016." Department of Justice, Office of Justice Programs.

———. 2019. "Table 3: Employment Status of the Civilian Noninstitutional Population by Age, Sex, and Race." *Current Population Survey*.

———. 2022. "Employment Projections: Education Pays." https://www.bls.gov/emp/chart-unemploy ment-earnings-education.htm.

———. 2023. "What Data Does the BLS Publish on Family Leave?" March. https://www.bls.gov/ebs /factsheets/family-leave-benefits-fact-sheet.htm.

Burga, Solcyre. 2023a. "California Is the Latest State Where a School Board Is Requiring Staff to Potentially Out Trans Kids." *Time*, September 30. https://time.com/6316006/school-boards-policies-outing -transgender-students/.

———. 2023b. "What to Know About Florida's New 'Don't Say Gay' Rule That Bans Discussion of Gender for All Students." *Time*, April 20. https://time.com/6273364/florida-dont-say-gay-expansion/.

Burrows, Charlotte. 2023. "A Message from EEOC Chair Charlotte A. Burrows for 2023 Equal Pay Day and Women's History Month." US Equal Employment Opportunity Commission. https://www.eeoc

.gov/wysk/message-eeoc-chair-charlotte-burrows-2023-equal-pay-day-and-womens-history-month #:~:text=The%20National%20Committee%20on%20Pay,had%20made%20the%20prior%20year.

Butler, Judith. 1999. *Gender Trouble: Feminism and the Subversion of Identity.* New York: Routledge.

A Call to Men. 2019. "Embrace a Healthy, Respectful Manhood." http://www.acalltomen.org/impact-healthy-manhood.

Cantor, David, Bonnie Fisher, Susan Chibnall, and Reanne Townsend. 2015. "Report on the AAU Campus Climate Survey on Sexual Assault and Sexual Misconduct." Association of American Universities.

Cantor, David, Bonnie Fisher, Susan Chibnall, Reanne Townsend, Hyunsik Lee, Carol Bruce, and Gail Thomas. 2017. "Report on the AAU Campus Climate Survey on Sexual Assault and Misconduct." Association of American Universities. https://www.aau.edu/sites/default/files/AAU-Files/Key-Issues/Campus-Safety/AAU-Campus-Climate-Survey-FINAL-10-20-17.pdf.

Cappelletti, Joey, and Ed White. 2022. "2 Men Convicted in Plot to Kidnap Michigan Gov. Whitmer." Associated Press. August. https://apnews.com/article/elections-presidential-michigan-gretchen-whitmer-grand-rapids-9ad8f100d32e7d5883b1be9d6c4cb8d5.

Carlson, Steven, Joseph Llobrera, and Brynne Keith-Jennings. 2021. "More Adequate SNAP Benefits Would Help Millions of Participants Better Afford Food." Center on Budget and Policy Priorities. July 15.

Carmichael, Sarah Green. 2017. Women Dominate College Majors That Lead to Lower-Paying Work. *Harvard Business Review*, April 19. https://hbr.org/2017/04/women-dominate-college-majors-that-lead-to-lower-paying-work.

Carnevale, Anthony P., Nicole Smith, and Kathryn Peltier Campbell. 2019. "May the Best Woman Win? Education and Bias against Women in American Politics." Georgetown University, Center on Education and the Workforce. https://cew.georgetown.edu/wp-content/uploads/Women_in_Politics.pdf.

Carrazana, Chabeli. 2021. "The Paycheck Fairness Act to Close the Gender Wage Gap Failed in Congress. What Comes Next?" *19th News*, June 10. https://19thnews.org/2021/06/paycheck-fairness-act-fails/.

Carter, Delphine. 2023. "Carry as You Climb: How to Be an Ally to Other Women in Business." *Forbes*, November 27. https://www.forbes.com/sites/forbesbusinesscouncil/2023/11/27/carry-as-you-climb-how-to-be-an-ally-to-other-women-in-business/?sh=74074c4c3f13.

Cater, Franklyn. 2020. "Federal Judge Dismisses US Women's Soccer Team's Equal Pay Claim." National Public Radio. May 2. https://www.npr.org/2020/05/02/849492863/federal-judge-dismisses-u-s-womens-soccer-team-s-equal-pay-claim.

CBS News. 2019. "Billy Bush: The Access Hollywood Tape Was 'Weaponized.'" September 10. https://www.cbsnews.com/news/billy-bush-access-hollywood-tape-everybody-knew-says-donald-trump-tape-was-going-to-be-weaponized-exclusive-interview/.

Center for American Women in Politics (CAWP). 2020. "Women in US Congress 2020." Rutgers University. https://cawp.rutgers.edu/women-us-congress-2020.

———. 2023. "2022 Election Results Tracker." Rutgers University. https://cawp.rutgers.edu/election-watch/2022-election-results-tracker.

———. 2024. "Women in Elective Office 2024." https://cawp.rutgers.edu/facts/levels-office/congress/women-us-congress-2024.

Center for Relationship Abuse Awareness. 2023. "Barriers to Leaving an Abusive Relationship." https://stoprelationshipabuse.org/educated/barriers-to-leaving-an-abusive-relationship/.

Centers for Disease Control and Prevention (CDC). 2010. "NISVS: An Overview of 2010 Findings on Victimization by Sexual Orientation." National Center for Injury Prevention and Control. https://www.cdc.gov/violenceprevention/pdf/cdc_nisvs_victimization_final-a.pdf.

———. 2019. "Intimate Partner Violence: Prevention Strategies." October 8. https://www.cdc.gov/violenceprevention/intimatepartnerviolence/prevention.html.

———. 2020a. "Preventing Teen Dating Violence." January 27. https://www.cdc.gov/violenceprevention/intimatepartnerviolence/teendatingviolence/fastfact.html#.

———. 2020b. "Violence Prevention." April 27. https://www.cdc.gov/violenceprevention/publichealthissue/index.html.

———. 2022. "Preventing Intimate Partner Violence." https://www.cdc.gov/violenceprevention/intimatepartnerviolence/index.html.

———. 2023a. "Pregnancy Mortality Surveillance System." https://www.cdc.gov/reproductivehealth/maternal-mortality/pregnancy-mortality-surveillance-system.htm.

———. 2023b. "US Teen Birth Rate Reached Another Historic Low in 2022." National Center for Health Statistics, June 1. https://www.cdc.gov/nchs/pressroom/nchs_press_releases/2023/20230601.htm.

Chenoweth, Erica, and Jeremy Pressman. 2017. "This Is What We Learned by Counting the Women's Marches." *Washington Post*, February 7. https://www.washingtonpost.com/news/monkey-cage/wp/2017/02/07/this-is-what-we-learned-by-counting-the-womens-marches/

Christenson, Josh. 2023. "Nearly 6,000 Public Schools Hide Child's Gender Status from Parents." *New York Post*, March 8. https://nypost.com/2023/03/08/us-public-schools-conceal-childs-gender-status-from-parents/.

Cilluffo, Anthony, and Richard Fry. 2019. "An Early Look at the 2020 Electorate." Pew Research Center. January 30. https://www.pewsocialtrends.org/essay/an-early-look-at-the-2020-electorate/.

Cimpian, Joseph. 2018. "How Our Education System Undermines Gender Equity." Brookings. April 23. https://www.brookings.edu/articles/how-our-education-system-undermines-gender-equity/.

Cimpian, Joseph. Sarah T. Lubienski, Jennifer D. Timmer, Martha B. Makowski, and Emily K. Miller. 2016. "Have Gender Gaps in Math Closed? Achievement, Teacher Perceptions, and Learning Behaviors Across Two ECLS-K Cohorts." *AREA* Open, 2(4). https://journals.sagepub.com/doi/full/10.1177/2332858416673617.

Clancy, Maggie. 2022. "Exhausted Mom Gives an Example of 'Hurtful Helping' and Default Parenting in Viral Video." *Scary Mommy*, August 29. https://www.scarymommy.com/parenting/tiktok-nurse-default-parenting-husband-hands-mom-crying-baby?fbclid=IwAR3CQLfbggCP5gvcREVLYqJTCirGG8Ti_2lzRsde75JQ9fgWzfGZTTYrj9I.

Clark, Lauren. 2023. "Could Gabby Petito's Death Have Been Prevented?" CBS News, May 28. https://www.cbsnews.com/news/gabby-petito-domestic-violence-could-her-death-have-been-prevented/.

Clark-Flory, Tracy. 2010. "Yale Fraternity Pledges Chant About Rape." *Salon*, October 15. https://www.salon.com/2010/10/15/yale_fraternity_pledges_chant_about_rape/.

Cleveland Clinic. 2023a. "Gender Affirmation (Confirmation) or Sex Reassignment Surgery." https://my.clevelandclinic.org/health/treatments/21526-gender-affirmation-confirmation-or-sex-reassignment-surgery.

———. 2023b. "Intersex." *Cleveland Clinic*. https://my.clevelandclinic.org/health/articles/16324-intersex.

Clinton, Hillary. 2016. "Hillary Clinton's Concession Speech (Full Text). CNN Politics. November 9. https://www.cnn.com/2016/11/09/politics/hillary-clinton-concession-speech/.

Cohen, Philip N. 2021. *The Family*, 3rd ed. New York: W.W. Norton & Company.

Collins, Patricia Hill. 2004. *Black Sexual Politics: African Americans, Gender and the New Racism*. New York: Routledge.

Colwell, Rita. 2020. "Women Scientists Have the Evidence about Sexism." *The Atlantic*, August 30. https://www.theatlantic.com/ideas/archive/2020/08/women-scientists-have-evidence-about-sexism-science/615823/?fbclid=IwAR1PySDwsXhBAcWciwysmqcsrZlgb5D9FFn4g-zPRkO56OQIOcVXYGlht7o.

Conly, Dalton. 2020. *You May Ask Yourself*, 7th ed. New York: W.W. Norton.

Connellan, Shannon. 2020. "#MeToo Founder Tarana Burke Explains the Link between Sexual Violence and Police Brutality." *Mashable*, June 25. https://mashable.com/video/tarana-burke-samantha-bee-sexual-violence-police/?fbclid=IwAR3IPuVAG67lJnfn_86_NU0q5RBRpVBplr-7jq3YU8aYveoOmaTJhM21X_Q.

Conroy, Meredith. 2019. "Are Americans More Divided on #MeToo Issues?" *FiveThirtyEight*, April 16. https://fivethirtyeight.com/features/are-americans-more-divided-on-metoo-issues/.

Coombs, Jefferson. 2019. "A Call to Action: Get the Health Coverage You Need." Human Rights Campaign. December 10. https://www.hrc.org/blog/a-call-to-action-get-the-health-coverage-you-need.

Coontz, Stephanie. 2015. "The Way We Weren't." *Phi Kappa Phi Forum*, 91(1): 22.

Cornell University. 2016. "What Does the Scholarly Research Say about the Link Between Family Acceptance and LGBT Youth Well-Being?" What We Know Project. https://whatweknow.inequality.cornell.edu/topics/lgbt-equality/what-does-the-scholarly-research-say-about-the-acceptancerejection-of-lgbt-youth-2/.

Cowen, Jill. 2023. "The Latest Target for California Conservatives? Local School Boards." *New York Times*, October 30. https://www.nytimes.com/2023/10/30/us/california-school-transgender-policy.html.

Cox, Daniel A. 2023. "From Swiping to Sexting: The Enduring Gender Divide in American Dating and Relationships." Survey Center on American Life. February 9. https://www.americansurveycenter.org/research/from-swiping-to-sexting-the-enduring-gender-divide-in-american-dating-and-relationships/.

Creamer, Jon, Emily A. Shrider, Kalee Burns, and Frances Chen. 2022. "Poverty in the United States: 2021." United States Census Bureau. September. https://www.census.gov/content/dam/Census/library/publications/2022/demo/p60-277.pdf.

Cromer, Sara J., Kristin M. D'Silva, and Neelam A. Phadke. 2022. "Gender Differences in the Amount and Type of Student Participation During In-Person and Virtual Classes in Academic Medicine Learning Environments." *JAMA Network Open*, 5(1). https://jamanetwork.com/journals/jamanetworkopen/fullarticle/2787980.

Cruz, Caitlin. 2021. "Oklahoma Woman Sentenced to 4 Years for Manslaughter after Miscarriage." *Jezebel*, October 15. https://jezebel.com/oklahoma-woman-sentenced-to-4-years-for-manslaughter-af-1847874545.

Dado, Natasha. 2019. "Michigan Governor Signs Bill to Protect Victims of Domestic Violence." *Click On Detroit*, November 8. https://www.clickondetroit.com/news/2019/11/09/michigan-governor-signs-bill-to-protect-victims-of-domestic-violence/.

Dalrymple, Amy, and Chistin Landivar. 2020. "7 Stats about Working Women to Celebrate the Women's Bureau Centennial." US Department of Labor blog. June 5. https://blog.dol.gov/2020/06/05/7-stats-to-celebrate-the-womens-bureau-centennial.

Daniels, Kimberly, and Joyce C. Abma. 2020. "Current Contraceptive Status among Women Aged 15–49: United States, 2017–2019. Centers for Disease Control and Prevention, NCHS Data Brief No. 388, October. https://www.cdc.gov/nchs/products/databriefs/db388.htm.

Das, Andrew. 2019a. "US Women's Soccer Team Granted Class Status in Equal Pay Lawsuit." *New York Times*, November 18. https://www.nytimes.com/2019/11/08/sports/uswnt-equal-pay-lawsuit.html.

———. 2019b. "US Women's Soccer Team Sues US Soccer for Gender Discrimination." *New York Times, March 8.* https://www.nytimes.com/2019/03/08/sports/womens-soccer-team-lawsuit-gender-discrimination.html?searchResultPosition=1.

Dastagir, Alia E. 2020. "Domestic Violence in the Age of Coronavirus: What Happens When You're Stuck at Home, but Home Isn't Safe?" *USA Today*, March 18. https://www.usatoday.com/story/news/health/2020/03/18/coronavirus-domestic-violence-shelters-prepare-hotlines-open/5067349002/.

Department of Health and Human Services. 2020. "Learn about FVPSA." April 21. http://www.learnaboutfvpsa.com/state-territory.

Dernberger, Brittany, and Joanna R. Pepin. 2020. "Gender Flexibility, But Not Equality: Young Adults' Division of Labor Preferences." *Sociological Science*, 7(2).

Desilver, Drew. 2023a. "In Places Where Same-Sex Marriages Are Legal, How Many Married Same-Sex Couples Are There?" Pew Research Center. June 13. https://www.pewresearch.org/short-reads/2023/06/13/in-places-where-same-sex-marriages-are-legal-how-many-married-same-sex-couples-are-there/.

———. 2023b. "What the Data Says about Food Stamps in the US" Pew Research Center. July 19. https://www.pewresearch.org/short-reads/2023/07/19/what-the-data-says-about-food-stamps-in-the-u-s/.

DeWard, Sarah. 2010. "Nature and Dynamics of Domestic Violence." Principles of Practice. New York State Coalition Against Domestic Violence.

Dewey, Caitlin. 2014. "The Only Guide to Gamergate You Will Ever Need to Read." *Washington Post*, October 14. https://www.washingtonpost.com/news/the-intersect/wp/2014/10/14/the-only-guide-to-gamergate-you-will-ever-need-to-read/.

DeWolf, Mark. 2017. "12 Stats about Working Women." US Bureau of Labor Statistics. March 2. https://www.bls.gov/blog/2017/12-stats-about-working-women.htm.

Diamant, Jeff, and Besheer Mohamed. 2023. "What the Data Says about Abortion in the US" Pew Research Center, January 11. https://www.pewresearch.org/short-reads/2023/01/11/what-the-data-says-about-abortion-in-the-u-s-2/.

Diaz, Jaclyn. 2021. "Police Foiled an Ohio Incel's Plot to Kill Women in a Mass Shooting, Prosecutors Say." National Public Radio, July 22. https://www.npr.org/2021/07/22/1019089834/police-foiled-an-ohio-incels-plot-to-kill-women-in-a-mass-shooting-prosecutors-s?fbclid=IwAR0A-d4FbdOgLoDqLuJnWlp_pm20FcPMjmKku8C7fpuRtmBF4X5BFsVOlYI.

Dick, Kirby, and Amy Ziering. 2019. *The Hunting Ground* (documentary). https://www.thehuntinggroundfilm.com/story.html.

Dickerson, Caitlyn, Seth Freed Wessler, and Miriam Jordan. 2020. "Immigrants Say They Were Pressured into Unneeded Surgeries." *New York Times*, September 29. https://www.nytimes.com/2020/09/29/us/ice-hysterectomies-surgeries-georgia.html.

Dittmar, Kelly. 2015. *Navigating Gendered Terrain: Stereotypes and Strategy in Political Campaigns.* Philadelphia: Temple University Press.

———. 2017. "Finding Gender in Election 2016: Lessons from Presidential Gender Watch." Presidential Gender Watch. http://presidentialgenderwatch.org/wp-content/uploads/2017/05/Finding-Gender-in-Election-2016_Highlights.pdf.

Dolan, Eric. 2020. "Men Are More Likely than Women to Perceive Face Masks as Infringing on Their Freedom." PsyPost. October 24. https://www.psypost.org/2020/10/men-are-more-likely-than-women

-to-perceive-face-masks-as-infringing-on-their-freedom-58359?fbclid=IwAR3fnqKeopy-z4WHAVOJ4Vn8SNITJAqe8v5EpurAa33OtOAJmqrbvqAbdbk.

Doyne, Shannon. 2023. "Should Award Shows Eliminate Gendered Categories?" *New York Times*, March 6. https://www.nytimes.com/2023/03/06/learning/should-award-shows-eliminate-gendered-categories.html.

Dular, Nicole. 2020. "Boy Bye: A Feminist Defense of Ghosting" in *College Ethics: A Reader on Moral Issues that Affect You*, 2nd ed. New York: Oxford University Press.

Dutt, Kuhelli, Danielle L. Pfaff, Ariel F. Bernstein, Joseph S. Dillard, and Caryn J. Block. 2016. "Gender Differences in Recommendation Letters for Postdoctoral Fellowships in Geoscience." *Nature Geoscience*, 9: 805–8.

Dwyer, Colin. 2020. "US Agrees to Pause Deportations for Women Alleging Abuse at ICE Facility." National Public Radio, November 24. https://www.npr.org/2020/11/24/938456423/u-s-agrees-to-pause-deportations-for-women-alleging-abuse-at-ice-facility?fbclid=IwAR1Tp7hJL7glWCbVwS9CoJlP04BtzSrEbosOqf4W_cBTunzCoMl13WD25io.

Economic Policy Institute. 2019. "Latinas Face a Double Pay Penalty for Their Ethnicity and Gender." https://www.epi.org/files/uploads/LatinaWomenGenderPayDay5.pdf.

Edelman, Adam. 2022. "Thomas Wants the Supreme Court to Overturn Landmark Rulings that Legalized Contraception, Same-Sex Marriage." NBC News, June 24. https://www.nbcnews.com/politics/supreme-court/thomas-wants-supreme-court-overturn-landmark-rulings-legalized-contrac-rcna35228.

Edelman, Amelia. 2019. "It's Official: Gen Z Is Rejecting the Gender Binary & the World Needs to Follow Suit." *SheKnows*, October 18. https://www.sheknows.com/parenting/articles/2117014/gender-identity-gen-z/.

Ehrenhalt, Jey. 2019. "Let's Talk About Nonbinary." *Learning for Justice*, January 30. https://www.learningforjustice.org/magazine/lets-talk-about-nonbinary.

Emba, Christine. 2019. "Men Are in Trouble. 'Incels' Are Proof." *Washington Post*, June 7. https://www.washingtonpost.com/opinions/men-are-in-trouble-incels-are-proof/2019/06/07/8d6ad596-8936-11e9-a870-b9c411dc4312_story.html.

———. 2023. "Opinion: Men Are Lost. Here's a Map Out of the Wilderness." *Washington Post*, July 10. https://www.washingtonpost.com/opinions/2023/07/10/christine-emba-masculinity-new-model/?fbclid=IwAR2h3eJYEkx1nFKzURv6U78YT5sLvTZdkDGNxPfPlBMeoq0Aa-CRe2p2STY.

End Rape On Campus. 2019. "Get Political." https://endrapeoncampus.org/action-center/get-political/ .

ERA Coalition. 2016. "Americans—by 94%—Overwhelmingly Support the Equal Rights Amendment (ERA)." June 17. https://www.prnewswire.com/news-releases/breaking-americansby-94---overwhelmingly-support-the-equal-rights-amendment-era-300286472.html.

Faludi, Susan. 1991. *Backlash: The Undeclared War against American Women*. Danvers, MA: Crown Publishing Group.

———. 2020. "Trump's Thoroughly Modern Masculinity." *New York Times*, October 29. https://www.nytimes.com/2020/10/29/opinion/trump-masculinity-femininity.html?fbclid=IwAR0eS2PS6iFHDf2F4obU8OUMKL39Dl_x0FRDzpiUdvTGrlfMYyqUkTlyMNA.

Fang, Marina. 2019. "Survivor in Brock Turner Case Reveals Her Name in New Memoir." *Huffington Post*, September 4. https://www.huffpost.com/entry/chanel-miller-brock-turner-stanford-sexual-assault_n_5d6fa547e4b0cdfe0578964d?fbclid=IwAR2OX6cYlfL_LLZrdA86y3nNIHjoBd3-UeV843irhAOkvwK5GN80uzcbqxk.

Fanslow, Janet L., Brooklyn M. Mellar, Pauline J. Gulliver, and Tracey K. D. McIntosh. 2023. "Evidence of Gender Asymmetry in Intimate Partner Violence Experience at the Population-Level." *Journal of Interpersonal Violence*, 38(15–16).

Federal Burean of Investigation (FBI). 2012. "Crime in the United States 2012. Table 42: Arrests by Sex, 2012." Criminal Justice Information Services Division. https://ucr.fbi.gov/crime-in-the-u.s/2012/crime-in-the-u.s.-2012/tables/42tabledatadecoverviewpdf/table_42_arrests_by_sex_2012.xls.

———. 2017. "National Incident-Based Reporting System, 2012–2016." Federal Bureau of Investigation.

———. 2022. "Hate Crime Statistics." Uniform Crime Report. US Department of Justice. https://www.justice.gov/hatecrimes/hate-crime-statistics.

Felix, Kwolanne. 2020. "Street Harassment Did Not Get the Memo about COVID-19." *Ms. Magazine*, June 16. https://msmagazine.com/2020/06/16/street-harassment-did-not-get-the-memo-about-covid-19/?fbclid=IwAR32ktZM__OACU7Hpcg-08ninjx8ipF3jDFCim8eeqnNtVJjuHxJE4Q_IDQ.

Fensome, Ali. 2022. "Gender Wage Gap Bot." https://genderpaygap.app.

Ferguson, Stephanie, and Isabella Lucy. 2022. "Data Deep Dive: A Decline of Women in the Workforce." US Chamber of Commerce. April 27. https://www.uschamber.com/workforce/data-deep-dive-a-decline-of-women-in-the-workforce.

FindLaw. 2020. "Domestic Violence." February 4. https://criminal.findlaw.com/criminal-charges/domestic-violence.html.

Fitzsimons, Tim. 2019. "A Very LGBTQ Decade: Gay Marriage, Trans Rights, and a 'Rainbow Wave.'" NBC News, December 29. https://www.nbcnews.com/feature/nbc-out/very-lgbtq-decade-gay-marriage-trans-rights-rainbow-wave-n1107901?fbclid=IwAR1g1FjsKK7y1XKT9WWIAIGnIRkuDKNwClf-gfV1QZWuSTZxwgDuJm4CELA.

Fleischer, Katie. 2020. "Equal Pay for Moms during COVID-19." *Ms. Magazine*, June 30. https://msmagazine.com/2020/06/03/equal-pay-for-moms-during-covid-19/?fbclid=IwAR2TaAve91yGuPnsCaprGE9GKiFeENoclUML8U-wv6k6-jc94-2eUBZZ9JY.

Ford, Rebecca. 2023. "America Ferrera Did That Epic *Barbie* Monologue '30–50 Times.'" *Vanity Fair*, July 24. https://www.vanityfair.com/hollywood/2023/07/america-ferrera-barbie-monologue-30-to-50-times.

Foubert, John D., Angela Clark-Taylor, and Andrew F. Wall. 2020. "Is Campus Rape Primarily a Serial or One-Time Problem? Evidence From a Multicampus Study." *Violence Against Women*, 26(3–4): 296–311. https://doi.org/10.1177/1077801219833820.

Foubert, John D., Matthew W. Brosi, and R. Sean Bannon. 2011. "Effects of Fraternity Men's Pornography Use on Bystander Intervention, Rape Myth Acceptance and Behavioral Intent to Commit Sexual Assault." *Sexual Addiction & Compulsivity: The Journal of Treatment & Prevention*, 212–31.

Framke, Caroline. 2021. "How Jazz Jennings Changed the World for Trans Youth Simply by Being Herself." *Variety*, June 2. https://variety.com/2021/tv/features/jazz-jennings-i-am-jazz-trans-legislation-1234985248/.

Framke, Caroline, and Constance Grady. 2017. "The Explosive Sexual Harassment Case Against Hollywood Mogul Harvey Weinstein, Explained." *Vox*, October. https://www.vox.com/culture/2017/10/6/16431674/harvey-weinstein-allegations-explained.

Franceschet, Susan, and Karen Beckwith. 2018. "Spain's Majority-Female Cabinet Embodies Women's Global Rise to Power." *The Conversation*, July 28. https://theconversation.com/spains-majority-female-cabinet-embodies-womens-global-rise-to-power-98433.

Frey, William H. 2022. "Midterm Exit Polls Show That Young Voters Drove Resistance to the 'Red Wave.'" Brookings. November 18. https://www.brookings.edu/articles/midterm-exit-polls-show-that-young-voters-drove-democratic-resistance-to-the-red-wave/.

Fridal, Emma E. and James Allen Fox. 2019. "Gender Differences in Patterns and Trends in US Homicide, 1976–2017." *Violence and Gender*, 6(1): 27–36.

Friedersdorf, Conor. 2022. "11 Reader Views on Class Prejudice in America." *The Atlantic*, August 1. https://www.theatlantic.com/newsletters/archive/2022/08/us-classism-economic-bias/671016/.

Fry, Richard. 2019. "US Women Near Milestone in the College-Educated Labor Force." Pew Research Center. June 20. https://www.pewresearch.org/fact-tank/2019/06/20/u-s-women-near-milestone-in-the-college-educated-labor-force/?utm_source=AdaptiveMailer&utm_medium=email&utm_campaign=19-06-20%20women%20in%20labor%20force%20FT&org=982&lvl=100&ite=4253&lea=983257&ctr=0&par.

Fuller, Thomas. 2016. "Court Papers Give Insight into Stanford Sex Assault." *New York Times*, June 12. https://www.nytimes.com/2016/06/13/us/brock-turner-stanford-rape.html.

Fung, Katherine. 2020. "What the New Title IX Rules Will Mean for Campus Sexual Assault Cases." *Newsweek*, May 7. https://www.newsweek.com/what-new-title-ix-rules-will-mean-campus-sexual-assault-cases-1502439?fbclid=IwAR2uMHgxjkaaZXHe1xwQXBQ3S7gMmV5SAMwkG7McMt7R-H4gj7-nh7xm_n8.

Gallagher Robbins, Katherine, and Rebecca Vallas. 2019. "5 Reasons Why Strengthening the EITC and CTC Is the Kind of Tax Reform America Needs." Center for American Progress. April 19. https://www.americanprogress.org/article/5-reasons-strengthening-eitc-ctc-kind-tax-reform-america-needs/.

Ganesh, Chandi. 2019. "College Mom Pens Letter Begging Girls to Stop Wearing Leggings So They Don't 'Tempt Her Sons.'" *Scoop* at Upworthy. October 2. https://scoop.upworthy.com/college-mom-pens-letter-begging-girls-to-stop-wearing-leggings-so-they-dont-tempt-her-sons?fbclid=IwAR2tTTWuFx2VXS3qwnHMw10ucZlX5PTLQjTiV18NoTgOmTBE52ckMw0P_T8.

Ganley, Colleen M., Casey E. George, Joseph R. Cimpian, and Martha B. Makowski. 2017. "Gender Equity in College Majors: Looking Beyond the STEM/Non-STEM Dichotomy for Answers Regarding Female Participation." *American Educational Research Journal,* 55(3). https://journals.sagepub.com/doi/abs/10.3102/0002831217740221.

Ganna, Andrea, Karin J. Verweij, Michel G. Nivard, Robert Maier, Robbee Wedow, Alexander S. Busch, Abdel Abdellaoui, Shengru Guo, J. Fah Sathirapongsasuti, and Brendan P. Zietsch. 2019. "Large-Scale GWAS Reveals Insights into the Genetic Architecture of Same-Sex Sexual Behavior." *Science*, 365(6456).

Garcia, Isabella. 2019. "Ending Domestic Violence Requires Working with Those Who Harm, Too." *Yes Magazine*, October 30. https://www.yesmagazine.org/social-justice/2019/10/30/men-domestic-violence-victims-healing.

Garcia-Navarro, Lulu. 2018. "#MuteRKelly Co-Founder on The Moment, Her Movement and Its Momentum." National Public Radio. May 6. https://www.npr.org/2018/05/06/608802024/-muterkelly-gathers-momentum.

Gates, Melinda French. 2019. "Melinda Gates: Here's Why I'm Committing $1 Billion to Promote Gender Equality." *Time*, October 5. https://time.com/5690596/melinda-gates-empowering-women/?fbclid=IwAR1LPE9AGqb7Um2G2qrUt00wftNgTQqJzzWuqi-H1k5SRP4ofKDmlRr5H6w.

Gay, Lesbian, and Straight Education Network (GLSEN). 2023. "GLSEN: Our Work." https://www.glsen.org/our-work.

Gendler, Alex. 2014. "The History of Marriage." TedEd Animations. https://www.youtube.com/watch?v=ZZZ6QB5TSfk.

Gillette, Hope. 2022. "The 4 Stages of the Cycle of Abuse: From Tension to Calm and Back." Psych-Central, July 15. https://psychcentral.com/health/cycle-of-abuse.

Gilson, Dave. 2018. "You Can't Understand White Supremacists without Looking at Masculinity." *Mother Jones*, July/August. https://www.motherjones.com/politics/2018/07/men-white-racist-extremism-michael-kimmel/?fbclid=IwAR37Bc-DIENqBugeNhq_I8TTpQKFOIvDDPge-1OKOtZsEkPEGYsyah1AVDk.

GLAAD. 2019. "GLAAD Media Reference Guide—Terms to Avoid." Gay and Lesbian Alliance Against Defamation. https://glaad.org/reference/.

———. 2023. "About GLAAD." https://glaad.org.

Glasmeier, Amy K. 2023. "Living Wage Calculator." Massachusetts Institute of Technology. https://livingwage.mit.edu.

Glenza, Jessica. 2019a. "Rate of US Abortions Drops to Lowest Level Since 1973." *The Guardian*, September 18. https://www.theguardian.com/world/2019/sep/18/us-abortion-rate-stats-lowest-since-roe-v-wade.

———. 2019b. "US Abortion Rate Is Lowest in Nine Years, New Data Shows." *The Guardian*, November. https://www.theguardian.com/world/2019/nov/27/us-abortion-rate-drops-data-shows?fbclid=IwAR3NousdphRcV01gu5N8OAJLhbRZNmrXrBlfoQf6K2dEKI5OyPAP_t8tTTQ.

Glezerman, Marek. 2016. *Gender Medicine: The Groundbreaking New Science of Gender- and Sex-Related Diagnosis and Treatment*. New York: Overlook Press.

Global Boyhood Initiative. 2024. "Representations of Masculinity in Boys' Television." Global Boyhood Initiative. https://www.boyhoodinitiative.org/resources/representations-masculinity-boys-television.

Golash-Boza, Tanya. 2021. *Race and Racisms: A Critical Approach*, 3rd ed. New York: Oxford University Press.

Goldar, Mita, Christopher Ryan, and Ahu Yildirmaz. 2019."*Rethinking Gender Pay Inequity in a More Transparent World*." ADP Research Institute. January 1. https://www.adp.com/resources/articles-and-insights/articles/r/rethinking-gender-pay-inequity-in-a-more-transparent-world.aspx.

Goldstein, Amy. 2021. "Biden Administration Revives Anti-Bias Protections in Health Care for Transgender People." *Washington Post*, May 10. https://www.washingtonpost.com/health/transgender-protection-hhs/2021/05/10/0852ce88-b17d-11eb-a980-a60af976ed44_story.html?fbclid=IwAR0evdiK_KlVXofu5ASQhmhAMMcJUhTyZJlmaptniuw8gMNTwlYoO-bQoMo.

Golshan, Tara. 2016. "Hillary Clinton's Concession Speech Full Transcript: 2016 Presidential Election." *Vox*, November 9. https://www.vox.com/2016/11/9/13570328/hillary-clinton-concession-speech-full-transcript-2016-presidential-election.

Goodman, Amy. 2020. "When Home Isn't Safe: Shelter-in-Place Is Putting Domestic Violence Survivors in a 'Dire Situation.'" *Democracy Now!* March 27. https://www.democracynow.org/2020/3/27/domestic_violence_coronavirus_katie_ray_jones.

Goodman, Lizzy. 2019. "The Best Women's Soccer Team in the World Fights for Equal Pay." *New York Times Magazine*, June 10. https://www.nytimes.com/2019/06/10/magazine/womens-soccer-inequality-pay.html.

Gould, Elise. 2019. "Latina Workers Have to Work Nearly 11 Months into 2019 to Be Paid the Same as White Non-Hispanic Men in 2018." Economic Policy Institute. November 19. https://www.epi.org/blog/latina-pay-gap-2019/?fbclid=IwAR2bMn0Kr97rZ-KF1G6mwu3uH8N60aSpx9nyZSEADdo_K3tu0E3IGaz-6Mw.

Grady, Constance. 2017. "Rose McGowan's Relentless Fight Against the Harvey Weinsteins of Hollywood." *Vox*, October 17. https://www.vox.com/culture/2017/10/19/16484728/rose-mcgowan-harvey-weinstein.

Grant, Jaime, Lisa Mottet, Justin Tanis, Jack Harrison, Jody Herman, and Mara Keisling. 2011. "Injustice at Every Turn: A Report of the National Transgender Discrimination Survey." National Center for Transgender Equality and the National Gay and Lesbian Task Force. February 3. https://www.thetaskforce.org/resources/injustice-every-turn-report-national-transgender-discrimination-survey/.

Green, Jeff, and Tiffany Stecker. 2022. "California Passes Law Requiring Companies to Post Salary Ranges on Job Listings." Bloomberg. August 30. https://www.bloomberg.com/news/articles/2022-08-30/california-passes-law-requiring-companies-like-meta-disney-to-post-salary-range.

Greenwood, Max. 2020. "Biden Says He Will Pick a Woman as VP." *The Hill*, March 15. https://thehill.com/homenews/campaign/487722-biden-says-he-will-choose-a-woman-as-his-running-mate-if-he-wins-nomination.

Gu, Jacob. 2020. "Deadliest Mass Shootings Are Often Preceded by Violence at Home." Bloomberg. June 30. https://www.bloomberg.com/graphics/2020-mass-shootings-domestic-violence-connection/?in_source=embedded-checkout-banner.

Guttmacher Institute. 2020. "Contraceptive Use among Adolescents in the United States." Guttmacher Institute Fact Sheet, April. https://www.guttmacher.org/fact-sheet/contraceptive-use-among-adolescents-united-states#:~:text=Among%20sexually%20experienced%2015%E2%80%9319,last%20time%20they%20had%20sex.

Haan, Katherine. 2023. "Gender Pay Gap Statistics in 2024." *Forbes*, February 27. https://www.forbes.com/advisor/business/gender-pay-gap-statistics/.

Hagan, Pat. 2013. "Don't Bottle Up Your Emotions— It'll Knock Years Off Your Life and Raise Cancer Risk by 70 Percent." *Daily Mail*, September 6. http://www.dailymail.co.uk/health/article-2414537/Dont-bottle-emotions—itll-knock-years-life-raise-cancer-risk-70-percent.html.

Hahn, Alicia. 2023. "2024 Student Loan Debt Statistics: Average Student Loan Debt." *Forbes Advisor*, July 16. https://www.forbes.com/advisor/student-loans/average-student-loan-debt-statistics/.

Hannon, Elliot. 2019. "Trump Wonders Why Coin Commemorating 100th Anniversary of Women's Suffrage Wasn't 'Done a Long Time Ago.'" *Slate*, November 26. https://slate.com/news-and-politics/2019/11/trump-coin-commemorative-coin-centennial-100-year-anniversary-womens-suffrage.html?fbclid=IwAR2Q1QQtR6RKA8sEZtSeuScm4noeCjXMQypiCgQ-RHOBZzxwdxb_gWsn2EU.

Hartocollis, Anemona. 2024. "Florida Eliminates Sociology as a Core Course at Its Universities." *New York Times*, January 24. https://www.nytimes.com/2024/01/24/us/florida-universities-sociology.html#:~:text=In%20November%2C%20the%20board%20of,a%20period%20of%20public%20comment.

Healy, Rachael. 2020. "'Women Are Tired of Having to Walk Men through It': The Male Comics Standing Up for #MeToo." *The Guardian*, October 27. https://www.theguardian.com/stage/2020/oct/27/standup-comedys-me-too-reckoning-male-comedians-women?fbclid=IwAR0KPI9uhAszNIDKZrRY0-nj2Xbu3ZAntTbSsGDs1tfjtsl4Ryf2fD7WSa8.

Heelan-Stanzoine, Melissa. 2019. "Law School Enrollment Up Overall, But Not for Minorities." Bloomberg Law. December 12. https://news.bloomberglaw.com/us-law-week/law-school-enrollment-up-overall-but-not-for-minorities.

Hemmings.com. 2023. "Sold—Crown of the Realm: 1983 Rolls-Royce Corniche Convertible." July 15. https://www.hemmings.com/auction/1983-rolls-royce-corniche/sold#:~:text=The%20base%20price%20of%20the,to%20%24400%2C000%20in%20today%27s%20dollars.

Hendrix, Steve. 2019. "He Always Hated Women. Then He Decided to Kill Them." *Washington Post*, June 7. https://www.washingtonpost.com/graphics/2019/local/yoga-shooting-incel-attack-fueled-by-male-supremacy/.

Hernandez, Joe. 2022a. "The US Men's and Women's Soccer Teams Will Be Paid Equally under a New Deal." National Public Radio. May 18. https://www.npr.org/2022/05/18/1099697799/us-soccer-equal-pay-agreement-women.

———. 2022b. "US Citizens Can Now Choose the Gender 'X' on Their Passport Applications." National Public Radio, April 11. https://www.npr.org/2022/04/11/1092000203/gender-x-us-passport-applications?fbclid=IwAR0fSvUG3_VD4i5KFjY6PPFjGSVCQ5FFdCniE7n19FGTDmSTRbacaknli2A.

Herr, Jane, Radha Roy, and Jacob Alex Klerman. 2020. "Gender Differences in Needing and Taking Leave." US Department of Labor, November. https://www.dol.gov/sites/dolgov/files/OASP/evaluation/pdf/WHD_FMLAGenderShortPaper_January2021.pdf?utm_source=npr_newsletter&utm_medium=email&utm_content=20230820&utm_term=8904071&utm_campaign=money&utm_id=63532678&orgid=310&utm_att1=.

Hesse, Monica. 2020. "Joe Biden's Very Manly Campaign." *Washington Post*, September 11. https://www.washingtonpost.com/lifestyle/style/joe-bidens-very-manly-campaign/2020/09/10/d20e2548-eed1-11ea-99a1-71343d03bc29_story.html?fbclid=IwAR26fVT6JclFQdLRu_pZodYLydtzkhE5GxNAPelOQgwWBvr6lqr16Awpt-Y.

Hetler, Amanda. 2023. "Facing the Edge: The Glass Cliff at a Glance." TechTarget. July 7. https://www.techtarget.com/whatis/infographic/Facing-the-edge-The-glass-cliff-at-a-glance#:~:text=A%20recent%20example%20of%20a,or%20facing%20a%20glass%20cliff.

Heyboer, Kelly. 2020. "Princeton U. Agrees to Pay Nearly $1.2 million to Female Professors after Feds Find Men Earned More." NJ.com, October 12. https://www.nj.com/education/2020/10/princeton-u-agrees-to-pay-nearly-12-million-to-female-professors-after-feds-find-men-earned-more.html.

Heymann, Jody, Amy Raub, and Aleta Sprague. 2020. "The US Has Fallen Behind on Equality of the Sexes." CNN News, January 14. https://www.cnn.com/2020/01/14/opinions/equal-rights-amendment-heymann-raub-sprague/index.html?fbclid=IwAR3oAfIwFPJqc_ZjHHtKWBq3xg8f9v8KDZsK4k7sZ3MPlGsnWrfwCfu23qc.

Heymann, Jody, Altea Sprague, and Amy Raub. 2020. *Advancing Equality: How Constitutional Rights Can Make a Difference Worldwide.* Berkeley: University of California Press.

Hidalgo Bellows, Kate. 2021. "How Social Media Is Fueling Protests against Campus Sexual Assault." *The Chronicle of Higher Education*, September 21. https://www.chronicle.com/article/how-social-media-is-fueling-protests-against-campus-sexual-assault.

Hill, James, and Bill Hutchinson. 2020. "Judge Rejects R. Kelly's Request to be Released from Jail Over Coronavirus Fears." ABC News, April 07. https://abcnews.go.com/Health/judge-rejects-kellys-request-released-jail-coronavirus-fears/story?id=70025508.

Hillman, Jennifer. 2022. "Lifetime Prevalence of Intimate Partner Violence and Health-Related Outcomes among Transgender Adults Aged 50 and Older." *The Gerontologist*, 62(2): 212–22.

Hirschel, David. 2008. "Domestic Violence Cases: What Research Shows about Arrest and Dual Arrest Rates." Office of Justice Programs, July 25. https://www.ncjrs.gov/pdffiles1/nij/222679.pdf.

Hochschild, Arlie Russell. 1989. *The Second Shift.* New York: Viking Penguin.

Hoffman, Candace. 2020. "Covid-19: Universal Masking, Even Indoors May Be Needed to Mitigate Spread." *Physician's Weekly*, June 1. https://www.physiciansweekly.com/covid-19-universal-masking-even-indoors-may-be-needed-to-mitigate-spread/.

hooks, bell. 2000. *Feminism Is for Everybody.* Cambridge, MA: South End Press.

Hopcroft, Rosemary L. and David O. Martin. "Parental Investments and Educational Outcomes: Trivers-Willard in the US." *Frontiers in Sociology*, March 31. https://www.frontiersin.org/articles/10.3389/fsoc.2016.00003/full.

Hope Shores Alliance. 2020. "Dating Violence Is Also." March 1. https://www.facebook.com/HopeShoresAlliance/.

Horowitz, Juliana Menasce. 2017. "About One-in-Seven Americans Don't Think Men Should Be Able to Take Any Paternity Leave." Pew Research Center, March 27. https://www.pewresearch.org/short-reads/2017/03/27/about-one-in-seven-americans-dont-think-men-should-be-able-to-take-any-paternity-leave/?utm_source=npr_newsletter&utm_medium=email&utm_content=20230820&utm_term=8904071&utm_campaign=money&utm_id=63532678&orgid=310&utm_att1=.

———. 2022. "More than Half of Americans in Their 40s Are 'Sandwiched' Between an Aging Parent and Their Own Children." Pew Research Center, April 8. https://www.pewresearch.org/short-reads/2022/04/08/more-than-half-of-americans-in-their-40s-are-sandwiched-between-an-aging-parent-and-their-own-children/.

Horowitz, Juliana Mensce, and Ruth Igielnik. 2020. "A Century after Women Gained the Right to Vote, Majority of Americans See Work to Do on Gender Equality." Pew Research Center. July 7. https://www.pewsocialtrends.org/2020/07/07/a-century-after-women-gained-the-right-to-vote-majority-of-americans-see-work-to-do-on-gender-equality/.

Houchins, Miranda. 2015. "This Day in History: Equal Pay Trailblazer Lilly Ledbetter Turns 77." White House. April 15. https://obamawhitehouse.archives.gov/blog/2015/04/14/day-history-equal-pay-trailblazer-lilly-ledbetter-turns-77.

Hsieh, Ning, and Hui Liu. 2019. "Marriage Could Be Good for Your Health—Unless You're Bisexual." *The Conversation*, September 20. https://theconversation.com/marriage-could-be-good-for-your-health-unless-youre-bisexual-121865.

Hsu, Andrea. 2020. "'This Is Too Much': Working Moms Are Reaching the Breaking Point during the Pandemic." National Public Radio. September 20. https://www.npr.org/2020/09/29/918127776/this-is-too-much-working-moms-are-reaching-the-breaking-point-during-the-pandemi?fbclid=IwAR1YXa-z5f5A6eOyNxVpLwr0bUu-UaVUJZEED4oy_cV0-t8Jp7AVqZU5Wrw.

Human Rights Campaign. 2023. "Our Work: Count Me In." https://www.hrc.org/campaigns/count-me-in.

Human Rights Watch. 2023. "Saudi Arabia: Law Enshrines Male Guardianship." Human Rights Watch, March 8. https://www.hrw.org/news/2023/03/08/saudi-arabia-law-enshrines-male-guardianship.

Hurst, Kiley and Richard Fry. 2023. "Women Have Gained Ground in the Nation's Highest- Paying Occupations, but Still Lag Behind Men." Pew Research Center. November 2. https://www.pewresearch.org/short-reads/2023/11/02/women-have-gained-ground-in-the-nations-highest-paying-occupations-but-still-lag-behind-men/.

Hutchings, Abigail. 2019. "Meet the College Student Exposing an Anti-Abortion Counseling Center in Colorado." Rewire News, December 20. https://rewire.news/article/2019/12/20/meet-the-college-student-exposing-an-anti-abortion-counseling-center-in-colorado/?fbclid=IwAR29ImS51PbRlUudAonMeGPIPPee_mspa37cFPAifXy4SJDned6jEqIRbel.

Hyman, Dylan. 2019. "Woman Who Called 911 to Order Pizza Was Really Reporting Domestic Violence Incident." WTAE ABC 4. November 22. https://www.wtae.com/article/woman-who-called-911-to-order-pizza-was-really-reporting-domestic-violence-incident/29897124#.

Hymes, Clare, Graham Kates, and Katrina Kaufman. 2024. "The Second Trial between Donald Trump and E. Jean Carroll Is Underway. Here's What to Know." CBS News, January 16. https://www.cbsnews.com/news/trump-e-jean-carroll-trial-what-to-know/#.

Igielnik, Ruth. 2022. "Most Americans Who Are Familiar with Title IX Say It's Had a Positive Impact on Gender Equality." Pew Research Center. April 22. https://www.pewresearch.org/short-reads/2022/04/21/most-americans-who-are-familiar-with-title-ix-say-its-had-a-positive-impact-on-gender-equality/.

Illinois Coalition against Sexual Assault. 2019. "Rape Myths." November 12. http://www.icasa.org/docs/rapemyths_fact_sheet.pdf.

Ingraham, Christopher. 2021. "Homes in Poor Neighborhoods Are Taxed at Roughly Twice the Rate of Those in Rich Areas, Study Shows." *Washington Post*, March 12. https://www.washingtonpost.com/business/2021/03/12/property-tax-regressive/?fbclid=IwAR0gnFHjM3AHqYG1fFDvpr9SRW9NIP8OomdeeN56N-oZwe_BDgoqlOm94qk.

Institute for Research on Poverty. 2020. "Involved Fathers Play an Important Role in Children's Lives." University of Wisconsin–Madison. February. https://www.irp.wisc.edu/resource/involved-fathers-play-an-important-role-in-childrens-lives/.

Institute for Women's Policy Research (IWPR). 2016. "Briefing Paper: Poverty, Gender, and Public Policies." February. https://iwpr.org/poverty-gender-and-public-policies/.

———. 2023a. "Native Women Will Not Reach Pay Equity with White Men until 2144." Institute for Women's Policy Research. November 21. https://iwpr.org/native-womens-wage-gap-fact-sheet/.

———. 2023b. "Women Earn Less thanMen Whether They Work in the Same or in Different Occupations." Institute for Women's Policy Research. March. https://iwpr.org/wp-content/uploads/2023/03/Gender-Wage-Gaps-2023-003.pdf.

Ipsos. 2019. "Nominating Woman or Minority Come Second to Nominating Candidate Who Can Beat Trump." *Ipsos*, June. https://www.ipsos.com/sites/default/files/ct/news/documents/2019-06/daily-beast-gender-topline-2019-06-17-v2.pdf.

Iqbal, Nosheen. 2019. "No Lust at First Sight: Why Thousands Are Now Identifying as 'Demisexual.'" *The Guardian*, September 7. https://www.theguardian.com/society/2019/sep/07/no-lust-at-first-sight-day-i-finally-realised-i-was-a-demisexual?fbclid=IwAR2g7metcAS076tfy7dXwsbE7sqfVsudoonlz_Lz3HEqDg_BiiRGvK0FYXc.

It's On Us. 2019. "The Story of Our Movement." *It's On Us*. https://www.itsonus.org/history/.

Izadi, Elahe, and Kayla Epstein. 2019. "'Squad' Jumped from Pop Culture to Become the Most Politically Polarizing Word of the Year." *Washington Post*, July 27. https://www.washingtonpost.com/lifestyle/style/squad-jumped-from-pop-culture-to-become-the-most-politically-polarizing-word-of-the-year/2019/07/27/6cfdd468-acbb-11e9-a0c9-6d2d7818f3da_story.html.

Jackson, Jon. 2022. "Christine Blasey Ford Death Threats Resurface Amid Kavanaugh Protests." *Newsweek*, May 09. https://www.newsweek.com/christine-blasey-ford-brett-kavanaugh-protests-supreme-court-roe-v-wade-1704942.

Jenkins, Morgan. 2019. "The Way Forward for Me Too, According to Tarana Burke." Vox, October 15. https://www.vox.com/identities/2019/10/15/20910298/tarana-burke-morgan-jerkins?fbclid=IwAR0Ep5gLzsw49dl_-UkxHU-fFKMDrF6pucHGqQn5yCdW2C5bUjDmLL5nvXk.

Jerkovich, Katie. 2023. "Matt Walsh Slams 'Anti-Man' 'Barbie' Film, Says Marketing Pulled a Fast One on Audience." *Daily Wire*, July 24. https://www.dailywire.com/news/matt-walsh-slams-anti-man-barbie-film-says-marketing-pulled-a-fast-one-on-audience.

Jhally, Sut, director. 2010. *Killing Us Softly 4: Advertising's Image of Women* (motion picture).

Johnson, Allan G. 2005. *The Gender Knot: Unraveling Our Patriarchal Legacy.* Philadelphia: Temple University Press.

Johnson, Jenna. 2019. "On Day One, Kirsten Gillibrand Faces the 'Likable' Question." *Washington Post*, January 16. https://www.washingtonpost.com/politics/on-day-one-kirsten-gillibrand-faces-the-likable-question/2019/01/16/568cb58c-1922-11e9-9ebf-c5fed1b7a081_story.html.

Johnston, Joni E. 2019. "The Most Disturbing Red Flag of Domestic Violence." *Psychology Today*, October 20. https://www.psychologytoday.com/us/blog/the-human-equation/201910/the-most-critical-red-flag-of-domestic-violence.

Joint Center for Housing Studies. 2023. "The State of the Nation's Housing." Harvard University. https://www.jchs.harvard.edu/state-nations-housing-2023.

Jones, Anetta, Tom Silverstone, Max Duncan, Jess Gormley, and Chris Michael. 2019. "'There's Food . . . It's Just Not Real Food': Inside America's Hunger Capital." *The Guardian*, November 20. https://www.theguardian.com/cities/video/2019/nov/20/theres-food-its-just-not-real-food-inside-americas-hunger-capital-video.

Jones, Jeffrey M. 2022. "Middle-Class Identification Steady in US." Gallup. May 19. https://news.gallup.com/poll/392708/middle-class-identification-steady.aspx.

———. 2023. "More Say Birth Gender Should Dictate Sports Participation." Gallup. June 12. https://news.gallup.com/poll/507023/say-birth-gender-dictate-sports-participation.aspx.

Joseph, Jisha. 2020. "Artist Portrays Michelle Obama, Hilary Clinton, and Other Icons as Victims of Gender-Based Violence." Upworthy. February 3. https://scoop.upworthy.com/artist-portrays-michelle-obama-hillary-clinton-victims-of-gender-domestic-violence.

Kaiser Family Foundation. 2019. "Medicaid's Role for Women" First Focus on Children. March. https://firstfocus.org/wp-content/uploads/2019/11/Fact-Sheet-Medicaids-Role-for-Women.pdf.

Kapralau, Marina. 2020. "Salma Hayek Explores Healthy Masculinity with 'The Boyhood Initiative.'" The Things, June 25.

Katella, Kathy. 2023. "Maternal Mortality Is on the Rise: 8 Things to Know." Yale Medicine, May 22. https://www.yalemedicine.org/news/maternal-mortality-on-the-rise.

Katz, Debra and Lisa Banks. 2019. "Setting the Record Straight: Dr. Christine Blasey Ford's Legal Team Speaks Out." *Ms. Magazine*, October 9. https://msmagazine.com/2019/10/09/setting-the-record-straight-dr-christine-blasey-fords-legal-team-speaks-out/?fbclid=IwAR2cZ7AjAMVI53AtANIc9njucCVxJpH04__divPLNhfbz72sVex3wDmt3UM.

Katz, Jackson. 1995. *The Invention of Heterosexuality.* New York: Dutton.

———. 2006. *The Macho Paradox. Sourcebooks, Inc*: Naperville, Illinois.

———. 2019. "The Masculinity Politics of Impeachment." *Medium*, November 21. https://medium.com/@jackson_14012/the-masculinity-politics-of-impeachment-26fee6b01f23.

———. 2020. "What Donald Trump Understands about American Men." *Ms. Magazine*, October 22. https://msmagazine.com/2020/10/22/donald-trump-patriarchy-masculinity-men-male-voters/?fbclid=IwAR2bobN_YFk_NwI4HWDF5SA87dZ0-7WEETnIFoEUIFc1XtUhRtsbDQbKbec.

Katz-Wise, Sabra L. 2021. "Misgendering: What It Is and Why It Matters." Harvard Health Publishing, Harvard Medical School. July 23. https://www.health.harvard.edu/blog/misgendering-what-it-is-and-why-it-matters-202107232553.

KFF. 2023. "Maternal Deaths and Mortality Rates per 100,000 Live Births." https://www.kff.org/other/state-indicator/maternal-deaths-and-mortality-rates-per-100000-live-births/?currentTimeframe=0&sort

Model=%7B%22colId%22:%22Maternal%20Mortality%20Rate%20per%20100,000%20live%20Births%22,%22sort%22:%22desc%22%7D.

Khazan, Olga. 2016. "The Unintended Consequences of Purity Pledges." *Atlantic*, May 4. https://www.theatlantic.com/health/archive/2016/05/the-unintended-consequences-of-purity-pledges/481059/?fbclid=IwAR0z6H8dXzynIYR2wlYQPUDS5_IQBTZ7A4ff6BwbwoyHg8kNzkjC5ZAmccE.

Kight, Stef W. 2019. "Deep Dive: 2020's New Voters Will Usher in an Age of Demographic Transformation." *Axios*, December 14. https://www.axios.com/2020s-new-voters-demographic-transformation-9da0acc7-0a30-447d-a4a2-4ef66640eee9.html.

Killerman, Sam. 2019. "Breaking through the Binary: Gender Explained Using Continuums." *It's Pronounced Metrosexual*. https://itspronouncedmetrosexual.com/2011/11/breaking-through-the-binary-gender-explained-using-continuums/.

Killoy, Andrew, Jason Young, Jeremy Earp, and Sut Jhally, directors. 2007. *Dreamworlds 3: Desire, Sex, & Power in Music Video* (motion picture).

Kimmel, Michael. 2013. *The Gendered Society*. Oxford: Oxford University Press.

———. 2018. *Healing from Hate*. Oakland: University of California Press.

Kimmel, Michael S., and Michael A. Messner. 2013. *Men's Lives*, 9th ed. London: Pearson.

King-Miller, Lindsay. 2019. "Why Gender Reveal Parties Have Been So Widely Embraced—and Reviled." *Vox*, July 31. https://www.vox.com/the-goods/2019/7/31/20708816/gender-reveal-party-social-media-game-pink-blue-fire.

Kini, Aditi Natasha. 2018. "Feminists Have Been Warning the World about 'Incels.' Ignoring Online Misogyny Has Deadly Consequences." *Washington Post*, April 30. https://www.washingtonpost.com/news/posteverything/wp/2018/04/30/feminists-were-right-ignoring-online-misogyny-has-deadly-consequences/.

Kinsey, Alfred C. 1948. *Sexual Behavior in the Human Male*. Philadelphia: W.B. Saunders Company.

Kitroeff, Natalie, and Jessica Silver-Greenberg. 2019. "Pregnancy Discrimination Is Rampant Inside America's Biggest Companies." *New York Times*, February 19. https://www.nytimes.com/interactive/2018/06/15/business/pregnancy-discrimination.html?fbclid=IwAR2ub5ItlWWVmvSMo6SuOLxzbjOwuhgP4BrhFy2nYPElUJygVUZh0hSgpBc.

Knott, Katherine. 2023. "Biden Administration Hears from 132,000 and Counting on Title IX Rule." *Inside Higher Ed*, May 15. https://www.insidehighered.com/news/government/2023/05/15/biden-administration-hears-132000-and-counting-title-ix-rule.

Ko, Lisa. 2016. "Unwanted Sterilization and Eugenics Programs in the United States." *Independent Lens*, January 29. https://www.pbs.org/independentlens/blog/unwanted-sterilization-and-eugenics-programs-in-the-united-states/.

Kober, Nancy, and Diane Stark Rentner. 2020. "History and Evolution of Public Education in the US." Center on Education Policy. George Washington University. https://files.eric.ed.gov/fulltext/ED606970.pdf.

Kortsmit, Katherine, Antoinette T. Nguyen, Michele G. Mandel, Elizabeth Clark, Lisa M. Holler, Jessica Rodenhizer, and Maura K. Whiteman. 2022. "Abortion Surveillance—United States, 2020." Centers for Disease Control and Prevention, November 25. https://www.cdc.gov/mmwr/volumes/71/ss/ss7110a1.htm#T3_down.

Krook, Mona L. 2020. "'That Woman from Michigan': Gretchen Whitmer and Violence against Women in Politics." October 26. https://genderpolicyreport.umn.edu/that-woman-from-michigan-gretchen-whitmer-and-violence-against-women-in-politics/.

Kurtzleben, Danielle. 2019. "Democrats Consider: Is a White, Straight Man the Safe Bet against Trump?" National Public Radio. April 23. https://www.npr.org/2019/04/23/715967411/democrats-consider-is-a-white-straight-man-the-safe-bet-against-trump.

Lakritz, Talia. 2021. "8 Transgender Politicians Who Are Changing Politics." *Emerge*, June 7. https://emergeamerica.org/8-transgender-politicians-who-are-changing-politics/.

Lamendola, Courtney, and Steph Scaglia. 2023. "2023 Gender Parity Index." Represent Women. August. https://www.representwomen.org/report_2023_gender_parity_index.

Lamont, Ellen. 2020. "The Puzzling Persistence of Gendered Dating." *The Society Pages*, February 18. https://thesocietypages.org/ccf/2020/02/18/2220/?fbclid=IwAR1LcGnx588asTO4fVfVGzX62g2QQe3BRMivCbyG3P49FnJxi6LzdB43nfw.

Lange, Jessica. 2022. "21 Characteristics of a Good Mom." *Organized Motherhood*, March 17. https://www.organizedmotherhood.com/characteristics-good-mom/#:~:text=She%20is%20someone%20who%20can,means%20being%20a%20great%20listener.

Langone, Alex. 2018. "#MeToo and Time's Up Founders Explain the Difference Between the 2 Movements— and How They're Alike." *Time*, March 22. https://time.com/5189945/whats-the-difference-between-the-metoo-and-times-up-movements/.

Lawless, Jennifer L., and Kathryn Pearson. 2008. "The Primary Reason for Women's Underrepresentation? Reevaluating Conventional Wisdom." *Journal of Politics*, 70(1): 67–82.

Lazarus, Amit, and Hadas Mandel. 2023. "The Allocation of Housework in Same- and Different- Sex Partnerships: Recent Evidence from the US" *Sex Roles*, 89, 394–408.

Lee, Chelsea. 2019. "Welcome, Singular 'They.'" American Psychological Association. October. https://apastyle.apa.org/blog/singular-they?fbclid=IwAR11RVDOx0wXpLPbHt42K2jfW4YhkXi7njmbYLmDq-DcPSehN9lsyLp9Z5g.

Leemis, Ruth W., Norah Friar, Srijana Khatiwade, May S. Chen, Marcie-jo Kresnow, Sharon G. Smith, Sharon Caslin, and Kathleen Basile. 2022. "The National Intimate Partner and Sexual Violence Survey: 2016/2017 Report on Intimate Partner Violence." Centers for Disease Control and Prevention. October. https://www.cdc.gov/violenceprevention/pdf/nisvs/nisvsreportonipv_2022.pdf.

Leraas, Bethany C., Nicole R. Kippen, and Susan J. Larson. 2018. "Gender and Student Participation." *Journal of Scholarship of Teaching and Learning*, 18(4). https://files.eric.ed.gov/fulltext/EJ1200685.pdf.

Levenson, Eric, del Valle, Morgan, and Sonia Moghe. 2020. "Harvey Weinstein Sentenced to 23 Years in Prison After Addressing His Accusers in Court." CNN, March 11. https://www.cnn.com/2020/03/11/us/harvey-weinstein-sentence/index.html?fbclid=IwAR0wf18Luy3mKK63VlVg2HoXryuCCQAi6jettCLZTOf7VQNzxk3SaWTCPHQ.

Levin, Dan. 2019. "North Carolina Reaches Settlement on 'Bathroom Bill.'" *New York Times*, July 23. https://www.nytimes.com/2019/07/23/us/north-carolina-transgender-bathrooms.html.

Lewis, Helen. 2020. "*The Coronavirus Is a Disaster for Feminism.*" *The Atlantic*, March 19. https://www.theatlantic.com/international/archive/2020/03/feminism-womens-rights-coronavirus-covid19/608302/utm_source=facebook&utm_medium=social&utm_campaign=share&fbclid=IwAR3Uht0kQTkGHV-29CXGYn_k6h8hyV7vAFwt5Kw7NbcyrwLeo0Jg5crj2tU.

Li, David K. 2022. "Man Sentenced to 16 Years for Plotting to Kidnap Michigan Gov. Gretchen Whitmer." NBC News, December 27. https://www.nbcnews.com/news/us-news/man-sentenced-16-years-plotting-kidnap-michigan-gov-gretchen-whitmer-rcna63327.

Liang, Fan. 2023. "Top Surgery (Chest Feminization or Chest Masculinization)." John Hopkins Medicine. https://www.hopkinsmedicine.org/health/treatment-tests-and-therapies/top-surgery#:~:text=What%20is%20top%20surgery%3F,nipples%20for%20an%20affirming%20look.

Lin, Luona. 2023. "About 8 in 10 Women in Opposite-Sex Marriages Say They Took Their Husband's Last Name." Pew Research Center, September 7. https://www.pewresearch.org/short-reads/2023/09/07/about-eight-in-ten-women-in-opposite-sex-marriages-say-they-took-their-husbands-last-name/.

Little, Becky. 2021. "How Early Suffragists Left Black Women Out of Their Fight." History.com. January 29. https://www.history.com/news/suffragists-vote-black-women.

Livingston, Gretchen, and Deja Thomas. 2019. "Why Is the Teen Birth Rate Falling?" Pew Research Center, August 19. https://www.pewresearch.org/short-reads/2019/08/02/why-is-the-teen-birth-rate-falling/.

Lockman, Darcy. 2019. "What 'Good' Dads Get Away With." *New York Times*, May 4. https://www.nytimes.com/2019/05/04/opinion/sunday/men-parenting.html?fbclid=IwAR27DdpKvfQrWx445Oxk3vDBE7Te8U2YYQyH0BZ6htXPyNL0ZG-LDioYj8Y.

Loofbourow, Lili. 2019. "Why Society Goes Easy on Rapists." *Slate*, May 30. https://slate.com/news-and-politics/2019/05/sexual-assault-rape-sympathy-no-prison.html?fbclid=IwAR0q2mCRSh_4KIUVOtqWdp3jX3kVjWxxkI6zPx3bA7d_xlzF7GpoLmln6ns.

Lorber, Judith. 1994. *Paradoxes of Gender.* New Haven, CT: Yale University Press.

———. 2020. "Gendered COVID-19 Research." *Gender & Society* blog, June 16. https://gendersociety.wordpress.com/2020/06/16/gendered-covid-19-research/

Lowe, Claire. 2017. "Why 80 Percent of New Jersey's Domestic Violence Cases Are Dismissed." *The Press of Atlantic City,* April 11. https://pressofatlanticcity.com/news/crime/why-80-percent-of-new-jerseys-domestic-violence-cases-are-dismissed/article_d9878dce-e162-5f98-8d6a-95eee8cb8884.html.

Lu, Yuan-Chiao, Regine Walker, Patrick Richard, and Mustafa Younis. 2019. "Inequalities in Poverty and Income between Single Mothers and Fathers." *International Journal of Environmental Research and Public Health* 17(1): 135. https://www.ncbi.nlm.nih.gov/pmc/articles/PMC6982282/.

Lyons, Patrick J., Maggie Astor, and Maya Salam. 2020. "Why the Equal Rights Amendment Is Back." *New York Times*, January 15. https://www.nytimes.com/2020/01/15/us/what-is-equal-rights-amendment.html.

Macias, Amanda, and Lora Kolodny. 2023. "Elon Musk Says Twitter Cash Flow Is Negative Due to Ad Revenue Declines, 'Heavy Debt.'" CNBC, July 15. https://www.cnbc.com/2023/07/15/elon-musk-says-twitter-cash-flow-remains-negative-with-heavy-debt-.html.

Madgavkar, Anu, Olivia White, Mekala Krishnan, Deepa Mahajan, and Xavier Azcue. 2020. "COVID-19 and Gender Equality: Countering the Regressive Effects." McKinsey & Company. July 15. https://www.mckinsey.com/featured-insights/future-of-work/covid-19-and-gender-equality-countering-the-regressive-effects#.

Mahdawi, Arwa. 2020. "Men Are Less Likely to Wear Masks—Another Sign that Toxic Masculinity Kills." *The Guardian*, May 16. https://www.theguardian.com/commentisfree/2020/may/16/men-masks-coronavirus-protests-masculinity-kills?fbclid=IwAR3Pcl28f1FEzewQSLUVkUcsofR9sbtDoVvuAHCNcao2BYUZEjY7olxkrcM

Malone, Dana M. 2022. "The Pandemic Makes the Second Shift Visible." *Women in Higher Education*, January 27. https://www.wihe.com/article-details/215/the-pandemic-makes-the-second-shift-visible/.

March of Dimes. 2022. "Nowhere to Go: Maternity Care Deserts across the US" March of Dimes. https://www.marchofdimes.org/sites/default/files/2022-10/2022_Maternity_Care_Report.pdf.

Marcotte, Amanda. 2019. "The 2010s in Feminism: Two Steps Forward and a Big Shove Back." *Salon*, December 14. https://www.salon.com/2019/12/14/the-2010s-in-feminism-two-steps-forward-and-a-big-shove-back/?fbclid=IwAR3sipl7XzjB3Ed2blFxARKbPeqWrOH5QGcN4_bm1fyu97zRoiWTMEq1egE.

Marino, Katharine. 2023. "The International History of the US Suffrage Movement." National Park Service. https://www.nps.gov/articles/the-internationalist-history-of-the-us-suffrage-movement.htm.

Mark, Nicholas D. E., and Lawrence L. Wu. 2022. "More Comprehensive Sex Education Reduced Teen Births: Quasi-Experimental Evidence." *Proceedings of the National Academy of Sciences of the United States of America*, 119(8).

Marowski, Steve. 2020. "Student Was Drugged, Raped at University of Michigan Frat Party, Lawsuit Says." *MLive*, October 2. https://www.mlive.com/news/ann-arbor/2020/10/student-was-drugged-raped-at-university-of-michigan-frat-party-lawsuit-says.html?fbclid=IwAR0xCmhsRjQ3sbb96SMmHL46WBHYkJvlw3m1Q29naQ2HTBBfnP6PVQGGUb4.

Matson, Erin. 2020. "Abortion Rights Opponents Are Terrified of the Equal Rights Amendment." Rewire News, January 21. https://rewire.news/article/2020/01/21/abortion-rights-opponents-are-terrified-of-the-equal-rights-amendment/?fbclid=IwAR3a_c7_gEwKhADw475voZ5dG-VvKJGFghoWjQiGa1aES8zJzhTE7bwF_TY.

Matthews, Alex Leeds. 2023. "Fertility Rates Dip, People Are Having Babies Later: The State of Birth Rates in the US." CNN Health, June 1. https://www.cnn.com/2023/05/31/health/fertility-rates-still-down-after-pandemic-rebound-dg/index.html.

McCann, Michael. 2020. "Why US Soccer Prevailed in USWNT's Gender Discrimination Lawsuit." *Sports Illustrated*, May 1. https://www.si.com/soccer/2020/05/02/uswnt-equal-pay-lawsuit-decision-analysis.

McCollum, Jennifer. 2023. "The Double Bind for Women—Being a Razor Blade and a Cupcake." SHRM. October 8. https://www.shrm.org/topics-tools/news/inclusion-equity-diversity/viewpoint-the-double-bind-for-women-being-a-razor-blade-and-a-cupcake.

McCulloch, Heather. 2017. "Closing the Women's Wealth Gap: What It Is, Why It Matters, and What Can Be Done about It." Closing the Women's Wealth Gap initiative. January. https://womenswealthgap.org/wp-content/uploads/2017/06/Closing-the-Womens-Wealth-Gap-Report-Jan2017.pdf.

McEvoy, Jemima. 2020. "Investigation into Claims of Mass Hysterectomies, Poor Covid-19 Care at ICE Detention Center." *Forbes*, September 15. https://www.forbes.com/sites/jemimamcevoy/2020/09/15/pelosi-calls-for-investigation-into-claims-of-mass-hysterectomies-poor-covid-19-care-at-ice-detention-center/?fbclid=IwAR260Jpk_kwPAYjyYykh9BO5mPSl36ylofy_YenjFwXwnE3ytbTPHrP43_A&sh=56e3430c5f7c.

McKee, Alan, Angela Dawson, and Melissa Kang. 2023. "The Criteria to Identify Pornography That Can Support Healthy Sexual Development for Young Adults: Results of an International Delphi Panel." *International Journal of Sexual Health*, 35(1): 1–12.

McKinsey & Company. 2023. "Women in the Workplace 2023." Lean In. https://leanin.org/women-in-the-workplace#key-findings-2023.

McShane, Julianne. 2020. "Race, Gender Dominated Coverage of Harris's VP Announcement, Report Finds." NBC News, October 14. https://www.nbcnews.com/news/nbcblk/racism-sexism-dominated-coverage-harris-s-vp-announcement-report-finds-n1243402?fbclid=IwAR0xCmhsRjQ3sbb96SMmHL46WBHYkJvlw3m1Q29naQ2HTBBfnP6PVQGGUb4.

Meckler, Laura. 2022. "Gender Identity Lessons, Banned in Some Schools, Are Rising in Others." *Washington Post*, June 3. https://www.washingtonpost.com/education/2022/06/03/schools-gender-identity-transgender-lessons/.

Melaku, Tsedale. 2019. *You Don't Look Like a Lawyer: Black Women and Systemic Gendered Racism.* Lanham, MD: Rowman & Littlefield.

MenCare. 2023. "Guiding Principles." MenCare: A Global Fatherhood Campaign. https://mencare.org/about-mencare/guiding-principles/.

Mendel, Richard. 2021. "Back-to-School Action Guide: Re-engaging Students and Closing the School-to-Prison Pipeline." The Sentencing Project. August 31. https://www.sentencingproject.org/reports/back-to-school-action-guide-re-engaging-students-and-closing-the-school-to-prison-pipeline/.

Merriam-Webster. 2017. "Merriam-Webster's 2017 Words of the Year." https://www.merriam-webster.com/words-at-play/word-of-the-year-2017-feminism/feminism.

Michals, Debra. 2015. "Ruby Bridges." National Women's History Museum. https://www.womenshistory.org/education-resources/biographies/ruby-bridges.

A Mighty Girl. 2017. "100 Years Ago, Women Were Beaten and Tortured for the Right to Vote." Blog. November 14. https://www.amightygirl.com/blog?p=16987&fbclid=IwAR3EHauXbBeTAfn5izC9W7ig0ReH4xwijKa7won1GqFrRhfEacDI66DLEhs.

Miller, Claire C. 2017. "*The Gender Pay Gap Is Largely because of Motherhood.*" *New York Times*, May 13. https://www.nytimes.com/2017/05/13/upshot/the-gender-pay-gap-is-largely-because-of-motherhood.html.

———. 2023a. "A Tradition Going Strong: Brides Who Take Their Husbands' Names." *New York Times*, September 12. https://www.nytimes.com/2023/09/12/upshot/maiden-names-change.html?fbclid=IwAR3_BxokHgZuU8CscNxLR8tsS643InhFLY9OfHaJwEWe4RyYVtrqIlVKs2A.

———. 2023b. "The World 'Has Found a Way to Do This': The US Lags on Paid Leave." *New York Times*, June 22. https://www.nytimes.com/2021/10/25/upshot/paid-leave-democrats.html.

Miller, Mahala. 2023. "The Unexpected Variability of Parental Happiness." *The Society Pages*, April 5. https://thesocietypages.org/discoveries/2023/04/05/surprising-patterns-of-parental-happiness-and-unhappiness/.

Millhiser, Ian. 2023. "The Lawsuits Seeking to Keep Drag Queens Legal, Explained." *Vox*, September 7. https://www.vox.com/2023/9/7/23860447/supreme-court-drag-shows-ban-tennessee-montana-texas-florida-queens.

Mineo, Liz. 2022. "'Shadow Pandemic' of Domestic Violence." *Harvard Gazette*, June 29. https://news.harvard.edu/gazette/story/2022/06/shadow-pandemic-of-domestic-violence/.

Minkin, Rachel, and Anna Brown. 2021. "Rising Shares of US Adults Know Someone Who Is Transgender or Goes by Gender-Neutral Pronouns." Pew Research Center, July 27. https://www.pewresearch.org/short-reads/2021/07/27/rising-shares-of-u-s-adults-know-someone-who-is-transgender-or-goes-by-gender-neutral-pronouns/.

Minsky, Adam. 2024. "$132 Billion in Student Loan Forgiveness Approved: Who Qualifies, and What's Next." *Forbes*, January 5. https://www.forbes.com/sites/adamminsky/2024/01/05/132-billion-in-student-loan-forgiveness-approved-who-qualifies-and-whats-next/?sh=63d0648a4a01.

Moms F1rst. 2023. "About." https://momsfirst.us/about/.

Montoya-Galvez, Camilo. 2022. "Investigation Finds Women Detained by ICE Underwent 'Unnecessary Gynecological Procedures' at Georgia Facility." CBS News, November 15. https://www.cbsnews.com/news/women-detained-ice-unnecessary-gynecological-procedures-georgia-facility-investigation/.

Morgan, Rachel E., and Barbara A. Oudekerk. 2019. "Criminal Victimizations, 2018." Bureau of Justice Statistics. September. https://bjs.ojp.gov/content/pub/pdf/cv18_sum.pdf.

Moriarty, Erin. 2023. "Living an Intersex Life." CBS News, October 29. https://www.cbsnews.com/news/living-an-intersex-life/.

Murray, Conor. 2023. "'Barbie' Largely Praised for Feminist Themes—But Draws Anger from the Anti-Woke." *Forbes*, July 26. https://www.forbes.com/sites/conormurray/2023/07/21/barbie-largely-praised-for-feminist-themes-but-draws-anger-from-the-anti-woke/?sh=7fca3f0858bd.

Mustian, Jim. 2020. "Prosecutors Charge 3 with Threatening Women in R. Kelly Case." ABC News, August 12. https://abcnews.go.com/Entertainment/wireStory/prosecutors-charge-threatening-women-kelly-case-72329670.

My Brother's Keeper Alliance. 2022. "MBK Alliance: What Works." June 22. https://www.obama.org/my-brothers-keeper-alliance/news/what-works/.

Myers, Justin. 2022. "This Is Siri's New Gender-Neutral Voice in Apple's iOS 15.4 for iPhone." *Gadget Hacks*, March 14. https://ios.gadgethacks.com/how-to/is-siris-new-gender-neutral-voice-apples-ios-15-4-for-iphone-0384979/.

National Alliance to End Homelessness. 2023. "Domestic Violence." https://endhomelessness.org/homelessness-in-america/what-causes-homelessness/domestic-violence/.

National Archives. 2024a. "Plessy v. Ferguson (1896)." https://www.archives.gov/milestone-documents/plessy-v-ferguson#:~:text=The%20ruling%20in%20this%20Supreme,numerous%20laws%20passed%20by%20Congress.

———. 2024b. "Brown v. Board of Education (1954)." https://www.archives.gov/milestone-documents/brown-v-board-of-education.

National Center for Education Statistics. 2018. "Table 318.10: Degrees Conferred by Postsecondary Institutions, by Level of Degree and Sex of Student: Selected Years, 1869–70 through 2028–29." *Digest of Education Statistics*.

National Council on Crime and Delinquency. 2019. "And Justice for Some: Differential Treatment of Youth of Color in the Juvenile System." Gault Center.

National Institute of Mental Health. 2019. "Suicide." https://www.nimh.nih.gov/health/statistics/suicide.shtml.

National Institutes of Health. 2023. "Understanding the Impact of Misgendering and Deadnaming." NIH Office of Intramural Training & Education, July 31. https://oitecareersblog.od.nih.gov/2023/07/31/understanding-the-impact-of-misgendering-and-deadnaming/.

National Low Income Housing Coalition (NLIHC). 2022. "Out of Reach: The High Cost of Housing." https://nlihc.org/oor.

National Network to End Domestic Violence (NNEDV). 2019. "Violence Against Women Reauthorization Act (VAWA) 2019." June. https://nnedv.org/wpcontent/uploads/2019/10/Library_Policy_VAWA_reauthorization_2019.pdf.

———. 2020. "Violence Against Women Act." April 22. https://nnedv.org/content/violence-against-women-act/.

———. 2022. "NNEDV Applauds Final Passage of the VAWA Reauthorization." March 10. https://nnedv.org/latest_update/nnedv-applauds-senate-passage-vawa-reauthorization/

National Responsible Fatherhood Clearinghouse. "About Us." Office of Family Assistance. https://www.fatherhood.gov/about-us.

National Sexual Violence Resource Center (NSVRC). 2012. "False Reporting." https://www.nsvrc.org/sites/default/files/Publications_NSVRC_Overview_False-Reporting.pdf.

National Women's Law Center (NWLC). 2012. "Fact Sheet: The Battle for Gender Equity in Athletics in Colleges and Universities." June. https://nwlc.org/wp-content/uploads/2015/08/battle_in_college_athletics_final_6.14.12_231.pdf.

———. 2019a. "How the Paycheck Fairness Act Will Strengthen the Equal Pay Act." January 27. https://nwlc.org/resource/how-the-paycheck-fairness-act-will-strengthen-the-equal-pay-act/

———. 2019b. "Unemployment Insurance and Protections Are Vital for Women and Families." December. https://nwlc.org/wp-content/uploads/2019/12/UI-Factsheet-2019.pdf.

———. 2021a. "Motherhood Wage Gap for Mothers Overall: 2021 State Rankings." April 29. https://nwlc.org/resource/motherhood-wage-gap-for-mothers-overall/.

———. 2021b. "The Wage Gap: The Who, How, Why, and What to Do." September 24. https://nwlc.org/wp-content/uploads/2019/09/Wage-Gap-Who-how.pdf

———. 2022. "Press Release: In 2021, More than 12 million Women and Girls Lacked Health Insurance; Poverty Rates Still Adversely Affected Women of Color at Higher Rates than Their White Counterparts, and the Wage Gap Has for Women Overall Widened to 84 Cents." September 13. https://nwlc.org/press-release/in-2021-more-than-12-million-women-and-girls-lacked-health-insurance-poverty-rates-still-adversely-affected-women-of-color-at-higher-rates-than-their-white-counterparts-and-the-wage-gap-has-for-wom/https://nwlc.org/resource/the-wage-gap-the-who-how-why-and-what-to-do/.

———. 2023. "Trans, Queer & Underpaid: Emerging LGBTQI+ Pay Gap Data." National Women's Law Center. June 15. https://nwlc.org/resource/trans-queer-underpaid-emerging-lgbtqi-pay-gap-data/.

Nduagbo, Kieran Chidi. 2020. "How Gender Disparities Affect Classroom Learning." Association of Supervision and Curriculum Development. *EL Magazine*, July 23. https://www.ascd.org/el/articles/how-gender-disparities-affect-classroom-learning.

Ness, Debra. 2019. "Parental Leave for Federal Government Employees Advances the Fight for Paid Leave." National Partnership for Women and Families. December 9. https://www.nationalpartnership.org/our-impact/news-room/press-statements/parental-leave-for-federal-employees-advances-paid-leave.html.

New York Times. 2023. "Tracking Abortion Bans across the Country." August 23. https://www.nytimes.com/interactive/2022/us/abortion-laws-roe-v-wade.html.

Newsom, Jennifer S., dir. 2015. *The Mask You Live In* [motion picture].

Newsom, Jennifer Siebel. 2019. "It's Time to Stop Treating Parenting as a Mom's Burden and a Dad's Adorable Hobby." *Glamour*, October 10. https://www.glamour.com/story/jennifer-siebel-newsom-gavin-newsom-parenthood-partnership?fbclid=IwAR3UwM2IGNu-XamEDblGFRiZyNcHMq4Q3ZqcTAc43DGOWjj8PZnGhTK4Eg0.

Nilsen, Ella. 2019. "The House Just Passed a Bill to Close the Gender Pay Gap." *Vox*, March 27. https://www.vox.com/2019/3/27/18282775/paycheck-fairness-act-gender-pay-gap-pelosi.

Nonko, Emily. 2019. "The Study Group Bringing bell hooks to Prisons." Next City. April 3. https://nextcity.org/daily/entry/the-study-group-bringing-bell-hooks-to-prisons?fbclid=IwAR2MtdZKGc-trl-Cg-RV9h57pbg8ltxxW-YC4Sn3yzi2wfQix-p4UM9cagw.

North, Anna. 2017. "For Every Harvey Weinstein, There's a Hundred More Men in the Neighborhood Who Are Doing the Exact Same Thing." *Vox*, October 28. https://www.vox.com/2017/10/28/16563668/me-too-tarana-burke-harvey-weinstein-harassment-assault.

———. 2019. "What's Next for #Metoo? This College Might Have the Answer." *Vox*, October 10. https://www.vox.com/identities/2019/10/10/20885824/me-too-movement-sexual-assault-college-campus?fbclid=IwAR0cNdld6vtg0oYXhMqCEw4yMzFnMEQP2LT_hrRmqpNlhVrlXoGAX0sYka4.

Office of Civil Rights. 2023. "Title IX and Sex Discrimination." US Department of Education. https://www2.ed.gov/about/offices/list/ocr/docs/tix_dis.html.

Office of Family Violence Prevention and Services. 2016. "Domestic Violence and Homelessness: Statistics." US Department of Health and Human Services. https://www.acf.hhs.gov/ofvps/fact-sheet/domestic-violence-and-homelessness-statistics-2016#:~:text=According%20to%20multiple%20studies%20examining,had%20previously%20experienced%20domestic%20violence.

Oliveira, Diego, Yifang Ma, Teresa Woodruff, and Brian Uzzi. 2019. "Comparison of National Institutes of Health Grant Amounts to First-Time Male and Female Principal Investigators." *JAMA*, March 5: 898–900. https://jamanetwork.com/journals/jama/fullarticle/2726973.

Onu, David. 2022. "Qualities of a Good Father That Will Transform Your Family Now." September 9. https://davidonu.com/qualities-of-a-good-father/#.

Ordoñez, Franco. 2023. "Book Bans Are on The Rise. Biden Is Naming a Point Person to Address That." National Public Radio, June 8. https://www.npr.org/2023/06/08/1180941627/biden-pride-month-book-bans.

Oremus, Will. 2014. "Here Are All the Different Genders You Can Be on Facebook." *Slate*, February 13. https://slate.com/technology/2014/02/facebook-custom-gender-options-here-are-all-56-custom-options.html.

Orenstein, Peggy. 2019. "The Miseducation of the American Boy." *The Atlantic*, December 20. https://www.theatlantic.com/magazine/archive/2020/01/the-miseducation-of-the-american-boy/603046/?fbclid=IwAR13xJbDP0aylivjjnlBp_9BIVDMBmeGqlSwxstU5WWYTx0Ifc1juR9IVUs#Update1.

Organisation for Economic Co-Operation and Development (OECD). 2022. "Health Status: Maternal and Infant Mortality." https://stats.oecd.org/Index.aspx?ThemeTreeId=9#.

Pampel, Fred. 2011. "Cohort Changes in the Socio-Demographic Determinants of Gender Egalitarianism." *Social Forces*, 89(3): 961–82.

Paoletti, Jo B. 2012. *Pink and Blue: Telling Girls from Boys in America*. Bloomington: Indiana University Press.

Parker, Annise. 2024. "Out for America 2023: An Overview of LGBTQ+ Elected Officials in the US." LGBTQ+ Victory Institute. https://victoryinstitute.org/out-for-america-2023/.

Parker, Kim. 2021. "What's Behind the Growing Gap Between Men and Women in College Completion?" Pew Research Center. November 8. https://www.pewresearch.org/short-reads/2021/11/08/whats-behind-the-growing-gap-between-men-and-women-in-college-completion/.

Parker, Kim, Juliana Menasce Horowitz and Anna Brown. 2022. "Americans' Complex Views on Gender Identity and Transgender Issues." Pew Research Center. June 28. https://www.pewresearch.org/social-trends/2022/06/28/americans-complex-views-on-gender-identity-and-transgender-issues/?fbclid=IwAR3ZKEEGZUzr9FTDQiKh4jt7KXSzgFf6x0i8fKlCim6ZhLOzbhnf2qbVJVU.

Parker, Kim, and Rachel Minkin. 2023. "Public Has Mixed Views on the Modern American Family." Pew Research Center, September 14. https://www.pewresearch.org/social-trends/2023/09/14/public-has-mixed-views-on-the-modern-american-family/.

Patton, Elaina. 2023. "'Every Body' Puts Faces to the Long-Silenced Intersex Community." NBC News, June 30. https://www.nbcnews.com/nbc-out/out-pop-culture/every-body-puts-faces-long-silenced-intersex-community-rcna91992.

Paul, Larisha. 2023. "Demi Lovato Re-adopted 'She/Her' Pronouns because Explaining 'They/Them' Was 'Exhausting.'" *Rolling Stone*, June 14. https://www.rollingstone.com/music/music-news/demi-lovato-explains-only-using-they-them-pronouns-was-exhausting-1234771153/.

Pawlowski, Agnes. 2019. "Women Make Up the Majority of US Medical Students for the First Time." Today. December 13. https://www.today.com/health/women-make-majority-u-s-medical-students-first-time-t169922?yptr=yahoo.

Peck, Emily. 2019a. "Half the Men in the US Are Uncomfortable with Female Political Leaders." *Huffington Post*, November 19. https://www.huffpost.com/entry/half-us-men-uncomfortable-with-female-political-leaders_n_5dd30b73e4b0263fbc993674.

———. 2019b. "Women at Ernst & Young Instructed on How to Dress, Act Nicely around Men." *Huffington Post*, October 21. https://www.huffpost.com/entry/women-ernst-young-how-to-dress-act-around-men_n_5da721eee4b002e33e78606a?fbclid=IwAR3SvnXpOS0bEOKNr0Nl7cR-JtdsoctVEavHhbdONGSGo5ientBXV8YphJo.

Perales, Francisco, Ella Kuskoff, Michael Flood, and Tania King. 2023. "Like Father, Like Son: Empirical Insights into the Intergenerational Continuity of Masculinity Ideology." *Sex Roles*, 88: 399–402.

Perez-Pena, Richard, and Vivian Yee. 2019. "Saudi Women's Rights Activists Granted Release, but Their Trial Continues." *New York Times, March 28.* https://www.nytimes.com/2019/03/28/world/middleeast/saudi-arabia-women-rights-activists.html.

Perrin, Liese M. 2001. "Resisting Reproduction: Reconsidering Slave Contraception in the Old South." *Journal of American Studies*, 35(2): 255–74.

Perry, Todd. 2020. "A Twitter Misogynist Called Feminists 'Unhappy' and Got Burnt to a Crisp in His Responses." Upworthy. January 30. https://www.upworthy.com/a-twitter-misogynist-called-feminists-unhappy-and-got-burnt-to-a-crisp-in-his-responses.

Petts, Richard J., and Daniel L. Carlson. 2019. "If I [Take] Leave, Will You Stay? Paternity Leave and Relationship Stability." *The Society Pages*, November 19. https://thesocietypages.org/ccf/2019/11/19/if-i-take-leave-will-you-stay-paternity-leave-and-relationship-stability/?fbclid=IwAR1Brx9adyqquH6PuGTrcR5TpTK7Jw1wlUn446zK2_AovTm9xgl3F7pOqNM.

Pew Research Center. 2013. "A History of Key Abortion Ruling of the US Supreme Court." Pew Research Center, January 16. https://www.pewforum.org/2013/01/16/a-history-of-key-abortion-rulings-of-the-us-supreme-court/.

———. 2022. "Majority of Public Disapproves of Supreme Court's Decision to Overturn Roe v. Wade." Pew Research Center, July 6. https://www.pewresearch.org/politics/2022/07/06/majority-of-public-disapproves-of-supreme-courts-decision-to-overturn-roe-v-wade/?utm_content=buffer2a47f&utm_medium=social&utm_source=twitter.com&utm_campaign=buffer.

Phelps, Steven W., and Robbee Wedow. 2019. "What Genetics Is Teaching Us about Sexuality." *New York Times*, August 29. https://www.nytimes.com/2019/08/29/opinion/genetics-sexual-orientation-study.html?fbclid=IwAR08E3ycooR8gIe75VtizuWiDTDzha0OUJPplCmLJ4OVNgYGri111jMCcyY.

Phillips, Dave. 2016. "North Carolina Bans Local Anti-Discrimination Policies." *New York Times*, March 23. https://www.nytimes.com/2016/03/24/us/north-carolina-to-limit-bathroom-use-by-birth-gender.html?module=inline.

Phillips, Rod. 2023. "When Did Humans Start Getting Divorced?" TED-Ed Animations. https://ed.ted.com/lessons/a-brief-history-of-divorce-rod-phillips?fbclid=IwAR1WT9ieH82NRM-3SXnVLDKJX7zXzrawl2785Zo-7LKC1QXlxNR5-KUeaQo.

Pierre-Bravo, Daniela. 2023. "Latinas Need to Work until They're 90 to Earn What White Men Make by Age 60." MSNBC, October 4. https://www.msnbc.com/know-your-value/business-culture/latina-equal-pay-day-2023-latina-workers-get-paid-52-n1307275.

Plataforma SINC. 2008. "Medical Textbooks Use White, Heterosexual Men as a 'Universal Model.'" *Science Daily*. https://www.sciencedaily.com/releases/2008/10/081015132108.htm.

Powell, Kevin. 2020. "Confessions of a Recovering Misogynist." In *Gender Through the Prism of Difference*, edited by Maxine Baca Zinn, Pierrette Hondagneu-Sotelo, and Michael. A. Messner. New York: Oxford University Press.

Powell, Tiffany. 2019. "Institutions of Higher Violence: The Influence of Pornography on College Sexual Assault." National Center on Sexual Exploitation, March 20. https://endsexualexploitation.org/articles/institutions-of-higher-violence-the-influence-of-pornography-on-college-sexual-assault/#:~:text=Of%20the%2050%20most%20common,and%2049%25%20contained%20verbal%20aggression.

Powers, Ashley. 2019. "'I Would Take Out $40, $50 at a Time and Put It in This Duffel Bag.' The Cost of Leaving an Abusive Relationship." *California Sunday Magazine*, October 3. https://story.californiasunday.com/escape-domestic-violence/.

Preisner, Klaus, Franz Neuberger, Ariane Bertogg, and Julia Schaub. 2019. "Does Having Kids Make You Happier?" *Gender & Society Blog*, October 7. https://gendersociety.wordpress.com/2019/10/07/does-having-kids-make-you-happier/?fbclid=IwAR0CU27GN3lNrcBU14FH8koN2NOC5bD8S1M4-JeOTtX6D70WenUuq2RXl4w.

Queally, James, and Richard Winton. 2019. "Harvey Weinstein Pleads Not Guilty to Two New Sexual Assault Charges in New York; Trial Delayed to 2020." *LA Times*, August 26. https://www.latimes.com/california/story/2019-08-26/harvey-weinstein-facing-two-new-sexual-assault-charges-in-new-york-trial-delayed-to-2020.

Quinlan, Casey. 2016. "The Beginning of 'Two Cultures': By Preschool, Boys and Girls Are Already Segregated." *Think Progress*, February 29. https://thinkprogress.org/the-beginning-of-two-cultures-by-preschool-boys-and-girls-are-already-segregated-219b6b4e76d0/.

Quinn, Melissa. 2023. "One Year after Roe v. Wade's Reversal, Warnings about Abortion Become Reality." CBS News, June 23. https://www.cbsnews.com/news/one-year-roe-v-wade-reversal-dobbs-decision-warnings-about-abortion-become-reality/.

Radde, Kaitlyn. 2022. "What Does the Respect for Marriage Act Do? The Answer Will Vary by State." National Public Radio. December 8. https://www.npr.org/2022/12/08/1140808263/what-does-the-respect-for-marriage-act-do-the-answer-will-vary-by-state.

Ravitz, Jessica. 2016. "The Surprising History of Abortion in the United States." CNN, June 27. https://www.cnn.com/2016/06/23/health/abortion-history-in-united-states/index.html.

Read, Max. 2012. "Wesleyan Sued Over 'Rape Factory' Frat House." *Gawker*, October 9. https://gawker.com/5950277/wesleyan-sued-over-rape-factory-frat-house.

Reagan, Leslie. 1996. *When Abortion Was a Crime*. Berkeley: University of California Press.

Redfield, Elana, Kerith J. Conron, Will Tentindo, and Erica Browning. 2023. "Report: Prohibiting Gender-Affirming Medical Care for Youth." UCLA School of Law Williams Institute. March. https://williamsinstitute.law.ucla.edu/publications/bans-trans-youth-health-care/.

Reese, Phillip. 2019. "When Masculinity Turns 'Toxic': A Gender Profile of Mass Shootings." *Los Angeles Times*, October 7. https://www.latimes.com/science/story/2019-10-07/mass-shootings-toxic-masculinity?fbclid=IwAR1LGop6bZ5AB7OeDwdwn-mq1vAYOYnJ4TW3ow3mMWBrrI5AEHy495Zh9eE.

Reilly, Katie. 2022. "Florida's Governor Just Signed the 'Stop Woke Act.' Here's What It Means for Schools and Businesses." *Time*, April 22. https://time.com/6168753/florida-stop-woke-law/.

Reiner, Andrew. 2023. "The 'Manning Up' of Boys Begins in the Cradle, But What Boys Really Need Is Emotional Support from Their Dads." National Public Radio. June 15. https://www.wbur.org/cognoscenti/2023/06/15/boys-in-crisis-masculinity-andrew-reiner?fbclid=IwAR2UIL0A431XzlRjLnX_Y8PATvUap94EdvKqfP5JODX4Xi5xVDZCT77AErQ.

Reinhart, R. J. 2021. "US: 9 in 10 See a Woman Leading the US in Ten Years." Gallup. March 8. https://news.gallup.com/poll/330530/u.s.-nine-woman-leading-u.s.-years.aspx.

Relman, Eliza. 2019. "The 25 Women Who Have Accused Trump of Sexual Misconduct." *Business Insider*, October 09. https://www.businessinsider.com/women-accused-trump-sexual-misconduct-list-2017-12.

Rennison, Callie Marie. 2002. "Rape and Sexual Assault: Reporting to Police and Medical Attention 1992–2000." Bureau of Justice Statistics. August. https://www.bjs.gov/content/pub/pdf/rsarp00.pdf.

Rennison, Callie, and Amy Bonomi. 2020. *Women Leading Change in Academia*. San Diego: Congnella Academic Publishing.

Representation Project. 2023. *Fair Play*. https://therepproject.org/films/fair-play/.

Richards, Libby, Melissa Franks, and Rosie Shrout. 2023. "Married Men Are Healthier than Everyone Else. Here's Why They Get the Best End of the Deal." *Fortune*, January 13. https://fortune.com/2023/01/13/why-are-married-men-healthier-on-average-women-gender-research/.

Rider, G. Nicole, Barbara J. McMorris, Amy L. Gower, Eli Coleman, and Marla E. Eisenberg. 2018. "Health and Care Utilization of Transgender and Gender Nonconforming Youth: A Population-Based Study." *Pediatrics*, 141(3). https://publications.aap.org/pediatrics/article-abstract/141/3/e20171683/37588/Health-and-Care-Utilization-of-Transgender-and?redirectedFrom=fulltext.

Riley, R. L. 2019. "Beauty Brands Want to Sell Queer Expression, But It Shouldn't Be for Sale." *Teen Vogue*, October 21. https://www.teenvogue.com/story/beauty-brands-queer-expression-makeup?fbclid=IwAR3HfGAwCVAC2WlMVwmYJa5o3IlhbvZv8MFZnwL8w_x2imumri9_LL8VKc8.

Rios, Victor M. 2020. "The Consequences of the Criminal Justice Pipeline on Black and Latino Masculinity." In *Gender Through the Prism of Difference*, edited by Maxine Baca Zinn, Pierrette Hondagneu-Sotelo, and Michael. A. Messner, 501–8. New York: Oxford University Press.

Roberts, Soraya. 2019. "How the Internet Killed Feminism." *Jezebel*. December 12. https://jezebel.com/how-the-internet-killed-feminism-1839983896?fbclid=IwAR24H1Q8qy_rcxlg61cOCbJE1kTUh271kmnBJoOUlf7Tt6U9j5_ZXqYFr0o.

Robinson, Carol. 2019. "Ex-Cop Surrenders after Estranged Wife Found Dead in Mountain Brook." Alabama.com, December 2. https://www.al.com/news/birmingham/2019/12/woman-found-dead-in-mountain-brook-was-selfless-servant-leader.html.

Rosalsky, Greg. 2023. "I'm a New Dad. Here's Why I'm Taking More Parental Leave than My Wife." *Planet Money*, August 22. https://www.npr.org/sections/money/2023/08/22/1194946948/im-a-new-dad-heres-why-im-taking-more-parental-leave-than-my-wife?fbclid=IwAR0wZUxArqo_QIE2Qq0G9zFNuCeFEPV7nQkcBi8wH32KfdKio3RQnM6JbTg.

Ross, Loretta. 2020. "What Is Reproductive Justice?" In *Reproductive Justice Briefing Book: A Primer on Reproductive Justice and Social Change*. Berkeley Law. https://www.law.berkeley.edu/php-programs/courses/fileDL.php?fID=4051.

Rothberg, Emma. 2023. "Laverne Cox." National Women's History Museum. https://www.womenshistory.org/education-resources/biographies/laverne-cox.

Ryan, Erin Gloria. 2014. "Infamous 'Rapebait' Frat Disbanded for Being Entirely Too Rapey." *Jezebel*, April 04. https://jezebel.com/infamous-rapebait-frat-disbanded-for-being-entirely-t-1558252895.

Ryan, Michelle K., and Alexander Haslam. 2005. "The Glass Cliff: Evidence that Women Are Over-Represented in Precarious Leadership Positions." *British Journal of Management, 16(2), 81–90.*

Ryle, Robyn. 2018. *Questioning Gender: A Sociological Exploration, 3rd ed.* Thousand Oaks. CA: Sage.

Saad, Lydia. 2020. "Americans Regard Gender Equality as Unfinished Business." Gallup News, August 10. https://news.gallup.com/poll/317009/americans-regard-gender-equality-unfinished-business.aspx?fbclid=IwAR1PySDwsXhBAcWciwysmqcsrZlgb5D9FFn4g-zPRkO56OQlOcVXYGlht7o.

Sadker, David, and Karen R. Zittleman. 2009. *Still Failing at Fairness: How Gender Bias Cheats Girls and Boys in School and What We Can Do about It.* New York: Simon & Schuster.

Saguy, Abigail C. and Juliet A Williams. 2019. "Why We Should All Use They/Them Pronouns." *Scientific American*, April 11. https://blogs.scientificamerican.com/voices/why-we-should-all-use-they-them-pronouns/.

Savage, Mark. 2020. "R. Kelly: The History of Allegations Against Him." BBC News, August 28. https://www.bbc.com/news/entertainment-arts-40635526.

Schilt, Kristen, and Matthew Wiswall. 2008. "Before and After: Gender Transitions, Human Capital, and Workplace Experiences." *B.E. Journal of Economic Analysis and Policy*, 8(1): article 39.

Schneider, Gregory S., Laura Vozzella, and Patricia Sullivan. 2020. "'A Long Time to Wait': Virginia Passes Equal Rights Amendment in Historic Vote." *Washington Post*, January 15. https://www.washingtonpost.com/local/virginia-politics/2020/01/15/0475d51a-36f1-11ea-9541-9107303481a4_story.html?fbclid=IwAR1WRNqH2pl-CvtL89BDWoNh3rzlrjjJMSVfyLFR2qCD0Cg1-g03Syz1T_I.

Schneider, Monica C., and Angela L. Bos. 2014. "Measuring Stereotypes of Female Politicians." *Political Psychology*, 35(2): 245–66.

Schoenbaum, Hannah. 2023. "Veto Overridden: Ban on Gender-Affirming Care for Minors Takes Effect in North Carolina." Associated Press. August 17. https://apnews.com/article/transgender-health-care-veto-override-north-carolina-536351cc360a92cdd21f298f6212e6d2.

Scimeca, Dennis. 2020. "Indie Developer Mocks GamerGate, Chased from Home with Rape and Death Threats." Daily Dot. March 1. https://www.dailydot.com/parsec/brianna-we-gamergate-threats/.

Seitz, Amanda. 2022. "Social Media Platforms Fail to Stop LGBTQ Hate Speech, according to GLAAD Report." *PBS News Hour*, July 13. https://www.pbs.org/newshour/nation/social-media-platforms-fail-to-stop-lgbtq-hate-speech-according-to-glaad-report.

Semega, Jessica. 2019. "Pay Is Up. Poverty Is Down. How Women Are Making Strides." Payday, Poverty, and Women, US Census Bureau. September 10. https://www.census.gov/library/stories/2019/09/payday-poverty-and-women.html.

Shadel, Molly Bishop, Sophie Trawalter, and J. H. Verkerke. 2022. "Gender Differences in Law School Classroom Participation: The Key Role of Social Context." *Virginia Law Review*, February 20. https://virginialawreview.org/articles/gender-differences-in-law-school-classroom-participation-the-key-role-of-social-context/.

Sharlach, Molly. 2022. "Study Points to Strategies for Closing the Participation Gender Gap in Engineering Courses." Phys.org. Princeton University. March 22. https://phys.org/news/2022-03-strategies-gender-gap-courses.html.

She Should Run. 2020. "We Help Women Explore the Possibility of a Run." May 23. https://www.sheshouldrun.org/what-we-do/.

She the People. 2024. "This Is Our Time." About Us. https://www.shethepeople.org/.

Shepardson, David. 2021. "Pete Buttigieg Becomes First Openly Gay Cabinet Secretary Confirmed by US Senate." Reuters. February 2. https://www.reuters.com/article/idUSKBN2A22IP/.

Shepherd, Katie. 2019. "A Former Police Officer Escaped Charged after Shooting His Wife in the Arm. Months Later, He Allegedly Murdered Her." *Washington Post*, December 5. https://www.washington

post.com/nation/2019/12/05/jason-bragg-mcintosh-megan-montgomery-murder-birmingham-alabama-cop/.

———. 2019. "She Needed to Fill Her Prescription for the Morning-After Pill. The Pharmacist Refused, She Alleges, Because of His 'Beliefs.'" *Washington Post*, December 13. https://www.washingtonpost.com/nation/2019/12/13/minnesota-woman-rejected-morning-after-pill-pharmacist-beliefs-birth-control/?fbclid=IwAR1iss3bnXUYvEkVxJ_6xelPJ_kwhaphhN8G-iJJVNI6nTbFeKP2A8Eq4fE.

Sherman, Mark. 2023. "The Supreme Court Rejects Biden's Plan to Wipe Away $400 Billion in Student Loan Debt." Associated Press. June 30. https://apnews.com/article/student-loan-forgiveness-supreme-court-653c2e9c085863bdbf81f125f87669fa.

Slagter, Martin. 2020. "New Cross-Examination Rule in Campus Sexual Assault Cases Reflects Past Court Rulings against University of Michigan." *MLive*, May 07. https://www.mlive.com/news/ann-arbor/2020/05/new-cross-examination-rule-in-campus-sexual-assault-cases-reflects-past-court-rulings-against-university-of-michigan.html?fbclid=IwAR0IdyM6lc23mTFB31_C8qaGvpxvxDe_wClnZ1xLWE1AkBSXr7_jtQT1VhY.

Smith, Sharon, Xinjian Zhang, Kathleen C. Basile, Melissa T. Merrick, Jing Wang, Marcie-jo Kresnow, and Jieru Chen. 2018. National Intimate Partner and Sexual Violence Survey (NISVS): 2015 Data Brief—Updated Release. National Center for Injury Prevention and Control, Centers for Disease Control and Prevention. https://www.nsvrc.org/resource/2500/national-intimate-partner-and-sexual-violence-survey-2015-data-brief-updated-release.

———. 2020. National Intimate Partner and Sexual Violence Survey: 2015 Data Brief. April 27. National Center for Injury Prevention and Control, Centers for Disease Control and Prevention.

Society of Family Planning. 2023. "#WeCount Report." Society of Family Planning, April 11. https://societyfp.org/wp-content/uploads/2023/10/WeCountReport_10.16.23.pdf.

Sorbara, Julia C., Lyne N. Chiniara, Shelby Thompson, and Mark Palmert. 2020. "Mental Health and Timing of Gender-Affirming Care." *Pediatrics*, 146(4). https://publications.aap.org/pediatrics/article/146/4/e20193600/79683/Mental-Health-and-Timing-of-Gender-Affirming-Care?searchresult=1.

Southern Poverty Law Center. 2020. "Male Supremacy." June 27. https://www.splcenter.org/fighting-hate/extremist-files/ideology/male-supremacy.

Sparks, Hannah. 2020. "Gender Reveal Party Inventor Begs for End to 'Toxic' Trend Amid Wildfires." *New York Post*, September 8. https://nypost.com/2020/09/08/gender-reveal-party-inventor-begs-for-end-to-trend-amid-wildfires/.

Specia, Megan. 2019. "Saudi Arabia Granted Women the Right to Drive. A Year On, It's Still Complicated." *New York Times*, June 24, https://www.nytimes.com/2019/06/24/world/middleeast/saudi-driving-ban-anniversary.html.

Stanford Poverty Law Center. 2019. "State of the Union 2018." *Pathways: A Magazine on Poverty, Inequality, and Social Policy*. https://inequality.stanford.edu/publications/pathway/state-union-2019.

Stein, Perry. 2018. "No Longer Just Male or Female: D.C. Schools to Give Families a Third Option With 'Non-Binary.'" *Washington Post*, November 12. https://www.washingtonpost.com/local/education/no-longer-just-male-or-female-dc-schools-to-give-families-a-third-option-with-nonbinary/2018/11/12/dc34d9e5-a70c-43a1-84b7-bcd6e3acd19b_story.html.

Steinmetz, Katy. 2020. "People Have Invented More than 200 Gender-Neutral Pronouns. Here's Why 'They' Is Here to Stay." *Time Magazine*, January 17. https://time.com/5763175/they-as-singular-pronoun/?fbclid=IwAR0kLN2zB7BkVRKr1y0iB4CE0G7GD2QFDgIUXoF_dp3hfAU7BMGhnVnowdM.

Stolberg, Sheryl Gay. 2021. "'This Is Politics': Dr. Rachel Levine's Rise as Transgender Issues Gain Prominence." *New York Times*, May 10. https://www.nytimes.com/2021/05/08/us/politics/rachel-levine-transgender.html.

Stracqualursi, Veronica. 2018. "Biden Says He Would 'Beat the Hell' Out of Trump If in High School." CNN News, March 21. https://www.cnn.com/2018/03/21/politics/joe-biden-donald-trump/index.html.

Sullivan, Kate. 2019. "Here Are the 4 Congresswomen Known as 'The Squad' Targeted by Trump's Racist Tweets." CNN News, July 16. https://www.cnn.com/2019/07/15/politics/who-are-the-squad/index.html.

Summers, D. J. 2022. "Which States Have Mandatory Arrests for Domestic Violence? What Are Their Impacts?" Fox 31. May 13. https://kdvr.com/news/data/which-states-have-mandatory-arrest-dv-laws-and-what-impact-do-they-have/.

Surgo Ventures. 2023. "Maternal Vulnerability in the US— A Shameful Problem for One of the World's Wealthiest Countries." Surgo Ventures. https://mvi.surgoventures.org.

Sussman, Anna Louie. 2023. "Why Aren't More People Marrying? Ask Women What Dating Is Like." *New York Times*, November 11. https://www.nytimes.com/2023/11/11/opinion/marriage-women-men-dating.html?fbclid=IwAR0T2BduL7ctcQC23nkVV9Wtyq7lCGfTU0hnfuk_iTdSE97DjyrouT0iL2k.

Sylvester, Elliott. 2023. "New Poll Emphasizes Negative Impacts of Anti-LGBTQ Policies on LGBTQ Youth." The Trevor Project, January 19. https://www.thetrevorproject.org/blog/new-poll-emphasizes-negative-impacts-of-anti-lgbtq-policies-on-lgbtq-youth/.

Taub, Amanda. 2020a. "A New Covid-19 Crisis: Domestic Abuse Rises Worldwide." *New York Times*, April 14. https://www.nytimes.com/2020/04/06/world/coronavirus-domestic-violence.html.

———. 2020b. "Pandemic Will 'Take Our Women 10 Years Back' in the Workplace." *New York Times*, September 26. https://www.nytimes.com/2020/09/26/world/covid-women-childcare-equality.html?fbclid=IwAR2bobN_YFk_NwI4HWDF5SA87dZ0-7WEETnIFoEUlFc1XtUhRtsbDQbKbec.

Thomson-DeVeaux, Amelia. 2019. "Gender Will Be an Issue for Men as Well as Women in 2020." FiveThirtyEight. August 08. https://fivethirtyeight.com/features/gender-will-be-an-issue-for-men-as-well-as-women-in-2020/.

Time's Up. 2020. "New TIME'S UP Now Report Finds Pervasive Sexist and Racist Bias in Media Coverage of Harris Selection as VP Pick." Time's Up Now.org. October 6.

Tirado, Fran. "*Queer Eye*'s Jonathan Van Ness: 'I'm Non-Binary.'" *Out Magazine*, June 10. https://www.out.com/lifestyle/2019/6/10/queer-eyes-jonathan-van-ness-im-nonbinary.

Toalson, Rachel. 2017. "A Dad Is Not a Babysitter or a Helper. He's a Parent." *Huffington Post*, December 6. https://www.huffpost.com/entry/a-dad-is-not-a-babysitter-or-a-helper_b_8911878.

Tolan, Casey. 2020. "Some Cities See Jumps in Domestic Violence During the Pandemic." CNN. April 4. https://www.cnn.com/2020/04/04/us/domestic-violence-coronavirus-calls-cases-increase-invs/index.html.

Topping, Alexandra. 2020. "Working Mothers Interrupted More Often than Fathers in Lockdown-Study." *The Guardian*, May 27. https://www.theguardian.com/world/2020/may/27/working-mothers-interrupted-more-often-than-fathers-in-lockdown-study?utm_term=RWRpdG9yaWFsX1RoZVdlZWtJblBhdHJpYXJjaHktMjAwNTMw&utm_source=esp&utm_medium=Email&utm_campaign=TheWeekInPatriarchy&CMP=weekinpatria.

Totenberg, Nina, and Sarah McCammon. 2022. "Supreme Court Overturns Roe v. Wade, Ending Right to Abortion Upheld for Decades." National Public Radio, June 24. https://www.npr.org/2022/06/24/1102305878/supreme-court-abortion-roe-v-wade-decision-overturn.

Trevor Project. 2023. "Explore Trevor: Our Work." https://www.thetrevorproject.org/explore/.

Tron, Gina. 2020. "Women Are Being Kicked Out of Domestic Violence Shelters for Self-Medicating the Trauma of Abuse." Rewire News Group. January 7. https://rewirenewsgroup.com/2020/01/07/women-are-being-kicked-out-of-domestic-violence-shelters-for-self-medicating-the-trauma-of-abuse/.

Trotta, Daniel. 2023a. "US Court Blocks Florida Law Restricting Drag Performances." Reuters, June 23. https://www.reuters.com/legal/us-court-blocks-florida-law-restricting-drag-performances-2023-06-23/#:~:text=June%2023%20(Reuters)%20%2D%20A,concern%20gender%20or%20LGBTQ%20matters.

———. 2023b. "US Court Strikes Down Florida Transgender Health Rule." Reuters, June 23. https://www.reuters.com/legal/us-court-strikes-down-florida-transgender-health-rule-2023-06-22/.

Truman, Jennifer L., and Rachel E. Morgan. 2022. "Violent Victimization by Sexual Orientation and Gender Identity, 2017–2020." Bureau of Justice Statistics, June. https://bjs.ojp.gov/library/publications/violent-victimization-sexual-orientation-and-gender-identity-2017-2020.

Tsioulcas, Anastasia. 2019a. "The #MuteRKelly Movement Takes Its Protest to the Steps of His Record Label." National Public Radio. January 16. https://www.npr.org/2019/01/16/685912752/the-muterkelly-movement-takes-its-protest-to-the-steps-of-his-record-label.

———. 2019b. "R. Kelly Pleads Not Guilty to Federal Charges in New York." National Public Radio. August 2. https://www.npr.org/2019/08/02/746684479/r-kelly-pleads-not-guilty-to-federal-charges-in-new-york

Tumin, Remy. 2023. "Title IX and the New Rule on Transgender Athletes Explained." *New York Times*, April 7. https://www.nytimes.com/article/title-ix-transgender-athletes-school-sports.html.

Turban, Jack L., Dana King, Julia Kobe, Sari L. Reisener, and Alex S. Keuroghlian. 2022. "Access to Gender-Affirming Hormones during Adolescence and Mental Health Outcomes among Transgender Adults." *PLOS ONE*, 18(6). https://journals.plos.org/plosone/article?id=10.1371/journal.pone.0261039.

Turner, Deborah. 2021. "Celebrating Black Women Who Helped Pave the Way for More Black Women in Politics." League of Women Voters. February 25. https://www.lwv.org/blog/celebrating-black-women-who-helped-pave-way-more-black-women-politics.

Ulaby, Neda. 2024. "'Barbie' Receives 8 Oscar Nominations, But Was That Kenough?" NPR. January 24. https://www.npr.org/2024/01/24/1226565927/barbie-oscar-snub-gerwig-robbie-gosling.

UN Women. 2019. "Facts and Figures: Leadership and Political Participation." UN Women, June. https://www.unwomen.org/en/what-we-do/leadership-and-political-participation/facts-and-figures.

UN Women; Inter-Parliamentary Union. 2019. "Women in Politics: 2019." UN Women. https://www.unwomen.org/en/digital-library/publications/2019/03/women-in-politics-2019-map#view.

US 116th Congress. 2019–2020. S.270—Paycheck Fairness Act. Washington, DC: https://www.congress.gov/bill/116th-congress/senate-bill/270.

US Congress Joint Economic Committee. 2011. "The Gender Wage Gap Jeopardizes Women's Retirement Security." US Senate, April 12. https://www.jec.senate.gov/public/_cache/files/f6fda396-2623-4e99-817e-bf9387360326/equal-pay-day-2011final.pdf.

US Department of Agriculture (USDA). 2022. "WIC Fact Sheet." Food and Nutrition Service, August 2. https://www.fns.usda.gov/wic/wic-fact-sheet.

———. 2023. "Snap Eligibility." https://www.fns.usda.gov/snap/recipient/eligibility.

US Department of Education. 2011. "Dear Colleague Letter." Washington, D.C., Office of Civil Rights. https://www2.ed.gov/about/offices/list/ocr/letters/colleague-201104.html.

JS Department of Health and Human Services. 2024. "Poverty Guidelines." https://aspe.hhs.gov/topics/poverty-economic-mobility/poverty-guidelines.

US Department of Housing and Urban Development. 2023a. "Glossary of Terms to Affordable Housing." https://archives.hud.gov/local/nv/goodstories/2006-04-06glos.cfm.

———. 2023b. "Rental Assistance." https://www.hud.gov/topics/rental_assistance.

US Department of Justice. 2019. "Usual Weekly Earning of Wage and Salary Workers Third Quarter 2019." Bureau of Labor Statistics. https://www.bls.gov/news.release/pdf/wkyeng.pdf .

US Department of State. 2023. "Selecting Your Gender Marker." Bureau of Consular Affairs. https://travel.state.gov/content/travel/en/passports/need-passport/selecting-your-gender-marker.html.

Us Weekly Staff. 2023. "Mark Ruffalo, Ryan Gosling and More Male Celebrities Who Are Proud Feminists." *Us Weekly*, March 8. https://www.usmagazine.com/celebrity-news/pictures/mark-ruffalo-ryan-gosling-male-celebrities-proud-feminists/.

Vagianos, Alanna. 2018. "The Rape Kit Backlog Shows Exactly How We Regard Women in This Country." *Huffington Post*, April 13. https://www.huffpost.com/entry/the-rape-kit-backlog-shows-exactly-how-we-regard-women-in-this-country_n_5acfb5e1e4b016a07e9a8c65.

Vagianos, Alanna, and Taryn Finley. 2022. "R. Kelly Found Guilty on All Counts in Sexual Abuse Trial." *Huffington Post*, July 10. https://www.huffpost.com/entry/r-kelly-trial-verdict-racketeering_n_614decf6e4b001641193bc02?fbclid=IwAR3tSu_sR34-f5TRxwOmDAphZQYnBFNuQ2aWS2AjavMw7oSU7IwonEhuGKs.

Van Dam, Andrew. 2023. "Millennials Aren't Having Kids. Here's Why." *Washington Post*, November 3. https://www.washingtonpost.com/business/2023/11/03/millennials-only-children/.

Vera, Amir. 2018. "Border Patrol Agent's Gender Reveal Party Ignited a 47,000 Acre Wildfire." CNN, October 2. https://www.cnn.com/2018/10/02/us/az-off-duty-border-patrol-agent-wildfire/index.html.

Vogels, Emily A., and Colleen McClain. 2023. "Key Findings about Online Dating in the US." Pew Research Center. February. https://www.pewresearch.org/short-reads/2023/02/02/key-findings-about-online-dating-in-the-u-s/.

Vogt, Emily, Charley Jiang, Quinton Jenkins, Maya Millette, Martina Caldwell, Kathleen Mehari and Erica Marsh. 2022. "Trends in US Emergency Department Use After Sexual Assault, 2006–2019." *JAMA Network Open*, October 20. https://jamanetwork.com/journals/jamanetworkopen/fullarticle/2797504?utm_source=For_The_Media&utm_medium=referral&utm_campaign=ftm_links&utm_term=102022.

Vote411. 2020. "About Us." May 23. https://www.vote411.org/about.

Wade, Lisa, and Mayra Marx Ferree. 2019. *Gender: Ideas, Interactions, Institutions*, 2 ed. New York: W.W. Norton & Company, Inc.

Wagner, John. 2019. "Joe Biden: I'll Challenge Trump to Do Push-Ups Onstage If He Makes Fun of My Age or Mental State." *Washington Post*, July 16. https://www.washingtonpost.com/politics/joe-biden-ill-challenge-trump-to-do-push-ups-on-stage-if-he-makes-fun-of-my-age-or-mental-state/2019/07/16/efe9d848-a7b3-11e9-a3a6-ab670962db05_story.html?fbclid=IwAR0cmDLURhE9y-f801BFXZ0z8-UVytKRsv4P5puFyb2sBQswjDV.

Wallace, Tim, and Alicia Parlapiano. 2017. "Crowd Scientists Say Women's March in Washington Had 3 Times as Many People as Trump's Inauguration." *New York Times*, January 22. https://www.nytimes.com/interactive/2017/01/22/us/politics/womens-march-trump-crowd-estimates.html.

Walsh, Kathleen. 2022. "Jennifer Lopez Affleck Responded to Critics of Her Name Change: 'It's a Power Move.'" *Glamour*, November 2022. https://www.glamour.com/story/jennifer-lopez-affleck-responded-to-objections-to-her-name-change.

Warburton, Moira. 2022. "US Congress Passes Landmark Bill Protecting Same-Sex Marriage." Reuters, December 8. https://www.reuters.com/world/us/us-congress-expected-pass-bill-protecting-same-sex-marriage-2022-12-08/.

We, As Ourselves. 2021. "We, As Ourselves: Shaping the Narrative about Black Survivors." https://weasourselves.org.

Weatherbed, Jess. 2023. "Greta Gerwig's 'Barbie' Blasts into the Blockbuster Record Books with $155 Million US Opening." *The Verge*, July 24. https://www.theverge.com/2023/7/24/23805370/barbie-greta-gerwig-oppenheimer-blockbuster-record-us-opening-weekend.

Weeden, Kim A., Dafna Gelbgiser, and Stephen L. Morgan. 2020. "Pipeline Dreams: Occupational Plans and Gender Differences in STEM Major Persistence and Completion." *Sociology of Education*, 93(4). https://journals.sagepub.com/doi/full/10.1177/0038040720928484?journalCode=soea.

Weisholtz, Drew. 2023. "David Beckham Roasts Victoria Beckham for Saying She's 'Working Class.'" October 5. https://www.today.com/popculture/tv/david-beckham-victoria-beckham-working-class-rcna118995.

Wenham, Clare, Julia Smith, and Rosemary Morgan. 2020. "COVID-19: the Gendered Impacts of the Outbreak." *The Lancet*, March 6. https://www.thelancet.com/journals/lancet/article/PIIS0140-6736(20)30526-2/fulltext?amp=1&fbclid=IwAR1qW0XujurXbsnylTjCuDuNRekrU8sT4bDS9IBXp-cyDKNPj3lv-yxENHU#.XnfFLsbHpcw.facebook.

Whaley, Natelgé. 2018. "3 Long-term Effects the Gender Pay Gap Has on Women." *Mic*, April 10. https://www.mic.com/articles/188833/3-long-term-effects-the-gender-pay-gap-has-on-women#.1jbSlvfwi .

White House. 2023a. "American Rescue Plan's Child Care Stabilization Funds Stabilized the Industry While Helping Mothers Return to Work." November 7. https://www.whitehouse.gov/cea/written-materials/2023/11/07/child-care-stabilization/#:~:text=November%2007%2C%202023-,American%20Rescue%20Plan%27s%20Child%20Care%20Stabilization%20Funds%20Stabilized%20the,Helping%20Mothers%20Return%20to%20Work&text=The%20Biden%2DHarris%20Administration%20provided,American%20Rescue%20Plan%20(ARP).

———. 2023b. "Fact Sheet: White House Calls on Congress to Support Critical Domestic Needs." October 25. https://www.whitehouse.gov/briefing-room/statements-releases/2023/10/25/fact-sheet-white-house-calls-on-congress-to-support-critical-domestic-needs/#:~:text=As%20Congress%20works%20to%20reach,or%20raise%20costs%20for%20families.

White, Alana. 2019. "The Legging Problem." *The Notre Dame Observer*, March 25. https://ndsmcobserver.com/2019/03/the-legging-problem/.

White, Kenneth. 2023. "The Majors of Transgender and Gender Diverse College Students." *Journal of LGBT Youth*. https://www.tandfonline.com/doi/abs/10.1080/19361653.2023.2268605?src=.

Whitmer, Gretchen. 2020. "#WomensEqualityDay." State of Michigan. April 19. https://www.michigan.gov/whitmer/news/proclamations/2020/08/26/august-26-2020-womens-equality-day.

Whitmire, Richard, and Susan McGee Bailey. 2023. "Gender Gap." *Education Next* (Fall). https://www.educationnext.org/gender-gap/.

Whittaker, Anna C., and Stephen Gallagher. 2019. "Caregiving Alters Immunity and Stress Hormones: A Review of Recent Research." *Current Opinion in Behavioral Sciences*, 28: 93–97. https://www.sciencedirect.com/science/article/abs/pii/S2352154618301827?via%3Dihub.

Wilcox, Brad, and Hal Boyd. 2020. "The Nuclear Family Is Still Indispensable." *The Atlantic*, February 21. https://www.theatlantic.com/ideas/archive/2020/02/nuclear-family-still-indispensable/606841/.

Williams, Pete. 2021. "Supreme Court Won't Hear Dispute over Bathrooms for Transgender Students." NBC News, June 28. https://www.nbcnews.com/politics/supreme-court/supreme-court-won-t-hear-dispute-over-bathrooms-transgender-students-n1272513?fbclid=IwAR1YHJE-Y4cjJaSya_K0ylzMBEEA9gOVs1bdUj-9EDCCSkwhYu2rlpPd4l4.

Williams, Vanessa. 2020. "After a Record Number of Female Presidential Candidates, It Would Be Odd If a Woman Doesn't Run the Next Time." *Washington Post*, March 6. https://www.washingtonpost.com/nation/2020/03/06/after-record-number-female-presidential-candidates-it-would-be-odd-if-woman-doesnt-run-next-time/.

Williamson, Molly Weston. 2023. "The State of Paid Family and Medical Leave in the US 2023." Center for American Progress. January 5. https://www.americanprogress.org/article/the-state-of-paid-family-and-medical-leave-in-the-u-s-in-2023/.

Wills, Amanda, Jacque Smith, and Casey Hicks. 2019. "*All the Countries That Had a Woman Leader before the US*" CNN Politics, January 28. https://www.cnn.com/interactive/2016/06/politics/women-world-leaders/.

Wilson, Casey. 2022. "Overcoming Motherhood Imposter Syndrome." *New York Times*, April 26. https://www.nytimes.com/2020/04/15/parenting/casey-wilson-motherhood.html?.

Wingfield, Adia Harvey. 2020. "Women Are Advancing in the Workplace, but Women of Color Still Lag Behind." Brookings Institute. October. https://www.brookings.edu/essay/women-are-advancing-in-the-workplace-but-women-of-color-still-lag-behind/?utm_source=feedblitz&utm_medium=FeedBlitzRss&utm_campaign=brookingsrss/topics/competitiveness.

Wong, Alia. 2019. "The US Teaching Population Is Getting Bigger, and More Female." *The Atlantic*, February 20. https://www.theatlantic.com/education/archive/2019/02/the-explosion-of-women-teachers/582622/.

Wright, Marisa. 2023. "How Student Loan Forgiveness Can Help Close the Racial Wealth Gap and Advance Economic Justice." Legal Defense Fund. April 17. https://www.naacpldf.org/student-loans-racial-wealth-gap/.

Wright, Paul J., and Robert S. Tokunaga. 2016. "Men's Objectifying Media Consumption, Objectification of Women, and Attitudes Supportive of Violence against Women." *Archives of Sexual Behavior*, 955–64.

Yentel, Diane. 2023. "The Gap: A Shortage of Affordable Homes." National Low Income Housing Coalition. March. https://nlihc.org/gap.

Zapata, Kimberly. 2021. "The Raw Truth about Being the Default Parent." *Scary Mommy*, August 18. https://www.scarymommy.com/parenting/default-parent-truth.

Ziv, Shahar. 2019. "3 Ways the Gender Pay Gap Is Even Bigger than You Think." *Forbes*, July 11. https://www.forbes.com/sites/shaharziv/2019/07/11/gender-pay-gap-bigger-than-you-thnk/#4426b8d47d8a.

Index

Milton Keynes UK
Ingram Content Group UK Ltd.
UKHW021021111224
452415UK00024B/413